**From Sacred Story
to Sacred Text**

Other Fortress Press Books
by James A. Sanders

Torah and Canon (1972)

God Has a Story Too: Sermons in Context (1979)

Canon and Community: A Guide to Canonical Criticism (1984)

Canon as Paradigm

From Sacred Story
to Sacred Text

James A. Sanders

FORTRESS PRESS   PHILADELPHIA

Library of Congress Cataloging-in-Publication Data

Sanders, James A., 1927–
  From sacred story to sacred text.

  Bibliography: p.
  1. Bible—Canon. I. Title.
BS465.S263 1987   220.1'2   85–45483
ISBN 0–8006–0805–4

1836G86 Printed in the United States of America 1–1901

For
our beloved grandchildren
Robin David Sanders, Jr.
and
Alexander Jonathon Sanders
gifts of the grace of God

Contents

Preface

Since I completed formal graduate work years ago I have continued to learn. In fact I am sure I have learned more per unit of time invested since those days than during them. Obviously we all continue to read and learn working alone in our studies and at our desks; and we learn by engaging in dialogue in our guilds. But, in my case at least, I have continued to have mentors right on through the years, students in the seminar setting and pastors in the parish setting.

One of the joys of teaching is learning from one's students. Working on compiling this book, which is made up of signposts along the route of development of the concept of canonical criticism, became a kind of celebration in memory of the various students along the way who have contributed to my thinking about how to extend critical study of the Bible beyond its current stage of focus on ancient individuals on into the historical process, even from earliest times, whereby these sacred stories became a sacred text. They helped me to see that canonization could not simply be seen as the final stage of literary formation of the Bible, where the textbooks have always left it. I have been blessed in having wonderful colleagues along the way as well, but almost invariably it was a student who would from time to time find just the right and timely way to put into "other words" what was really happening.

These students have come from many and varied backgrounds and thus had different kinds of "other words" whereby to help crystalize developing thoughts. They often provided just the perspective from another background we needed to clarify and move on, recapitulate and transcend, as the old expression in intellectual history puts it.

The title of this book I owe to Merrill Miller who was among my early graduate students at Union Theological Seminary/Columbia University, New York City. He first used it, to my knowledge, in a paper titled, "Reflections on Scripture as Midrash." I learn something from Miller nearly every time we talk or write. It was he who, after the publication of the presidential address to the Society of Biblical Literature, suggested I should press the observations I made there about the masoretic phenomenon back into the biblical Iron Age—hence the last chapter in this present volume (chap. 9).[1]

Another former student, Richard Weis, suggested a helpful metaphor for understanding the place and importance of Enlightenment or contextual study of the Bible, as well as how one can speak in a scholarly context about the Holy Spirit, or *Shekinah* for Jews, as a factor in the canonical process and the formation of the Bible as Scripture, not just as a body of literature. Weis suggested that the student who struggles with serious exegesis of Scripture, like Jacob at the Jabbok, at first must wrestle with a passage as one does with a human, later to find that he or she had been wrestling with God (Gen. 32:22–23).[2]

A current student, Steven Delamarter, was the one who came up with the expression of the Bible being a "compressed text" of all sorts of literature that had first arisen out of many different contexts. This has been a very helpful way of thinking about the Bible in its so-called final forms. Delamarter is also working out a way of discerning the conception of reality that lies behind a text, especially behind early versions of biblical texts, as a crucial factor in making text-critical judgments as well as in discerning more precisely the nuance most appropriate in a given text of a multivalent word or term.

Horace Allen, who earned his degree in another field but has been a long-time conversation partner in discerning the most effective function of Scripture critically perceived and understood in the exercise of worship and liturgy, was the person who called to my attention the book by John James on the structure of the cathedral at Chartres.[3]

Gary Wilson has been the student of late who has kept up with the bibliography in canonical criticism and it is to him that we owe thanks for the select bibliography attached to this volume. But more important, Wilson has frequently gone out of his way to come by or call to mention a particularly important article or other title that I might well otherwise have overlooked. His work on canonical criticism as the valid bridge between responsible exegesis and homiletics will, I am sure, be recognized as filling that gap really good preachers have had to fill alone, so far without much help from the academic guilds.

Other students I have mentioned elsewhere but wish to thank also in this context are: Paul Dinter, William Miller, Mary Howard Calloway, Jane Schaberg, David Balch, Sharon Ringe, Craig Evans, and Marvin Sweeney.[4] Current students who have provided stimulus also are Peter Pettit, Garth Moller, Gerald vander Hoek, David Carr, and Bret Lamberty.

Not only students in the academic setting have been helpful but also pastors in parish settings. I am dedicated to the principle of continuing education and have been involved in it for over thirty years in pastors' schools run by seminaries, church judicatories, and local ecumenical pastors' groups.

I am also dedicated to working with lay groups, mainly those organized by pastors of local congregations around the country. Much of what has developed in my thinking about canonical criticism has come out of such dialogues and discussions, especially out of seeing firsthand the immense need to close the gap between pulpit and pew, the seminary and the congregation.[5] The kind of education we have been providing the future pastors of mainline congregations has been patently inadequate to handle the question of the relation of Scripture to church, that is, canon to community of faith. My book, *Canon and Community,* was written to address the need. Canonical criticism attempts to focus as much on the contributions of ancient communities of faith to the formation of the canon as those of ancient individuals. As stressed there, the Bible reaches its full stature in church; that is its true *Sitz im Leben* (setting in life), not the university or even the pastor's study alone.

Even as I compose this Preface I am also doing basic research and intensive study of the role and function of Scripture, the Old Testament in Greek (that is, the Septuagint, LXX), in the composition and formation of Luke's Gospel and the Acts of the Apostles. I find that it had considerable formative influence on the way Luke wrote, considerably beyond what current commentaries suggest. It is full of rhetorical paraphrases of Scripture. Even the best current commentary on Luke—that indeed recognizes much of the influence of the Septuagint in it—not only fails to see a good bit that is there, but addresses it only in terms of its influence on Luke, as an individual, or on his sources.[6] The conceptual imagery in nearly all scholarship on the New Testament is that of individual authors at their desks. In my work I am shifting that imagery to Luke's work with his congregation, and it makes a considerable difference. What Luke wrote and passed on to us in his literary work undoubtedly reflects what went on in the educational and liturgical programs of the congregation.

I am convinced that early Christians underwent rather intensive programs of instruction in the faith upon conversion, and that at the center of such programs was the "churches' book," the Septuagint, or whatever scrolls of it they had access to. According to the best New Testament scholarship, they would also have had traditions, written and oral, about the life and ministry of our Lord. Those traditions would have included, in the case of Luke's congregation, a form of Mark, a collection of Jesus' teachings and Jesus stories called the unknown source, or Q (those passages where Luke and Matthew agree without dependence on Mark), and perhaps in Luke's case a special source, whether oral or written is hard to say. Much New Testament scholarship leaves the question of sources there. There was another and it was as influential perhaps as any of those outside Mark; that source was the Septuagint, that is, Scripture. The Septuagint had the advantage of already being accepted in the Hellenistic world generally as worthy literature, and in some non-Jewish quarters as being somewhat authoritative. For early Christians it was not so much Jewish as it was sacred. They knew it was read and recited in the local synagogue down the street, so to speak, in Hebrew with commentary in Aramaic, but for them it was primarily sacred in that it told of what God had been doing since creation up to God's work in Christ and in the early church.

In the educational program of the first-century congregation, such as Luke's, the few literate members would read aloud for the benefit of the whole group, and then they would undoubtedly discuss the "lesson" or reading of the day or week under the guidance of their teaching elder, such as Luke. Such discussions would have reflected the lessons retold *in their own words*, as requested or required by the instructor. Good pedagogy requires it, and we can undoubtedly assume it in the sociology of early Christian congregations. The sermon the following Sunday would undoubtedly have incorporated the terms of those discussions.[7] So would Luke's literary efforts of writing it all up at his desk, probably at their behest. Paraphrases of Scripture are commonplace in the literature of early Judaism, whether in the Targumim (Aramaic commentaries) or in other literature we call apocryphal, including the Qumran literature in the Dead Sea Scrolls. To limit the influence of Scripture on a Gospel like Luke's to strictly repeated phrases is to fly in the face of reality. On the other side of the question, of course, restraint must be practiced in the exercise; but I think that such a shift in contextual imagery on how the Gospels and epistles were formed should make a considerable difference in how we see the formation of the New Testament.

The conviction that the Bible *as canon* belongs in church, rather than in the scholar's or even pastor's study only, brings with it important consequences as to how biblical scholarship should be done. But it has also meant that the scholar who shares the conviction has to be involved rather directly in the life of the church at the congregational and pastoral levels, even while making adjustments for differences in cultural setting. That involvement has been a joy for me as well as a source of insight on how to read the Bible.

What we have included in this book, a sort of pilgrimage into canonical criticism, has been influenced both by my work with my students in the academic setting, and with pastors and lay people out there where the "called people of God" are struggling daily with the issues of faith and obedience, precisely with how to monotheize, that is, how to affirm the oneness and integrity of reality in the midst of all sorts of modern forms of polytheism and idolatry. It is my deepest hope that sharing in this way will enhance that struggle.

This has been my fourth opportunity to work with Fortress Press, and each has been a joy as a manuscript moved out of my hands through those of my colleagues and friends at the press to become a book. It has always been with the greatest confidence that I have entrusted each to their care, knowing that it would receive both the scrutiny and the nourishment it needed to become a book we could be pleased to share with others. Norman A. Hjelm had first encouraged me to begin the process of sharing the pilgrimage this book traces. Harold W. Rast and John A. Hollar sustained his encouragement. It is to John Hollar that I owe the most thanks of all for his dedication and determination that what I sent him would indeed become a book.

NOTES

1. Among Merrill Miller's publications pertinent here are "Targum, Midrash and the Use of the OT in the NT," *JSJ* 2 (1971): 29–82, and *IDBSup.*, s.v. "Midrash." See also Michael E. Stone's *Scriptures, Sects and Visions* (Philadelphia: Fortress Press, 1980), 116: "In Judaism there was a transition from sacred tradition to sacred book." The address referred to is in *JBL* 98 (1979): 5–29.

2. See Richard D. Weis, *A Handbook of OT Exegesis*, 2d rev. ed. (Claremont, Calif., 91711: 1983 [available only through the author]), esp. 1–7.

3. See Prologue, n. 3.

4. See James A. Sanders, *Canon and Community* (1984), 63 n. 5. It is most encouraging to see the ever-increasing number of NT scholars using canonical criticism in their work.

5. See James A. Sanders, "The Bible and the Believing Communities," in *The Hermeneutical Quest. Essays in Honor of James Luther Mays on His Sixty-fifth Birthday*, 145–57. Edited by Donald G. Miller (Allison Park, Pa.: Pickwick Publications, 1986).

6. Joseph A. Fitzmyer, S.J., *The Gospel According to Luke*, 2 vols., AB 28 and 28A (Garden City, N.Y.: Doubleday & Co., 1981, 1985).

7. Note the observation by William S. Kurz, S.J., in "Luke 22:14–38 and Greco-Roman and Biblical Farewell Addresses," *JBL* 104 (1985): 252–53: "I am not arguing that Luke used any one farewell speech as his exemplar. Rather, from his familiarity with many farewell speeches, he gave Luke 22 a 'biblical flavor' by alluding especially to Greek OT farewell speeches. A modern comparison might be the biblicism and King James English in some contemporary sermons." In a note appended to this felicitous observation Kurz stresses that while he in his study investigated both Jewish and Greco-Roman writers, "the evidence still suggests closer imitation of the biblical examples." I fully agree.

Acknowledgments

"Adaptable for Life," by James A. Sanders from *Magnalia Dei* by Frank Moore Cross, Werner E. Lemke and Patrick D. Miller. Copyright © 1976 by Frank Moore Cross. Reprinted by permission of Doubleday & Company, Inc.

"Torah and Christ." Reprinted by permission from *Interpretation: A Journal of Bible and Theology* 29 (1975): 372–90.

"Hermeneutics" by James A. Sanders excerpted from *The Interpreter's Dictionary of the Bible, Supplementary Volume*. Copyright © 1976 by Abingdon. [= chap. 3] Used by permission.

"Biblical Criticism and the Bible as Canon." Copyright © 1977 by James A. Sanders. This article originally appeared in *Union Seminary Quarterly Review* 32 (1977).

"Hermeneutics in True and False Prophecy" was previously published in *Canon and Authority: Essays in Old Testament Religion and Authority*, edited by George W. Coats and Burke O. Long. Philadelphia: Fortress Press, 1977. [= chap. 5]

"Torah" by James A. Sanders excerpted from *The Interpreter's Dictionary of the Bible, Supplementary Volume*. Copyright © 1976 by Abingdon. [= first part of chap. 6] Used by permission.

"Torah and Paul" by James A. Sanders from *God's Christ and His People: Studies in Honour of Nils Alstrup Dahl*, edited by Jacob Jervell and Wayne A. Meeks. Oslo: Universitetsforlaget, 1977. [= second part of chap. 6] Used by permission.

"Text and Canon: Concepts and Method" by James A. Sanders from *Journal of Biblical Literature* 98 (1979): 5–29.

"Canonical Context and Canonical Criticism" by James A. Sanders from *Horizons in Biblical Theology* 2 (1980): 173–97. Reprinted by permission of Pittsburgh Theological Seminary.

"From Sacred Story to Sacred Text" was originally written for and delivered at the international conference on "Sacred Texts: The Hermeneutics of Religious Literature in a Post-Holocaust Age," held October 17–19, 1982, at Indiana University, Bloomington. It is here published for the first time.

Abbreviations

AB	Anchor Bible
ANE	ancient Near East
ANQ	*Andover Newton Quarterly*
ARNA	*Aboth de Rabbi Nathan*, recension A
AT	Ancien Testament; Alten Testament
BA	*Biblical Archaeologist*
BHK	*Biblia hebraica*. Edited by R. Kittel. Stuttgart, 1929–.
BHS	*Biblia hebraica stuttgartensia*. Stuttgart, 1968–.
Bib	*Biblica*
BibB	Biblische Beiträge
BibSt	Biblische Studien (Neukirchen)
BJRL	*Bulletin of the John Rylands University Library of Manchester*
BTB	*Biblical Theology Bulletin*
BZAW	Beihefte zur *ZAW*
ca.	circa = about (with dates)
CBQ	*Catholic Biblical Quarterly*
CCen	*Christian Century*
CST	Contemporary Studies in Theology
CTM	*Concordia Theological Monthly*
DBSup.	*Dictionnaire de la Bible. Supplément*. Edited by F. Vigoroux.
EncJud	*Encyclopaedia Judaica*
ET	English translation
EvT	*Evangelische Theologie*
ExpTim	*Expository Times*
GBS	Guides to Biblical Scholarship
HBT	*Horizons in Biblical Theology*
HDG	*Handbuch der Dogmengeschichte*

HTR	*Harvard Theological Review*
HTS	Harvard Theological Studies
HUBP	Hebrew University Bible Project
HUCA	*Hebrew Union College Annual*
IDB	*Interpreter's Dictionary of the Bible.* New York and Nashville: Abingdon Press, 1962.
IDBSup.	*Interpreter's Dictionary of the Bible, Supplementary Volume.* Nashville: Abingdon Press, 1976.
IEJ	*Israel Exploration Journal*
Int.	*Interpretation*
JAAR	*Journal of the American Academy of Religion*
JAOS	*Journal of the American Oriental Society*
JB	*Jerusalem Bible.* Edited by A. Jones. Garden City, N.Y.: Doubleday & Co., 1966.
JBC	*Jerome Biblical Commentary.* Edited by R. E. Brown et al. Englewood Cliffs, N.J.: Prentice-Hall, 1969.
JBL	*Journal of Biblical Literature*
JBLMS	Journal of Biblical Literature Monograph Series. Atlanta: Scholars Press.
JBR	*Journal of Bible and Religion*
JNES	*Journal of Near Eastern Studies*
JR	*Journal of Religion*
JRT	*Journal of Religious Thought*
JSJ	*Journal of the Study of Judaism in the Persian, Hellenistic and Roman Period*
JSNTSup.	Journal for the Study of the New Testament, Supplement Series
JSOT	*Journal for the Study of the Old Testament*
JSS	*Journal of Semitic Studies*
JTC	*Journal for Theology and the Church (ZThK)*
JTS	*Journal of Theological Studies*
KKTS	Konfessionskundliche und kontroverstheologie Studien
LBS	Library of Biblical Studies
LexTQ	*Lexington Theological Quarterly*
LQ	*Lutheran Quarterly*
LW	*Luther's Works.* Edited by Jaroslav Pelikan, Hilton C. Oswald, Helmut Lehmann. Volumes 1–30—St. Louis: Concordia Publishing House, 1955–; volumes 31–55—Philadelphia: Fortress Press, 1957–.
LXX	Septuagint
McCQ	*McCormick Quarterly*
MT	Masoretic Text
NAB	New American Bible
NEB	New English Bible
NJV	New Jewish Version

NorTT	*Norsk Teologisk Tidsskrift*
N.S.	new series
NT	New Testament; Neues Testament; Nouveau Testament
NTA	*New Testament Abstracts*
OstKSt	*Ostkirchliche Studien*
OT	Old Testament
PCB	*Peake's Commentary on the Bible.* Edited by Matthew Black and H. H. Rowley. New York: Thomas Nelson & Sons, 1963.
RB	*Revue biblique*
RelLife	*Religion in Life*
RevExp	*Review and Expositor*
*RGG*³	*Religion in Geschichte und Gegenwart.* 3d ed.
RSV	Revised Standard Version
RThPh	*Revue de théologie et de philosophie*
SBLDS	Society of Biblical Literature Dissertation Series. Atlanta: Scholars Press.
SBLMasS	Society of Biblical Literature Masoretic Studies. Atlanta: Scholars Press.
SBT	Studies in Biblical Theology
SE	*Studia Evangelica*
SJLA	Studies in Judaism in Late Antiquity
SJT	*Scottish Journal of Theology*
SR	*Studies in Religion/Sciences religieuses*
ST	*Studia theologica*
SWJT	*Southwestern Journal of Theology*
TDNT	*Theological Dictionary of the New Testament.* Edited by G. Kittel and G. Friedrich. Grand Rapids: Wm. B. Eerdmans, 1964–.
Theol.	*Theology*
ThG	*Theologie der Gegenwart*
ThLZ	*Theologische Literaturzeitung*
ThPh	*Theologie und Philosophie*
ThZ	*Theologische Zeitschrift*
TOB	Traduction Oecuménique de la Bible
TS	*Theological Studies*
TToday	*Theology Today*
UBS	United Bible Societies
UBS-HOTTP	United Bible Societies Hebrew Old Testament Project
USQR	*Union Seminary Quarterly Review*
UUÅ	*Uppsala universitetsårsskrift*
VT	*Vetus Testamentum*
VTSup.	Vetus Testamentum, Supplements
WMANT	Wissenschaftliche Monographien zum Alten und Neuen Testament

YJS	Yale Judaica Series
ZAW	*Zeitschrift für die alttestamentliche Wissenschaft*
ZNW	*Zeitschrift für die neutestamentliche Wissenschaft*
ZThK	*Zeitschrift für Theologie und Kirche (JTC)*

**From Sacred Story
to Sacred Text**

Prologue

This volume is a complement and supplement to *Torah and Canon* (1972) and *Canon and Community* (1984). It is designed to trace a pilgrimage of over twenty years to understand the Bible as canon. Such a review is both informative and humbling, at least for the author.

An abstract with background information is provided for each chapter. I attempt to evaluate the place of each chapter in the pilgrimage from the standpoint of changes in thinking about the Bible as canon since each was written. The text of each of the eight previously published chapters is essentially the same as the original essay. The chapters appear in the chronological sequence in which I wrote them, though not necessarily in the exact sequence of publication; in one or two cases the manuscript was completed long before it was published.

Since the question of the principal stimuli to which canonical criticism has been a response is dealt with explicitly in chapters 4 and 8, no further attempt at that important exercise will be made here. Nor need I say much more now about the issue of original intentionality.

As explained in *God Has a Story Too*, I am something of a squirrel; that is, I rarely clean out my files, so that for each chapter I have raw material for reconstructing the history of the formation of each chapter, including what I thought I was doing at the time. Seen now in the light of what is included here, I can appreciate as never before the limited importance of an author's "original intention."

A Pilgrimage

I started out as a graduate student to study New Testament. I intended to do serious scholarly work, insofar as capable, in New Testament studies. When I had completed only two years of seminary at the Vanderbilt University Divinity School, it became clear to me that my vocation was to teaching and scholarship within the church, but not the parish ministry. James Philip

Hyatt, a student of Millar Burrows at Yale University, was my principal mentor. Another mentor was Kendrick Grobel, a student of Rudolf Bultmann, although he did not share Bultmann's views of the value of the Old Testament to the church nor of its relation to the New. Grobel, though professor of New Testament, was my first teacher of biblical Hebrew. Hyatt engendered in me the desire to work in New Testament with a thorough knowledge of the Hebrew Bible, as well as its ancient Greek translation, the Septuagint, and of early Judaism. I had applied for and received a Fulbright grant for study abroad so that I left seminary at Vanderbilt and did the third year of seminary at the Faculté Libre de Théologie Protestante and at the Ecole des Hautes Etudes in Paris during the year 1950–51. I intended to go on to Yale thereafter in New Testament.

Correspondence with Hyatt during the year in Paris convinced me that I should take a year of graduate work at the Hebrew Union College–Cincinnati before going to Yale, in order to improve my knowledge of Jewish backgrounds to the New Testament. In Paris I studied under André Dupont-Sommer in Aramaic texts and in the Dead Sea Scrolls, the first of which had just been published in the early spring of 1950. But most of my work was with Oscar Cullmann with whom I later spent the year 1972–73 at the Ecumenical Institute for Advanced Theological Study at Tantur in Jerusalem where we both served as fellows in its first full year of operation. In Paris I was also fortunate to study with Maurice Gaugel who at the time was eighty-four years old. Hyatt's advice was good, as usual.

I arrived with my bride in Cincinnati in the fall of 1951 anxious to get on with work in backgrounds to New Testament. There Samuel Sandmel became my principal mentor, along with Sheldon Blank. Hyatt and Sandmel were close friends from Sandmel's days as Hillel Professor at Vanderbilt before he went to the Hebrew Union College, so Sandmel knew my plans. Sandmel and Alexander Guttmann were my major professors in early Judaism, the one on the Hellenistic side and the other on the early rabbinic side. I also did considerable work with Blank on the prophets and with Isaiah Sonne on the Qumran scrolls. I considered myself a student of Scripture, acquiring the various necessary backgrounds and tools for further graduate work on the New Testament. Hyatt spent a semester on sabbatical leave while I was there, so that we studied together in classes on Ugaritic literature and rabbinic midrash.

I had gone to the Hebrew Union College–Cincinnati for one year but stayed three and received the Ph.D. degree with Sandmel as first reader and Blank as second. I was still on track, or so I thought, when a telephone call came in May 1954 from Wilbour Eddy Saunders, president of the Colgate Rochester Divinity School, asking if I would teach there one year while they looked for a successor to Bernhard W. Anderson, who had just decided to leave Colgate Rochester in order to become dean of the seminary at Drew University. I had finished the dissertation except for the final typing and was free to accept, though I was not inclined to do so. Mrs. Sanders and I had in-depth conversations about it with Nelson Glueck, president of the college, and with Sandmel about what to do. I finally agreed to take the job with the clear understanding that it was for one year only, so that I could get on with work in New Testament.

We stayed eleven. Because I was teaching what Christians ineptly call the Old Testament, I was thought of in the guild of scholarship as being "in Old Testament." And according to the protocols of Protestant biblical scholarship, either one is in Old Testament or one is in New Testament. Roman Catholics felicitously refer to Scripture scholars; but Protestants fall heir principally to German biblical study and with it a good measure of anti-Semitism.[1] Since my formation is largely French and Jewish I approach the New Testament first and foremost as but a part of Christian Scripture. Such an approach has provided me with a slightly different set of questions to put to the New Testament and to Scripture as a whole from that of many of my Protestant colleagues. And it has provided me with a heightened sense of the anti-Semitism in much Protestant, especially New Testament, scholarship.

The dissertation done at the Hebrew Union College was a study of the relationship in the Hebrew Bible, and in early Judaism, between judgment and hope. It focused on a single expression of the relationship, namely the concept of *musar*, or divine punishment of sin, but also as discipline toward Israel's transformation into what became known as Judaism. Much of my work to date has been in exploration of that relationship in numerous areas. There is only one theological relation between judgment and hope as expressed biblically, and that is in a monotheizing view of God as both Creator and Redeemer. What I learned in doing the dissertation has been extended in various ways but principally into research on canonical hermeneutics, those unrecorded hermeneutics that lie between all the lines of Scripture where any authoritative community tradition, or international wisdom accepted as authoritative, is cited or alluded to and re-presented.

The relationship so discerned between judgment and hope in the Bible in its monotheizing context led to further insight on the relation canonically expressed between God as Creator and God as Redeemer, as well as to God's freedom within commitments and promises to express God's grace not only through redemption but in creation.

A Metaphor

The Bible is a product of human history, the peculiar histories of early Judaism and Christianity, and one's study of the Bible can remain entirely on that level. But if one is to arrive at full appreciation of the true nature of the Bible as the book of certain believing communities, ancient and modern, then it is simply inadequate to remain wholly on that level even of the "scientific" study of it. The more one wrestles with the concept of the Bible as Scripture or sacred text, the more one realizes that the whole indeed exceeds the sum of the parts: there is another dimension. As argued in *Canon and Community*, the

Holy Spirit should be viewed not only as working with the individual contributors to the Bible, but also as working all along the path of its formation.[2]

And that dimension exceeds any purely humanist grasp at understanding or comprehension. To use a metaphor, it is somewhat like John James's understanding of the cathedral at Chartres. Chartres is surely the finest expression of Gothic cathedral architecture of all that exist. It is awe-inspiring and breathtaking to anyone with an aesthetic eye to see and heart to perceive: it is the finest such expression, perhaps, of joint human dedication and endeavor. And yet James, who spent years studying its every nook, cranny, and detail, says it is in actual fact "a mess."[3] It is the product of a long process. Numerous master masons and builders contributed to it over several generations, and it would be difficult indeed to express adequately what makes all its disparate parts Chartres! In a similar manner the Bible as canon, or as a whole, seems just such a glorious mess! Like Chartres, the parts seem disparate and sometimes disjointed. Serious study of the parts in themselves makes one wonder what the unifying factor is, and many attempts have been made to suggest what its unity is.

Our suggestion is that the only really unifying factor of the Bible is not in a theme or concept, such as covenant, promise and fulfillment, or any other such effort of the many that have been attempted. These efforts have all issued finally in failed attempts to attach a handle to Scripture whereby to tame it or manipulate it. Dietrich Bonhoeffer often used the word "Reality" (*die Realität*) in referring to God. Like Chartres, the one real unity or integrity of the Bible is the Integrity of Reality, the oneness of God, to which all the parts, in one way or another, when joined together, point and testify. The contributors to each, the cathedral or the canon, were all human, no matter how inspired we may consider them to have been. They had variant visions, diverse talents, and even convictions about what was really important; but they all, when their works are joined together, pursue the Integrity of Reality—God's ontological and ethical oneness. No one part alone, or grouping of parts, expresses what it is all about or testifies to that Integrity to which the whole witnesses. The glory of the architecture of either the cathedral or the Bible transcends all the parts and their joinings; their glory is that to which they witness.

The Bible as canon, particularly as a final, stabilized literary text, presents itself as a compressed record of some two thousand years of struggles of our ancestors in the faith over against the various sorts of polytheism confronted during that time span, from the Bronze Age to the Hellenistic-Roman. Brevard Childs's view of the Bible as canon stresses the value of what emerged from the compression, the stabilized text in its final form (see chap. 8). Childs stresses the interrelationship of the parts in their canonical shape (for the Old Testament the masoretic form). And that is important to a limited extent; as argued in *Torah and Canon* its value as a compressed text must be fully appreciated. But that dimension of the text, its final plane, so to speak, is only a part of its value for believing communities today. The tools of the Enlightenment permit us to honor the struggles of our ancestors in the faith diachronically, that is, all along the path of formation of the text so that we can actually reconstruct realistically how they met the challenges of life right in their own cultural contexts. This is one of the great gifts of Enlightenment, or contextual, study of Scripture: we now have the opportunity to look into various parts of Scripture to see how our ancestors in the faith put that faith to work in concrete situations. We need not be satisfied with only a final product, or synchronic plane, that is, with a compressed de-historicized body of literature, as valuable as that aspect of Scripture as canon may be. We can also learn from the many very real persons and communities of faith that contributed to the various layers of its formation.

The Enlightenment may be viewed as a gift of God in due season, in the fullness of time, if its limitations are carefully observed. We can appreciate and be thankful for the tools that now permit us to reconstruct ancient struggles to monotheize, at all the stages of formation of the Bible, without embracing the peculiar form of idolatry and polytheism of the Enlightenment, namely, humanism. Like Jacob we must first wrestle as with a human, but to be thorough that struggle must go on to a striving with the Integrity of Reality, God's oneness, to which the canon as a whole witnesses.

Another form of idolatry or polytheism that has emerged in Western Christianity in reaction, in part, to Enlightenment study of the Bible, and that needs also to be eschewed, is that of bibliolatry—viewing the Bible itself as somehow divine. God is divine, not the Bible! Hard-core fundamentalism and literalism, born in extreme reaction to contextual study of the Bible, have so idolized the Bible as to abuse it. Canonical criticism proposes to under-stand the Bible as canon not as a box of ancient jewels forever precious and valuable, but as a paradigm of the struggles of our ancestors in the faith over against the several forms of polytheism from the Bronze Age to the Roman Empire.

A Paradigm

The word "paradigm" comes from a classical Greek verb that means "show side by side" or "represent." The noun means "pattern, exemplar, or model," as in the expression "an architect's plan," found in Herodotus. The Bible as canon may best be understood as a paradigm on how to monotheize over against all kinds and sorts of polytheism, or fragmentations of truth, even those practiced today. Since the Bible comes to us cloaked in the idioms, mores, and cultural givens of the five culture eras through which it passed to get here, we must be careful not to generalize on or absolutize any of them but try to discern in and through all that the mode or modes by which our ancestors in the faith affirmed God's oneness, or integrity, in their day—then take that as inspiration and energy for going and doing likewise in our day. Because the Bible is so fraught with the cultural mores of the time-span from the age of Abraham, the Bronze Age, down to the beginning of the second century C.E., the period of the early church, called the Hellenistic-Roman era, we must be cautious not simply to haul them into our time. What is sacred and precious is the legacy of striving they did back there on our behalf. We do not live in Anathoth or Antioch, but we believe firmly that we can learn from those reflected in the Bible who did, how to resist all the various forms of idolatry and polytheism today. The triangle, explained in chapter 5, is a tool designed to help bring the paradigm into new situations; chapter 3 explains the importance of discerning cultural context and its needs before attempting to apply the paradigm. Actually, the order in which we have arranged the chapters is probably best for getting into the whole concept of how the Bible can function as effective paradigm for faith and obedience. A paradigm shows us how to conjugate verbs and decline nouns; the canonical paradigm instructs us in how to monotheize in a multitude of situations without having to live in those contexts or absolutize them.[4]

We need the literary and historical tools of Enlightenment study in order to learn from our ancestors in the faith how to engage in our own struggle today to monotheize or pursue the Integrity of Reality—both synchronically on the final, compressed shape of the whole and diachronically on all the layers contributed through its history of formation by the several individuals and communities all along the way. Enlightened reading of the layers can thus be corrected by enlightened reading of the whole, and vice versa. Each type of reading corrects and informs the other so that, for instance, no view of God, or Reality, that emerges from the reading of a single text or layer of text can be generalized or absolutized; and so that no view of God or Reality that any one generation or denomination attempts to construct allegedly on the whole can escape the challenge of those parts the construct cannot account for. For, in truth, this wonderful glorious mess is such that no theological construct built on it can escape—sooner or later—the Bible's own prophetic challenge.

Serious study of the late Bronze Age indicates that there were numerous migrations as well as slave rebellions in the same period as that of the Hebrew slaves in Egypt. A theocentric hermeneutic, learned in part from Enlightenment study of these texts, permits us to see that God chose one such slave rebellion, that of Moses and the Hebrew slaves, as paradigm whereby to perceive God's emancipation proclamation for all humanity and creation. A monotheizing hermeneutic, learned from these same texts, permits us to understand Pharaoh's point of view (seen as hardness of heart by the oppressed slaves) as well as that of Moses (seen as a murderer, a fugitive from justice, and a community organizer/agitator by the Egyptians). Pharaoh was no more a bad guy for attempting to protect his economy in the late Bronze Age than many American Christians have been bad guys for resisting efforts on the part of some citizens of this country to challenge a system that maintains cheap labor and thus improve their lot. I was born and grew up in the South and know Pharaoh's point of view and argument very well indeed: Hold on, you're moving too fast! Radical fundamentalism flourishes among those who hold such a view precisely because it prevents the Bible from being the prophetic voice and challenge that it can be to such a position or any position. The Bible, read with its own theocentric-monotheizing hermeneutic, says that God could work in and through Pharaoh's point of view as well as Moses' to effect God's, not Pharaoh's, emancipation proclamation (Torah) as paradigm for all humanity. If Pharaoh's heart had been soft, he might indeed have issued his own emancipation proclamation, but there would have been no Torah. This is a good point at which to stress the importance of theologizing before moralizing; to moralize only would issue in the absurdity that we should harden our hearts today so God can make some more Torahs.

Monotheizing pluralism is the affirmation of God's oneness, the Integrity (ontological and ethical) of Reality. The pluralism of the Bible's own glorious mess provides it with its own built-in self-corrective apparatus so that we do not absolutize the parts we like and ignore those that challenge our views of it. In addition, the Bible's monotheizing pluralism renders it a prophetic voice, precisely the Word of God, for the world today, if we read it on its own terms. And those terms, those hermeneutics, were signaled by Jesus himself in his answer to the lawyer who asked what he should do to be saved (instead of asking what God had done that he might be saved). Jesus responded by asking what was written in Torah and how the lawyer read it (Luke 10:26); the lawyer correctly answered by quoting Deut. 6:5 and Lev. 19:18. In the Matthean version of the dialogue it was Jesus who answered the question with the same quotations: "You shall love the Lord your God with all your heart, and with all your soul, and with all your mind. This is the great and first commandment. And a second is like it, You shall love your neighbor as yourself. On these two commandments depend all the Torah and the Prophets" (Matt. 22:37–40). In other words, Jesus is reported himself to have taught that all Scripture depends on theologizing first, loving God with all the self, and moralizing thereafter, loving neighbor as self. And the theologizing by which Scripture must first be read is also monotheizing; for Jesus' citation of Deut. 6:5 is a part of the *Shema'*, precisely the monotheizing commandment par excellence (Deut. 6:4ff.). And the two prongs of the hermeneutic together, love of God and love of neighbor, mean that love of God entails at least understanding the point of view of others, even Pharaoh's or Herod's.

Is it possible that God is working through our modern fears of total holocaust of this planet to get us to do just that? Is it possible that the Integrity of Reality is reaching through the information revolution, telecommunications, and the bomb to induce in humanity a change of mind-set (Jer. 31:33; Ezek. 36:26; Phil. 2:5–11)? Is it possible to attempt to obey that ultimate commandment of Christ's to love the enemy (Matt. 5:44), precisely to refuse to read the Bible or human history or our situation through the hermeneutics of good guys versus bad guys? Is it possible that God is working with, in, and through our own American hardness of heart (from the point of view of the poor and of much of the world), as well as through the fear we and the Russians engender in the rest of the world, in order to bring about a mutation of the human heart or mind-set? Is it possible that human humility, the ability to hear others and understand their hopes and fears, may become more important than our several tribal and denomi*national* notions of responsibility? Is it possible that now we may learn that true responsibility *is* humility, that same humility we Christians profess was incarnate in God's Christ? Hope, our true hope, lies in the faith perspective that reality *is* God's integrity, God's oneness, and that its desire is for us humans humbly to perceive our rightful but limited place in that integrity.

NOTES

1. The debate about Martin Luther's contribution to the problem continues. See, e.g., Kurt Aland's "Toleranz and Glaubensfreiheit im 16. Jahrhundert," in *Reformation and Humanismus*, ed. M. Greschat and J. Goeters (Luther-Verlag-Witten, 1969), 67–90; and Walther Bienert, *Martin Luther und die Jüden* (Frankfurt: Ev. Verlagswerk, 1982). As in all such debates one should go to the sources; in all fairness one should read Luther's essay, "That Jesus Christ Was Born a Jew," *LW* 45:195–229, as well as the oft-cited, "The Jews and Their Lies," *LW* 47:137–306 (Philadelphia: Fortress Press, 1962, 1971).

2. J. A. Sanders, *Canon and Community* (1984), xv–xviii. See also John Calvin, *Treatises Against the Anabaptists and Against the Libertines*, ed. and trans. B. W. Farley (Grand Rapids: Baker Book House, 1982), for a clear statement about the necessity of the work of the Spirit for proper understanding of Scripture.

3. John James, *Chartres: The Masons Who Built a Legend* (London: Routledge & Kegan Paul, 1982), 9: "When you examine the cathedral closely, you discover to your immense surprise that the design is not a well controlled and harmonious entity, but a mess."

4. Michael Fishbane's incisive and milestone work, *Biblical Interpretation in Ancient Israel* (Oxford: Clarendon Press, 1985), provides an excellent elaboration of the canonical paradigm in terms of what he calls scribal, legal, aggadic, and mantological exegesis within the Hebrew Bible. Norman K. Gottwald's article, "Social Matrix and Canonical Shape" (*TToday* 42 [1985]: 307–21), provides a good perspective on the need of exegeting the social and political context a biblical passage addressed in order to discern its full canonical value without absolutizing that ancient social context as though it itself were canonical—a critique I would have of some of Gottwald's earlier work.

1
Adaptable for Life: The Nature and Function of Canon

"Adaptable for Life" (1972) was written as a follow-up to *Torah and Canon* (1972) soon after the manuscript for the latter had gone off to press. There I had addressed the problem of why "Joshua" or, at least, the traditions it represents, did not end up in the Torah that Ezra brought back with him from Babylonia to Jerusalem (Nehemiah 8), whereas almost all the recitals of Israel's epic history in the prophets, psalms, and historiography included and often concluded with the entrance into the land. But I felt I needed to address an equally important question, and that was how the Ezra Torah could so quickly claim the authority it did, and, furthermore, how that same Torah could maintain that authority in and for Judaism for centuries to come.

In the introduction to *Torah and Canon* I had said, "This essay began as an effort to look at the Bible holistically—not to seek its unity (no one is doing that these days), but to describe its shape and its function. It soon became clear that the origin and essence of the Bible lay in the concept of Torah, those early traditions of ancient Israel which not only had a life of their own but gave life to those who knew them and molded their own lives around them. It was soon also clear that in that life process lay the meaning of canon" (pp. ix–x). But I had written the introduction, like all authors I think, after I had written the book. The introduction represented thinking already somewhat beyond the contents of the book. I felt I needed to address the question of authority in a really fresh way. "Adaptable for Life" was that attempt. It addresses both questions: how that authority arose and how it was thereafter maintained.

I knew I had to get away from the conscious intentions and decisions of early Jews in dealing with the question. There was also the other problem, dealt with to some extent in *Torah and Canon*, of how it was that only the Bible folk, the heirs of old Israel and Judah, survived the successive power flows of the late Iron Age before stability once more was assured, not this time by Egypt but rather by Persia. Why did Judaism alone survive? The Samaritan question could be bracketed for two reasons: the origin and early history of the Samaritans was and still is somewhat uncertain; but more important, they, too, were Torah folk. The others, Israel's neighbors, subject to the same power pressures for assimilation and therefore identity extinction, succumbed and disappeared.

Even so, it was not Israel and Judah that survived. It was a new Israel, Judaism, born out of the ashes of the old in exile. "Adaptable for Life" advances the *thesis* that the resurrection of Judaism out of the death of the old, was due to the *relecture*, the rereading or reciting of old preexilic traditions, indeed, preconquest or pre-identity-

9

with-the-land traditions, that gave survival power to those who elected because of that to keep what identity they could of their preexilic existence. Torah, indeed, had survival power. It was being read and reread all through the Diaspora by what we now know was a remnant, precisely those who retained the old, but adapted, identity. But that same power for life also transferred to the readers of those traditions: they refused to assimilate.

That death-and-life experience became thereafter indelibly imprinted on the corporate Jewish psyche or *lēb* (heart). It was serious reading and rereading of the old traditions that provided the staying power for that remnant. The nonremnant assimilated just as other national identities were dissipating and assimilating.

But that very act, or process, of reading and rereading in Diaspora—and even life in Palestine was a form of Diaspora under dominant Persia—where Ezra's Torah was edited and shaped, indicated the considerable malleability of the shaping of the traditions. There was a core. There was an essence. There was continuity or stability in those traditions. But there was also adaptability.

These observations raised the question of hermeneutics in a poignant way. Not hermeneutics in the way most exegetes, interpreters, and theologians were talking about hermeneutics in the early 1970s or since, but the hermeneutics of those very believing communities that experienced what Ezekiel called the resurrection (Ezekiel 37). How did they read the traditions that they yielded such existential power for them? The old traditions that survived and were shaped by the death-and-life experience of exile became Torah for all time, but a Torah adaptable and stable enough to be, indeed, not only a lamp and a light on life's pilgrimage, but also life in the land when Torah is not forgotten but rather is imprinted for joy on the heart (Ps. 119:105–12) just as Jeremiah had hoped (Jer. 31:31–34). Such was the origin, then, of the old Jewish concept of Torah being the Book of Life.

Its power for life, then, is not to be thought of in philosophical existentialist terms primarily; for its life-giving power, which had been "proved" in the resurrection experience, continued to nourish Judaism and to provide it with a sure guide to life style. It was not just a matter of survival; it was also a matter of life's ethos. The authority of such power was there for the remnant to behold and wonder at before that authority was expressed in terms of Mosaic authorship or acceptance by some sort of authoritative council. It was indelibly imprinted on the corporate soul of Judaism.

See especially the recent works of G. Wilson, *The Editing of the Hebrew Psalter* (Chico, Calif.: Scholars Press, 1985), and M. Wise, "The Dead Sea Scrolls, Part 1," *BA* 49 (1986): 140–55. (See also p. 85 n. 11, below.)

On the new impetus in the study of the Pseudepigrapha, see James H. Charlesworth, ed., *The OT Pseudepigrapha*, 2 vols. (Garden City, NY: Doubleday & Co., 1983, 1985). (See also p. 32 n. 13, below.)

I

The study of the canon of the Bible, and especially of the OT, is today in a state of flux. One senses this especially if one rereads, at the present moment, the standard introductions and handbooks on the subject. For the most part they exhibit consensus on the meaning of canon without broaching the problems of canon as they should be put today. Discrepancy in judgment may appear on how early or how late one may speak of closure of the three sections of the OT; but, save for a few hints otherwise, standard discussions of canon deal almost exclusively with last things in the canonical process rather than with the early factors that gave rise to the phenomenon of canon as Judaism inherited it.

The sense of flux comes in reading such discussions in the light of what has been happening in the last several years in biblical studies generally. Today, I am convinced, we cannot deal adequately with the question of the structure of canon, or what is in and what is out, until we have explored seriously and extensively the question of the function of canon. It is time to attempt to write a history of the early canonical process.[1] Out of what in ancient Israel's common life did the very idea of canon itself arise? The concept of canon is located in the tension between two poles: stability and adaptability; but discussions since Semler[2] in 1772 have dealt almost exclusively with the former and rarely with the latter. Hence, all the brave efforts to work on hermeneutics in the past fifteen years have failed, I think, for the lack of work on canonical criticism, for hermeneutics must be viewed as the midterm of the axis that lies between stability and adaptability.

Robert Pfeiffer's chapter in his introduction is one of the finest of the older liberal discussions of canon.[3] And yet, Pfeiffer started with the finding of the scroll in the temple in 621 B.C.E.: he started with the concept of stability and the necessary observations about Deut. 31:26. It seemed quite normal at the time, I am sure, and one can understand it today even though we are in a quite different Zeitgeist, to cast about for the earliest evidence of when a certain body of traditional literature became stabilized; and Deuteronomy seems to provide that evidence for the Pentateuch. The work of the exilic or priestly editors then is usually mentioned, followed by observations about the work of Ezra with evidence to substantiate it in the Chronicler. So much for the Law. In the case of the Prophets the discussions start with citations from Ben Sira 48 and 49, written about 190 B.C.E. to show that the books of the Three and the Dodecapropheton must have become by that time the prophetic corpus as we know it now—with a door left ajar to allow for the embarrassing results of literary and historical criticism, that some isolated passages in the Prophets may have dated from Ptolemaic, Seleucid, or even Maccabean times.

What is rather remarkable is the tendency to read back as far as possible the closure of some portions of the Writings. This has especially been the case for the Psalter. Before the discovery of the large Psalms scroll from Qumran Cave 11 a general consensus had been reached placing the stabilization of the masoretic collection of 150 psalms (give or take Psalm 151) in the late Persian period. Supported by what I suppose one might call a general neo-orthodox atmosphere, at least certainly a conservative one, conjoined with a growing nationalist hermeneutic in Jewish scholarship, assertions outreached the evidence for such a judgment. A review of the evidence advanced by even the greatest names in scholarship for such an early dating of the closure of the MT-150 Psalter exposes rather dramatically the paucity of basis for it, as well as the range played by impertinent data.[4] The only sound thesis that can be built on the now-available evidence is that while the MT-150 collection may well have stabilized for some sects in Judaism already in the middle of the second century B.C.E. (considerably after the Persian period), for other segments of the Jewish community the Psalter was open-ended well into the first century C.E. The prevailing view that the proto-MT text of the Law and the Prophets became the official text, and became largely stabilized, in the period of the some hundred years from Hillel to the fall of Jerusalem 69 C.E., may possibly be a parallel and analogous historical picture for what happened to the Psalter in that same all-crucial period.[5] At any rate, the question of the dates of the individual psalms remains uninfluenced by the independent question of the stabilization of the contents and order of the MT Psalter, just as the text-critical question of the individual variants for the several psalms has to be dealt with on its own methodic grounds.[6] Social and political factors were at work in the period of Roman hegemony which just simply had not been there in such degree before and which caused an intensive, concentrated amount of scholarly effort on the part of Palestinian Jews resulting in the sorts of evidence of stabilization in the period available to us today.

Despite the apparent lack of clear reference to Jabneh,[7] there is abundant indirect evidence for the convening, at the end of the first century C.E., of a group of rabbis who felt constrained by the compelling events of the day, largely the threat of disintegration due to the loss of Jerusalem and her religious symbols, to make decisions regarding the contents of the Hagiographa.[8] The remarkable thing about the assumed council at Jabneh is not that it did not settle absolutely all questions. The remarkable thing, in the light of the way the question of canon should be broached today, is that so few questions remained after Jabneh about what was in (soiled the hands) and what was out. When one looks at the whole question of canon, from its inception in preexilic days, the authority of the supposed council of Jabneh is remarkable indeed. And the fact that some scattered debate continued into the second century about the canonicity of Esther, Song of Songs, Ecclesiastes, and even Proverbs and Ezekiel, should, in that perspective, properly be viewed as minimal in the extreme. The effectiveness of the conciliar decisions at Jabneh (or what we extrapolate from the plethora of evidence for a Jabneh council) points as does very little else to the enormity of the fall of Jerusalem in 69 C.E. in the religious (not to speak of the social, economic, and political) history of Judaism. And it should caution us today against reading back in to the earlier period what Judaism became in the first century.[9] Dramatic changes took place in Judaism in the first century of the Common Era that affected the bottom end of the canonical process.

Current discussions of the canon of the OT have to begin, therefore, from a different perspective. This new approach to the question of canon I have called canonical criticism.[10] A new departure for the study of canon is necessary for a number of reasons: the need to move away from the peculiar views offered by the Jabneh mentality; the need to account for the fluidity (to a greater or lesser extent) both in text and content of the Prophets and Writings right up to the period of Pharisaic hegemony under Salome Alexandra;[11] the need to account for the great pluralism in Judaism in the early Jewish period; and the need to account for a basic shift in hermeneutic techniques in proto-Pharisaic circles away from contextual to atomistic midrash.[12]

Largely because of the recovery of the Qumran literature, but also in part because of the intensive review that recovery has caused scholarship to engage in of the other Jewish literature datable to early Judaism (including apocryphal, pseudepigraphic, and neotestamental),[13] we now know that the Jabneh mentality cannot dominate the way we must now think about the canonical process up to the first centuries B.C.E. and C.E. Not only is there no clear evidence of such punctiliar and conciliar decision making in the period before Jabneh,[14] there is also no evidence prior to the first century C.E. of the kind of standardization of norms by which that century is now so well characterized. A new attitude is indicated in thinking about the canonical process and must be at the heart of canonical criticism.

II

Current thinking on OT exhibits a kind of frustration about what is in and what is out of the canon. Behind the frustration is a tension between the Jabneh mentality and the modern question arising out of the ecumenical movement: what shall we say in answer to the question of what is canonical for church and synagogue today? Some of the deuterocanonical books which Roman Catholics value to some degree as authoritative but which Jews and most Protestants do not consider at all canonical, were quite clearly authoritative for many Jews in the pre-Jabneh period. Are they in or out? Should they be graded separately and individually? Nor do these questions touch on the very sensitive problem for us of what is in the canon in the Eastern churches.[15] These modern, "relevant" questions serve but to stress the need for canonical criticism to turn, for the present, to the other pole of the canonical process. Let us begin at the beginning. Exorcising the Jabneh mentality and turning our back on the frustrations it has engendered requires concentration on the basic concept of canon itself.

Because nearly all discussions of canon start with some etymological observation about the word "canon" (Qaneh-kanōn), the aspect of "normative rule" provides a mind-set from the beginning. Attention is drawn immediately to the question of the size of the rule. How long is it? Why is it that long? What were the criteria that determined its length? This is the pole of stability. But the other aspect of the idea of canon, always in tension with it, is not its length or structure, but rather its nature and function. And it is on the nature and function of canon that canonical criticism puts the prior emphasis. What does it do? How did it get started in the first place? A priori, the first consideration of canonical criticism is the phenomenon of repetition. Repetition requires that the tradition be both stable and adaptable. Minimally speaking, it is the nature of canon to be "remembered" or contemporized. The fact that begs explanation is that of the earliest rise of a tradition.

Otto Eissfeldt is right to begin his chapter on canon with what he calls prehistory. "It was only in the second century A.D. . . . that the formation of the Old Testament canon came to an end. But its prehistory begins centuries or even millennia earlier. Its starting-point is the belief that particular utterances of men are in reality the word of God and as such can claim for themselves special authority."[16] But because Eissfeldt limited himself in his prehistory to the concept of "word," he goes on only to speak of "Six different kinds of words which rank as divine words." And in doing so he further limits his thinking to three of them, judgment, word, and directive (mishpat, dabar, and torah), which narrows his cursive prehistory to collections of legal material and how they grew, "the replacement of older bodies of law by newer ones." And then, forthwith, he deals with the single aspect of inclusion-exclusion and leaves aside a discussion that could have been very fruitful indeed.

Aage Bentzen, in his introduction to the OT, has a very pregnant sentence in his chapter on canon which he, too, fails to develop: "Another germ of a formation of Canon is probably also found in what has been called 'the historical Credo of Israel.' "[17] Bentzen is surely right, for concentration on how little legal codes became larger legal codes is not only a Holzweg for understanding the canonical process in general, it overlooks the essential nature of the Torah itself in which those codes are embedded. Two of the essential observations one must make about the OT are (1) there are no laws, with the status of law, outside the Torah; and (2) the Torah itself is not primarily legal literature. It was in part to probe such observations that I wrote *Torah and Canon*, and I do not want to repeat all that here. But canonical criticism must deal with the observation that it is the Torah that gives authority to the laws within it, and not the other way around. Building on the observations of Gunnar Östborn, and on one's own unbiased reading, one must insist that a primary definition of Torah cannot be "law."[18] It is a story, first and foremost, with Yahweh, the God of Israel (in all his syncretistic make-up),[19] as the prime actor and speaker. Biblical scholarship has clearly shown that the laws in the Pentateuch actually date from widely varying times and were in some measure the common property of the ancient Near East. Ancillary observations such as that of the lack of laws in Joshua (despite the formulary introduction in 24:25ff.), or in Samuels or Kings, despite the insistence therein that Israel's kings constantly made judicial decisions and ruled largely by royal decree, simply force the question of why Eissfeldt's "collections of judgments" are to be found *only* in the Pentateuch. (Ezekiel's so-called Temple Torah in chaps. 40—48 did not make it in.)

III

The Torah is best defined as a story (*mythos*) with law (*ethos*) embedded in it.[20] The observation that has imposed itself most strongly in the past generation is that this Torah story is to be found in scattered places in the Bible, in shorter or longer compass—without the laws (or, to put it the way it is usually put, without Sinai). Gerhard von Rad has called these passages, especially those in Deut. 26:5–9 and Joshua 24, ancient Israel's ancient credo,[21] and George Ernest Wright has called them confessional recitals of God's mighty acts.[22] Touching directly on the question of the nature of canon, Wright calls the Bible the Book of the Acts of God.[23] Martin Noth in turn built on von Rad's thesis by a rather far-reaching tradition-critical study of the Pentateuch.[24]

The position generally shared by these three scholars and those that follow them is that the Pentateuch, or Torah, is the credo, or confessional recital, writ large. To it have been added, according to Noth, a number of other traditions including Sinai. Wright's position differs largely in his insistence that the Torah including Sinai stems from actual historical occurrence indicated (though not proved) by archaeology.

Von Rad's work on the credo, and his and Noth's form-critical and tradition-critical work on the Hexateuch, have come under careful scrutiny in recent years.[25] The bulk of the criticism is to the effect that the so-called credo is not ancient at all, but rather Deuteronomic, and that in form Deut. 26:5–9 is not a Gattung at all; but rather all such passages are historical summaries embedded within larger forms such as the covenantal formulary, or simply parts of prayers of thanksgiving, petition, catecheses, or the like.[26]

These main points of criticism are in large part justified, especially the observation that the recitals are not ancient in the *form* that we inherit them. Surely Deut. 26:5–9 is in every crucial turn of phrase Deuteronomic.[27] The neo-orthodox Zeitgeist of the 1930s permitted the use of the term "credo" without criticism until 1948.[28]

Wright's term "recital" is a far more felicitous word for, as the critics of von Rad have pointed out, the summaries seem to be largely catechetical in form. But criticism of the main point of the summaries must itself not be permitted to get out of hand. The history of scholarship shows that often the pendulum-swing from one Zeitgeist to the following tends to annihilate what ought to remain of earlier work as well as what was tenuous about it. (One wonders if some of the fine work done in the last ten years on Wisdom in the OT will be forced to languish for a while when the mood changes once more.) Critics of von Rad have seemed content to leave the impression, almost in the manner of assumptions made in the era of source criticism, that the Deuteronomists created the historical summary form without probing the question of where it had itself come from.

Without faulting Wright's term "recital," I prefer the term *mythos*, or "Torah story."[29] The idea of *mythos* admits of a wider range of questions concerning the function of the summaries. Form criticism is a useful tool in biblical criticism, or within any criticism of any literature, but it can never stand alone. The form of a literary passage cannot possibly answer all the questions necessary concerning it. Indeed, its form may be deceptive, for the ancient speaker or writer may well have intended to pour new wine into an old wineskin, precisely in order to make a point that literary conformity might not have permitted him or her to make.[30] But more than that, as in the case of the larger question of canon, one must always ask what function a literary piece served, originally as well as in its subsequent contexts. What did these recitals or Torah stories do? The answers to that question will, I think, preclude any suggestion or assumption that the school of Deuteronomy invented them. There can be little question that Deuteronomy underscored their importance, just as there is little question the intrusion of Deuteronomy into the old JE story line (between Numbers and Joshua, and then eventual displacement of Joshua) had a profound effect on Judaism and its ability in exile, by God, to arise out of the ashes of the old nationalist cult.[31]

IV

If one reflects on the basic idea of canon, what he or she must probe is the fact of repetition—a priori, the first time an idea was taken up again. It passed the immense barrier from a first telling to a second. One must dwell on that phenomenon above all others. My colleague Theodor Gaster insists that it may have been only for its entertainment or aesthetic value. And that is right, perhaps, in the case of songs and certain types of stories and proverbs. They afford distraction, release, or alter moods to some desired end. Aesthetics would clearly have been a determinant in the phenomenon of repetition.

But there are many collections of such materials that do not a canon make.[32] One then must add the other criterion, function. Whatever else canon does it serves to engage the two questions: who am I, or we, and what are we to do? This is the classical understanding of the function of canon, and it has not been improved on. Canon functions, for the most part, to provide indications of the identity as well as the life style of the ongoing community that reads it. The history of the biblical concept of canon started with the earliest need to repeat a common or community story precisely because it functioned to inform them who they were and what they were to do even in their later situation.

But in the case of identity stories (and it is out of some sort of self-understanding that life style is derived; a community's *ethos* issues from its *mythos*) it is most unlikely that there was ever a set form, either at the beginning or in the subsequent stages of repetition. Here Wright is surely correct: the basic elements in the recitals derive from history. And those basic elements were both the common property of the people and the constant factor in whatever form they might take, whether song, hymn, prayer, catechesis, covenant formulary, "creed," or what not. The more important such stories are to the life and existence of a people (that is, the more they are remembered or repeated) the less valuable they are apt to be to modern historians with *their* rather peculiar needs—since, of necessity, each repetition invites, so to speak, an increase of history, something from the period in which retold. Whenever a history belongs to the people and has existential value for them, it, of necessity, becomes *legendum* in some sense. Therefore, what we observe in the OT is that Israel had a story of existential value for them communally, a historial *mythos* that took on a number of forms, and that functioned for the people in certain types of reflective situations. Since there might be several different forms, the aesthetic factor in repetition was clearly at best secondary. A quest for the reason for repetition has to be sought elsewhere.

The primary authority of Israel's central tradition, that of the escape from Egypt and entrance into Canaan, lay in its power to help the people answer the two questions of self-understanding and life pattern. The fact that the story, in whatever form, passed the barrier from one generation to the following is, in this light, evidence enough of its validity. It spanned a generation gap at some point in Israel's early history. What scholars who try to meet their own needs (seeking answers to narrowly defined questions about history) must remember is that the needs of the people whom they study were for the most part quite different from theirs. And it is highly unlikely that a tradition arises and persists simply because there is a need to fill out a cultic order of service (the narrow sense of *Sitz im Leben*). As conservative as cults tend to be they were formed because of some gut-level existential need of the people they served, and from time to time demonstrated the ability to meet the people at that level again.

A story that succeeded in passing from one generation to another did so, therefore, not because it had a set form or primarily because it distracted the people, but because (1) it spoke to a majority of the community; (2) it communicated to them a power they sought; and (3) this power met a common need of the community, probably the need to recapitulate their common self-understanding and to transcend a challenge born to it. The challenge would have been some newness or strangeness that had to be dealt with—usually either by rejection or integration, by retaining a status quo, or by effecting some change. The challenge might range from the subtlest sort of threat to the existing societary structure, to a clear and present danger of its total disintegration.

In all such circumstances the imperative to any community is to review its understanding of who it is (1) to know if in the moment of the review (and according to its Zeitgeist) the society should or can adapt to the measure indicated (*shalom*), or (2) in the event of rejection and violence at the other extreme (*milḥamah;* cf. Jer. 28:8–9), to relearn, in the new situation presented by the threat, exactly who they are, so that when they emerge on the other side of the sword (Jer. 31:2) they will know (to put it very simply) if indeed they survived.

Survival is not a matter of living only, or breathing, or blood flowing through individual veins; for assimilation to another culture (which has another and different identifying *mythos*) is death as sure as slaughter is death. (What happened to the so-called northern ten tribes of Israel? They were assimilated into the dominant culture of the eighth-century neo-Assyrian Empire. The majority lost their identity, though most of the individuals involved survived and had children.)[33] So whether the whole of a society lives, or only a remnant, a dynamic source of identity provision is absolutely necessary for that measure of continuity, within discontinuity, that can mean survival. Other factors may seem of equal or greater importance at the moment, such as the foreign policy or statecraft of the threatening power: Assyria's sponsored disintegration of subject peoples, Babylonia's sponsored remnant or ghetto-type survival.[34] But statecraft in the sixth and fifth centuries was not, in fact, the more important factor; for many of the victims changed to such a point that many of the peoples existing in the Palestinian area from the late Bronze Age through the Iron Age simply passed from the scene under Babylonian and Persian hegemony.

Why did Israel survive? That is the immense historial question that begs explanation. That which happened to some of the other victim nations did not happen to Israel. Israel changed rather radically, to be sure, from being a nation with its own government and a highly nationalist cult, to being a dispersed religious community (whether in Palestine or outside it) called Judaism. But the point is that Israel survived whereas others did not.

V

Why? What was Israel's dynamic identity source? It would have been (1) an indestructible element in society, (2) a commonly available element, (3) a highly adaptable element, and, if necessary, (4) a portable element. It would have been indestructible or the likelihood of its own survival in the midst of violence is precluded or greatly reduced. It would have been commonly available so that widely scattered segments of a remnant emerging from violence could consult it wherever they might be. It would have been adaptable so that it sponsored survival in new and strange situations and did not preclude it. And it would have been portable so that territory loss or forced emigration could not sever the community from the survival power it needed.

Obviously a temple, or an elaborate cult, fails all four tests, though a portable shrine (Exodus 25—40) meets (4), and perhaps (3). An ark meets (3) and (4) beautifully, and in small communities that stay together may do for (2). Tradition affirms that the ark served identity purposes in the midst of violence very well indeed in Israel's early days.

But only a story meets all four criteria. It is, to the exclusion of all other religious "vessels," indestructible, commonly available to scattered communities, highly adaptable, and portable in the extreme.

The primary characteristic of canon, therefore, is its adaptability. Israel's canon was basically a story adaptable to a number of different literary forms, adaptable to the varying fortunes of the people who found their identity in it, adaptable to widely scattered communities themselves adjusting to new or strange idioms of existence but retaining a transnational identity, and adaptable to a sedentary or migratory life.

It is in this sense, therefore, that the study of canon cannot begin where the handbooks now start, with stability and the concept of inclusion-exclusion. There was no set creed, like Deut. 26:5–9, that was expandable. But there was a story existing in many forms from early days. In all likelihood, there were a number of such stories, but the Law and the Prophets as we inherit them highlight two basic themes, those we call the Mosaic and the Davidic.[35] Only these survived, other traditions adhering to them; and only the Mosaic, less the conquest, became the Torah. The nature of such an identifying story demanded that it be told in the words and phrases and sense-terms of the generation and local community reciting it. Adaptability, therefore, is not just a characteristic; it is a compulsive part of the very nature of the canonical story. The story, in some part, is probably quite old, though no one *form* of it surviving in the Bible need of necessity be.[36] It is at least as old as Amos (Amos 2:9–11; 3:1–2; 4:10–11; 5:25; 9:7; cf. 6:5; 9:11). But it is Amos's use of the story, as we shall see, that precludes any thought of its being invented by him or later inserted into the text of Amos.[37]

The second, and equally important character of a canonical story, is its ability to give life as well as survive in itself. One can characterize survival in any phenomenon as adaptability. And so canon. But that is only a part of the truth of canon. Another part is that canon is canon not only because it survives but because it can give its survival power to the community that recites it. It not only has survival qualities for itself; it shares those life-giving qualities with the community that finds identity in it.

Life, therefore, is the supreme character of canon. It has it and it gives it. It provides survival with identity to those who "remember" and repeat it, either in the essential demands of peace or the existential threat of upheaval. It can provide continuity within discontinuity because it offers to the community an essential identity that permits the people to adapt. Israel's story undoubtedly served this function many times from her origins until the Torah was shaped definitely in the exile, and the Torah, as we know it, emerged therefrom. But its power for life was so crucial to the remnant in Babylon in the sixth century B.C.E. that there was surely burnt into the community memory, indelibly, the knowledge that Torah both had life and gave life. To this Judaism in its later literature many times attests (cf. John 5:39; *pirqê abot* 2:8; 6:7).[38] Professor Lewis Beck, of the University of Rochester, is an excellent example of the modern philosopher who has purposefully abandoned his Christian origins. Beck is one of the best of the anti-Christian polemicists today.[39] But Beck often points out that Judaism and Christianity simply cannot die. Even, he says, if earthlings should find life on a distant planet, the Bible religions would adapt to the new knowledge and probably flourish in it.

This is, in part, due to the high pluralism resident in the Bible.[40] But the qualities of survival and adaptability date from the earliest repetition of the story that became the essence or core of Israel's self-understanding. Wright's concept of there being in the Bible a canon within the canon is rather inescapable.[41] Brevard Childs has attacked the notion and argued for thinking of the Bible's authority in terms of the full canonical context.[42] I have argued that they are both right.[43] A canon-within-the-canon idea that does not perceive its high adaptability as essential, or as put above, a compulsive part of its nature, but too much relegates other parts of the final closed canon (such as the Jamnian) as of less power or authority, overlooks the dynamic nature of the canon's adaptability.[44] A crucial part of the canonical process, at all stages, were the historical accidents that caused the people to put certain questions to the traditions and not others. They did not rest back and, like scholars, make choices as to which questions they would ask of the story. Theirs was an existential dialogue, ongoing, of greater or lesser moment, and no question, no part of that dialogue was, at the moment, of less importance or had less power than another. A full-canonical-context idea about the Bible, however, that does not appreciate the life-giving qualities of the central tradition and its own nature of adaptability that ultimately afforded the vast pluralism in the Bible can be misunderstood as a kind of unfortunate biblicism.[45]

VI

A new method of approach to the question of the relation between the Old and New Testaments is called comparative midrash.[46] If one studies the various ways in which Second Temple Judaism contemporized OT traditions, one can actually trace the history of such midrashic tendency back into the

OT itself. In fact, since the older discipline of tradition criticism has begun to include in its purview the question of *why* a tradition would be repeated, or taken up again in another form, it has begun to sound more and more like the study of midrash.[47] This raises the question of what the difference between them (and redaction criticism in certain phases) actually is. Geza Vermes rightly says the difference is canonization.[48] But that difference needs clarifying.

As stressed above, certain traditions in ancient Israel bore repeating. Among these traditions, allowing for some aesthetic factor, the most important were those that told Israel's story about who she was and what her salient characteristics were.[49] Even stories that had little or nothing to do with Israel originally (such as common ancient Near Eastern myth, Canaanite legend, etc.) became attached to the growing number of such traditions. They were adapted by the fourfold process (where and when needed) of depolytheizing, monotheizing, Yahwizing, and Israelitizing. Sometimes one or more of these treatments did not take too well and the scholar today easily perceives beneath only a very slight veneer the original non-Israelite and polytheistic shape of the material. Some of this material shows up in the OT more than once, and is hence available for tradition-critical work on it. The moment one asks why such material bore repeating, however, he or she is engaged in the question of authority. Such material, which met a need in one situation, was apparently able to meet another need in another situation. And that is precisely the kind of tradition that becomes canonical—material that bears repeating in a later moment both because of the need of the later moment and because of the value or power of the material repeated (the dialogue between them).

Early material repeated in this manner attains the status of tradition. Eventually it may attain the status of canon. Only the traditional can become canonical. One of the very real existential factors in the canonical process is that of the value or power of tradition, that is, material that had proved its worth in more than one situation had already shown a measure of historical transcendence in its ability to address itself to two or more space-time parameters. One observation that impresses itself time and again in the study of history is that in crisis situations only the old, tried and true has any real authority. Nothing thought up at the last minute, no matter how clever, can effect the necessary steps of recapitulation and transcendence needed by the threatened community, if it is to survive with identity. A new story will not do; only a story with old, recognizable elements has the power for life required, because it somehow can pierce beneath the immediate and apparent changes taking place to recover the irreducible core of identity left unthreatened, that which can survive the crisis. The early canonical process was precisely one of selectivity of such materials, and the major factor of selectivity was existential. In this sense may the criteria of antiquity, inspiration, and popularity be understood.[50] The older material, which had already shown its value in more than one situation, had in effect proved its status of being inspired. And certainly no private story or tradition would measure up in the breach: it had to have been widespread, or at least not esoteric.

The relationship, therefore, between the older (tradition-critical) materials within the OT and the later midrashic use of those traditions, as well as of anything else available in the final canonical mass, is obviously very close indeed. To put it another way, one can extend tradition-critical study of the OT well into postbiblical times simply by continuing on without an artificial or arbitrary halt. In the same manner, the student of midrash can push his or her work back into the earlier biblical period simply by continuing on without an artificial or arbitrary halt, even though he or she may be invading the tradition critic's territory.

And what both disciplines find above all else, throughout the whole biblical and postbiblical period, is that the major characteristic of canonical material is its adaptability—not its rigidity. One of the major results of the new method of approach to early Jewish literature, including Qumran and the NT, is the observation that adaptation of canonical material to a midrashic need (the old problem of "inaccurate quotation" that lies outside even new observations about fluidity in text criticism), far from being impious, was a sign of the greater piety of the period—especially for eschatological groups.[51] In the long period before the marked tendency toward stabilization and standardization became the dominant trend among proto-rabbinic Jews, convictions about God's activity in their own time brought them frequently to adapt the available text to the conviction. Again the salient character of canon was adaptability. And this was indeed its major trait from the earliest "moment" far back up the line in the canonical process until the other need, that of stabilization, became the more dominant in the later period.[52]

Morton Smith, in a book on the canonical process, stresses the political factor in selectivity almost to the exclusion of all others.[53] The existential factor may be thought of, academically, in political terms. That is, whenever a community or society has a need of any sort and tries, through one or more of its influential members or groups, to meet that need, there is without question a political situation in the broad sense. The difficulty with Smith's thesis is that it reads back a situation of fragmentary politics of a later period in the late Iron Age problem of whether old Israel ought not to have passed from the scene of history the way some of her neighbors did.[54] That is an existential problem, a life-and-death situation that informs the political, if not transforms it. Smith's political theory also does not allow sufficient appreciation for the theological or mythic dimension in the exilic process of canonization; this is in contrast to the existential which underscores it. Smith's other major observation, however, is correct. We should assume that what we inherit in the OT is only a fraction of what had been available, and that they were the needs of the community that shaped the surviving, earlier traditions into the Bible as we know it. I would see the process, however, dating well back into preexilic times and concentrating in the all-encompassing life-and-death situation of the sixth century B.C.E., instead of, with Smith, as beginning in postexilic times, for the most part, and concentrating in Hellenistic times.[55]

If adaptability was an abiding character of the canonical process well into Hellenistic times, and was completely overcome by the need for uniformity and stability of text only finally in the period of Roman occupation,[56] then von Rad's inability, in the light of all the recent criticism, either to establish a single form for his credo or to prove its high antiquity linguistically, should occasion no surprise. A basic story about a migration from Egypt to Canaan under Yahweh's tutelage pervades much of the literature of the OT.[57] It would be utterly and completely foolhardy to gainsay that basic attainment of the work of the past generation. And it is with such traditions that the work of canonical criticism proceeds.

At the heart of canonical criticism will be not those introductory questions of source and unity that have so occupied the tradition critics, but rather the questions of the nature and function of the tradition cited. When a tradent is deposited in a particular situation, we must assume that it was found useful to that situation: it had a function to perform there and that is the reason it was called upon. At the heart of canonical criticism are the questions of the nature of authority and the hermeneutics by which that authority was marshaled in the situation where needed. What was the need of the community and how was it met?

VII

One of the remarkable observations one has to make about early biblical canonical materials is that the manner in which they were called upon to meet the people's need was not necessarily popular. On the contrary, there is much evidence in the biblical process to indicate that authoritative traditions were used in particular situations to challenge the way the majority of the people and their political representatives, the establishment, or any political group, thought their needs ought to be met. (Did the phenomenon of the lectionary arise for this reason?)

Partly in response to Smith's otherwise very logical and cogent theory,[58] and partly in response to George Mendenhall's otherwise engaging theory about the place of the prophets in his five-part *schema* of OT history,[59] the balance of this essay will center in the question of how the great judgmental prophets of ancient Israel marshaled the authority by which they declaimed their messages of pending change in Israel's basic self-understanding. Clearly Smith is right that "Yahweh-only" thinking won the day at the crucial junctures of Israel's history, and especially in the all-important exilic period, with respect to what finally became canon. But two decisive factors must not be overlooked in that process: (1) it won the day not because of some unknown political clout certain parties may have had, but because the theological view they espoused most met the existential needs arising out of historical circumstance; and (2) the Law and Prophets as they emerged through that process (even though not stabilized for some time to come) do not present a single clear-cut political program. This second point is as important as the first. The Bible is highly pluralistic. A few years back many scholars were looking for the unity of the Bible, or of the OT. They did not succeed. Today, the challenge for any student who thinks he or she has found a definite system, especially political program, in the Bible, is to return to the Bible and locate its contrapositive. Politicans can always proof text their position from the Bible. That is one of the reasons, the historian must avow, that the Bible has lasted so long. And whatever cannot be found there by one set of hermeneutic rules can almost certainly be located by another. This is the history of biblical interpretation, from the beginnings until today. And every party or denomination seeking authority in the Bible has been "right."

In Mendenhall's five-stage *schema* there is much that is still valid. He, resting his case largely on the work of William F. Albright, names the five stages thus: Praeparatio (the Bronze Age or Genesis period), the Creative (or Mosaic) period, the Adaptive (or tribal federation–monarchic) period, the Traditional (or prophetic) period, and the period of Reformation (or exilic and early postexilic era).

Much of what Mendenhall writes is in reaction to an earlier emphasis on the prophets having been the principal creative force in Israel's history as well as in the OT as a whole. He scores the thinking of Wellhausen that the prophets introduced ethical monotheism into the religion of Israel. A historian might well say that Mendenhall was responding to the Zeitgeist of the neo-orthodox period by reacting to the Zeitgeist of the liberal period.[60] Be that as it may, Mendenhall is right to attribute both the monotheizing process in Israel's history and the concern for ethics to the so-called Mosaic period. And he is right to insist that the prophets were dependent on authoritative traditions they inherited from the earlier period. What is questionable is his limiting their contribution to "the preservation and transmission of a tradition which was necessary to the preservation of the group." One needs to explore carefully his assertion that "in all the furor and violence of the whole period, there is no reason, no evidence, for the belief that anything important was added to the religious tradition." This is so in part because Mendenhall himself says, in the same section of his own work, "The prophets were proclaiming the necessity of change in the unchangeable," and again, ". . . the prophets added much of value to the tradition through their message to their own time."

The resolution between these apparent contradictions can perhaps be found in Mendenhall's claim that the message of the prophets "consisted largely of the fact that a group which was called into existence (chosen) to serve Yahweh ceased to have any excuse for being when it ceased to serve."[61] The difficulty with such an assertion can be found in recent work on the so-called false prophets, or establishment prophets. For it is now abundantly clear that the so-called false prophets relied on the same authoritative traditions as the so-called true prophets in propounding their message of no-change, or status quo, or continuity. They claimed that Israel was serving Yahweh. The utterly engaging aspect of current study of the false prophets is that their arguments, based in large measure on the same traditions from the exodus-wanderings-entrance story, were very cogent and compelling.[62] And they apparently won the day!

The "false" prophets could and did cite Israel's story to support their view that the Yahweh who had brought Israel out of Egypt could surely maintain her in Palestine. On the basis of the same authority the "true" prophets argued the opposite—that the Yahweh who brought Israel out of Egypt could also take her out of Palestine.[63] Hananiah chided Jeremiah for not having enough faith in Yahweh's power to sustain his people (Jer. 28:2–11). The "false" prophets must not be viewed as having been somehow intrinsically wrong. They too believed in the "presence of God" and interpreted that presence to mean providence for continuity (Micah 2:6; 3:11; Jer. 5:12; 14:9; Isa. 36:15). The story itself was adaptable to whatever hermeneutics employed. Hermeneutics must be historically viewed as arising out of the need to keep a stabilized tradition adaptable. The difference between the hermeneutics of continuity and the hermeneutics of discontinuity, that is, between the hermeneutics of *shalom* and of *milḥamah* (Jer. 28:8–9 and 38:4) lay not so much between the Mosaic and Davidic views of the covenant with Yahweh, as between theological axioms.[64] Both the true and the false prophets offered hope, but the former held the higher view of God (Jer. 23:23; cf. Isa. 22:11) that he could offer continuity even in radically altered forms of the common life, that is, he could give by taking away. Amos rested his whole view of the taking away (Amos 1:3—2:8) on the authority of what God had done for Israel in the beginning (Amos 2:9–11; 3:1–2), as did Hosea (11:1–5; 13:4–8). Micah rested his three-point sermon on what Yahweh required of Israel out of the same Torah story (Micah 6:3–5) of what it was Yahweh had done for Israel, while Isaiah cited God's grace to David on giving him Jerusalem, precisely to give authority to his message of judgment and salvation (Isa. 1:21–27; 5:1–7; 22:2; 28:4; 28:21; 29:1–7; 32:13 et passim).[65] And Ezekiel, who had a developed view of what the old story meant (chap. 20) could adapt it with no difficulty to drive home his message of judgment (chaps. 16 and 23). And it was the same Torah story that was called on to support the prophetic view of salvation in judgment (Hosea 2:16–17; Isa. 1:21–27; 32:1–18; 33:1–22; Jer. 16:14–15; 23:7–8; 31:31–34).[66]

VIII

The perspective that is needed here is that of canonical criticism. When would the criterion of "popularity," or widespread acceptance, have come to play in the case of the judgmental prophets? Manifestly not in the preexilic period. There can be no doubt that these prophets had followers, or even small schools, to preserve their material. The family of Shaphan, as well as Baruch, would have been essential at the point of earliest preservation of the Jeremiah materials. And we must posit such small continuing groups, perhaps schools, for the others from Amos on. But, in contradistinction to Smith's thesis, I cannot see these groups as forming a political movement or group. If so, they were not strong enough to prevent Jeremiah's being tried twice and imprisoned several times during the sieges of Jerusalem in the early sixth century.[67] A few continuing followers convinced enough to preserve (and adapt) the records of their masters' words and deeds is the most the evidence suggests.

When then did what the prophets had to say come to be perceived for its great value for Israel? Clearly the answer is the exile when what they had predicted occurred.[68] But even a prediction-fulfillment phenomenon is not sufficient to understand the canonical process so vigorously at work in the disintegrative experience of the national existence in the sixth and early fifth centuries. For some of what they predicted did not take place, and yet it too was preserved. The first step surely was the recognition in adversity that these men had been "right." But the next step in the process, gradually dawning on and pervading the consciousness of the remnant, was the really crucial one. And here is where the positive-thinking message of the old so-called false prophets when recalled would have turned to bitterness in their mouths. Both groups, so-called true and so-called false, had offered hope.[69] And they had both offered hope based on the old traditions about what God had done so effectively in the past. The great difference was that the judgmental prophets had offered an existential understanding of "Israel" that could survive the death of the body politic and that offered the means whereby a new corporate life could be accepted, though radically changed in form and venue.

The POWs in Babylon after 586 B.C.E., under either Babylonian or Persian hegemony, had two alternatives: life or death, not so much for themselves individually, but in terms of communal identity. They could pass from the scene the way others were doing—by assimilation to the dominant culture. There is a good bit in the Bible to suggest that this is what happened to many normal, rational Jews (Ps. 137:1–4; Ezek. 8:12–13; 18:25; 33:17, 20; Jer. 17:15; Isa. 40:27 et passim; Mal. 2:17). The evidence was in: Yahweh was bested in a fair fight. Israel's ancient Holy Warrior was defeated. One could not fly in the face of such proof as the utter defeat of Zedekiah's forces and the destruction of Jerusalem and the temple, especially the latter, afforded.

But a few, stunned and bewildered, asked a very crucial question: 'Ek-nihyeh? "How shall we live?" (Ezek. 33:10). In what now does life obtain? All the symbols of the covenant relation were gone. What now? A fugitive ran with the message all the way from crumbling Jerusalem to the camp where Ezekiel was interned with the awful message, "The city has fallen" (Ezek. 24:26; 33:21). Some say the news arrived the morning after Mrs. Ezekiel had died (Ezek. 24:18). Be that as it may, Ezekiel used the occasion of the passing of the "delight of his eyes" to speak of the passing of the temple, which Ezekiel called the delight of the eyes of the people (24:21; cf. 7:24; 16:24). They felt that as long as the temple was standing there was still hope. Therefore, when the impossible and unthinkable happened, that hope was dashed, and they turned to the resident, judgmental prophet with the question, "How shall we live?" Ezekiel answered it in the way we should have expected him to: Israel lives, moves, and has its being in the judgments of God (Ezek. 33:10–16).[70] But following the thinking of Jeremiah (31:29–34), and his own development of that thought (Ezekiel 18), Ezekiel stressed the responsibility of the individual in the new dispersed situation. Between the thinking of Jeremiah and Ezekiel in this regard, the exiles had a real vehicle for understanding "Israel" corporately. Each stressed individual responsibility, but in two different ways: Jeremiah horizontally, as it were, and Ezekiel vertically. Jeremiah's new covenant idea provided the means for understanding how Israel could be scattered in far-flung places and still be Israel: because each person would be responsible, wherever he or she was, for being "Israel." Thinking of an individual as standing for the whole, wherever he or she was, was already a part of royal tradition.[71] Ezekiel then stressed the vertical aspect of individual responsibility, by generations, as it were. He spoke of how the child would not suffer for the parent's sin, and indeed, how within a generation each person had to maintain rather strict obedience.

These two views of individual responsibility provided the means for Israel to be Israel in Diaspora.

It is clear that a great deal of reflection went on, in agonizing reappraisal, of what Israel meant now that the temple and "holy city" were gone. A number of exiles reflected on the old story, the old adaptable canon. Whether or not they recited the Deuteronomic *form* of the *Arami 'obed 'avi* we do not know. But they surely came very close to it: "Abraham was one man and came into possession of the land. We are many: therefore the land is surely (all the more so) ours" (Ezek. 33:24; cf. Isa. 51:2). I have inserted the expression in parentheses to indicate that this is a typical midrashic *qal vaḥomer* (argument from lesser to greater) or *argumentum a fortiori*. If the old story, or authoritative tradition, started out talking about one man (wandering and perishing), then the disintegrative experience of defeat and dispersion may not be the end but yet another beginning.

I am quite convinced that it was precisely this kind of reflective dialogue, as indicated in Ezekiel 33 and Isaiah 51, that formed the remnant in Babylon (cf. Hab. 2:4). These would have been the ones whom Deutero-Isaiah addressed as "those who know righteousness, the people in whose heart is my law" (Isa. 51:7)—as over against those whom he addressed as "stubborn of heart, far away from righteousness" (Isa. 46:12).[72] Those who knew righteousness were those who could recognize a righteousness, that is, a mighty act of God, when they saw one, and had been able to affirm the sovereignty of Yahweh in Israel's terrible adversity and upheaval. They were also those who, like the earlier prison mates of Ezekiel, reflected on God's initial work through Abraham (Isa. 41:8–9) and figured that if God had done such things with Abraham he could surely do them with a remnant folk who remembered God's mighty acts well enough that they could recognize a new one if they saw it (Isa. 52:8).

It is in the light of such agonizing reflection (Ezek. 4:17 et passim) that the canonical process with respect to the earlier judgmental prophets must be understood. When the positive-thinking message that God would never, no never, let them go, or let them down—precisely because he was powerful enough—had turned bitter to the decimated folk, and they had turned either to worship the gods of the Babylonians, or to engage in the traumatic reappraisal of their faith and experience, then a few also asked, I think, to hear the messages of those earlier prophets whom they had called *meshuga'im* (Jer. 29:26), madmen, unpatriotic, blasphemous, seditious, and traitorous. I imagine that at some point after Ezekiel had given his famous answer to their existential question, one of the inquirers (Ezek. 36:37; contrast 14:7), asked to hear once more what they had so recently called unpalatable. Was there not a disciple of Amos around the camps the other day talking that nonsense again? And disciples of Hosea, Micah, Isaiah, and the others? Let us hear it once more, now.

And with the new ears to hear and the new eyes to see (every religious and national symbol now gone) they perceived in a way they had never been able to understand before. Was it that the prophets had predicted this? Yes, that was surely a primary factor. But within that was a far deeper element. For the messages of the madmen of God now offered a hope which no simple, magical prediction could possibly afford. For what they had said could not be fully appreciated until in the canonical process of agonizing reflection they were "heard" by many for what was existentially the first time: God was in charge of the adversity; God was challenging Israel's basic self-understanding; God was re-forming his Israel (Jer 18:1–11) and reshaping his people into a new Israel (Ezekiel 36—37). Those who embraced such an outrageous program before the discontinuity took place were viewed as traitorous, seditious, blasphemous, and mad. Does God want only masochists? But after the old national vessel had been broken to smithereens (Isa. 30:13–14), two options were open: either to join the First Church of Marduk (assimilate) or in agony to reflect on Israel's basic identity. To ask, who are we and what are we to do?

It was then also that the anticultic and antiroyalist strictures of the judgmental prophets made "canonical" sense. What the prophets had kept saying, in effect, was that the cultic and royal institutions and practices did not derive from the Torah *mythos*, that is, they were unauthorized by the tradition the prophets adhered to (Amos 5:25; Hosea 8:4 et passim; Micah 6:6–7; Isa. 1:12–17; Jer. 7:22; etc.) as authoritative.[73] In the preexilic period that simply represented one of two points of view that one might hold: either cult (as practiced) and palace were authentic and properly authorized in Israelite society, or they were not. But in the period of intensive canonical process these strictures took on a much different meaning. When you are a POW pondering the awful experience of destitution, and are squarely facing the choice of whether your identity as "Israel" should live or die, then the prophetic strictures provide a means of survival as Israel, without temple or palace. If they did not derive from the Torah story (preconquest) period, then they were not *essential* to identity. The community need not lose its identity because they were lacking. Because certain prophets had been saying this even when those institutions stood, their words bore all the more power for survival to those in destitution. *If need be*, Israel could be Israel even if reduced to one destitute man (Abraham, servant, Job, Christ). That this is canonical does not mean that Israel *should* be one destitute man, but it does mean that "Israel" can survive calamity with identity. The canon is adaptable to the worst and the best. It is for life.

IX

It is as though the old story, as well as the preexilic prophetic interpretations of it, were most vital in the death-and-resurrection experience of the exile.[74] That was the crucible for the old traditions, in which those that really spoke to the people's existential problems of identity and life style became the core of the canon. If one thinks of all that we have called the Yahwist tradition or cycle of materials (including both the Mosaic and Davidic traditions) out of the monarchical period of preexilic Israel, then the Torah as it received its basic shaping (neither its creation nor its final form) is surprisingly apocopated: it is all preconquest.[75] But it is precisely a Torah that would have offered life to a dispersed Israel, a transforming Israel, an emerging Judaism. The Joshua materials about the conquest are left to be the first book of the Prophets, a hope integral to Judaism and all it meant, but not a part of the basic canon within the canon—not in the Torah. This is the greatest surprise of the canonical process, since none of von Rad's or Wright's ancient recitals lacks the conquest as part of the confession. But it is understandable that it could be the new Israel anywhere at all. This did not preclude a return. Far from it. The return has been an integral part of the hope of Judaism.

From this point the canonical process continued. Whatever Ezra brought back with him from Babylonia, it was surely the essential Torah (though not yet closed) as we know it (Neh. 8:1–12). It had been shaped by and edited in the agonizing reflection, and out of the existential questions, of the crucible of exile. The major judgmental prophets were gathered, read, and reread in the light of the new perspective of the shedding of false hopes that the crucible provided. The canon of the prophets was not closed until much, much later. It is becoming more and more difficult to suggest a probable date for its closure, but the basic gestalt of the Law and the Prophets was being formed in the crucible.[76] Not only had some of the old traditions (some, but by no means all) survived, but they survived because they offered life in that crucial time. It was the old story reviewed in the shedding experience of exile that infused slain Israel with the spirit of life of which Ezekiel spoke (37:6). The whole of the passage on resurrection in Ezekiel 37 is told with the covenantal verbs of the old Exodus story (37:1, 2, 5–6, 11–14).[77] No one in antiquity who heard him would have missed the point Ezekiel was making: if Yahweh had created himself a people out of slaves in Egypt, he was now creating himself a renewed Israel. His use of those verbs was his authority for his idea of the resurrection.

It was surely in this same period that other old traditions took on new vibrant meaning: an old story about child sacrifice; whatever else Genesis 22 had said originally or in the preexilic period, it now said that the God who had given Isaac to the aged Abraham and the barren Sarah had every right to ask for him back; but instead, he gave the child a second time. Such a story, no matter what form criticism and source criticism can show it originally meant, to the exiles surely meant that the future of the believing community, of Israel, the question of the continuation of the people, the anxiety about whether there would be another generation, rested in the hands of the life-giver, of him who gives and gives again.[78] And no matter what form- and source-criticism can show the Garden of Eden story originally meant, to the exiles it was viewed in the light of their own expulsion from the garden of Canaan (Ezek. 36:35–36; cf. Isa. 5:1–7; Jer. 11:16–17; 12:10; Ezek. 28:12–19; Isa. 27:2–5). And no matter what must or must not be said about a Bronze Age Abraham, to the exiles when the canonical process was most decisively at work, he meant God's starting again: "Abraham was one man . . ." (Ezek. 33:23–29; Isa. 51:2).

Adaptability and stability. That is canon. Each generation reads its authoritative tradition in the light of its own place in life, its own questions, its own necessary hermeneutics. This is inevitable. Around this core were gathered many other materials, as time went on, adaptable to it.[79] There are many contradictions within the Bible; it is a highly pluralistic document. Hence, no tyranny can be established on its basis, for there is always something in it to challenge whatever is constructed on it. Its full context is very broad and very wide and sponsors serious dialogue.[80] No single program, political, social, economic, or otherwise can escape the challenge of something in it. As the rabbis say, in another context, "It is the book with everything in it." There appears to be only one certainly unchallenged affirmation derivable from it: a monotheizing tradition that emerges through the canonical process. It gives the impression that Israel always doggedly pursued the integrity or sovereignty of God, his oneness.[81] The Bible is replete with polytheism often only thinly veiled. But it was finally the affirmation of the old Mosaic story, as well as the judgmental-prophetic insistence on it, that God is one, both Judge and Savior, saving as he judges, that afforded the true hope that disintegrated Israel in exile needed *lemiḥyah*, for life (Gen. 45:5; Ezra 9:8–9). It is abundantly clear that once the crisis had passed and Judaism was established, internal, normal, fractious politics came once more to the fore in the decision-making process. But by that time the existential experience of death and resurrection had burned itself forever into the cultic memory of Judaism. Torah was for life.[82] And that, in the final analysis, is the authority of canon.

NOTES

1. In a manner of speaking George Ernest Wright has been doing this, from his perspective of a canon within the canon, all along. If one reviews his published work in biblical theology from 1937 to the present one witnesses a process at work: "Exegesis and Eisegesis in the Interpretation of Scripture," *ExpTim* 48 (1937): 353–57; "The Terminology of OT Religion and Its Significance," *JNES* 1 (1942): 404–14; "How Did Early Israel Differ from Her Neighbors?" *BA* 6 (1943): 1–10, 13–20; *The Challenge of Israel's Faith* (Chicago: Univ. of Chicago Press, 1944); "Neo-Orthodoxy and the Bible," *JBR* 14 (1946): 87–93; "Interpreting the OT," *TToday* 3 (1947): 176–91; "The Christian Interpreter as Biblical Critic," *Int.* 1 (1947): 131–52; *The OT Against Its Environment* (London: SCM Press, 1950); "The Unity of the Bible," *Int.* 5 (1951): 131–33, 304–17; *God Who Acts* (Chicago: Henry Regnery, 1952); "Wherein Lies the Unity of the Bible?" *JBR* 20 (1952): 194–98; *The Biblical Doctrine of Man in Society* (London: SCM Press, 1954); "The Unity of the Bible," *JRT* 13 (1955): 5–19; "The Unity of the Bible," *SJT* 8 (1955): 337–52; with R. H. Fuller, *The Book of the Acts of God* (Garden City, N.Y.: Doubleday & Co., 1957); *The Rule of God* (Garden City, N.Y.: Doubleday & Co., 1960); "History and Reality: The Importance of Israel's 'Historical' Symbols for the Christian Faith," in *The OT and Christian Faith*, ed. B. W. Anderson (New York: Harper and Row, 1963), 176–99; *The OT and Theology* (New York: Harper & Row, 1969).

A beginning on a history of the canonical process is attempted in J. A. Sanders, *Torah and Canon* (1972). From a different perspective but congruous in certain presuppositions and basic theses is Morton Smith's *Palestinian Parties and Politics that Shaped the OT* (New York: Columbia Univ. Press, 1971). From the NT perspective see Albert C. Sundberg, Jr., *The OT of the Early Church*, HTS 20 (Cambridge: Harvard Univ. Press, 1964); idem, "The 'OT'; A Christian Canon," *CBQ* 30 (1968): 143–55; idem, "Toward a Revised History of the NT Canon," *SE* (1968): 452–61. The trend of discussion on canon in NT can be seen in N. Appel, *Kanon und Kirche*, KKTS 9 (Paderborn: Bonifacius-Druckerei, 1965); Ernst Käsemann, "The Canon of the NT and the Unity of the Church," in *Essays on NT Themes* (London: SCM Press, 1964), 95–107; and esp. in Ernst Käsemann, ed., *Das Neue Testament als Kanon* (Göttingen: Vandenhoeck & Ruprecht, 1970). Käsemann's own contributions to the latter (pp. 336–410) are especially valuable. I would still insist that the problem of whether the OT was Christian did not arise in the church until the second century C.E. The problem of the first century, and hence of the NT, was whether the NT was biblical, i.e., whether God really had done another righteousness, in Christ. Brevard S. Childs, while intensely and rightly interested in the nature and function of canon, is not primarily interested in a history of the early canonical process; see below nn. 43–45.

2. Johann Salomo Semler, *Abhandlung von freier Untersuchung des Canon*, 2d ed. (1776). Cf. Gottfried Hornig, *Die Anfänge der historisch-kritischen Theologie; Johann Salomo Semlers Schriftverständnis und seine Stellung zu Luther* (Göttingen, 1961); and Wolfgang Schmittner, *Kritik und Apologetik in der Theologie J. S. Semlers* (1963).

3. Robert H. Pfeiffer, *Introduction to the OT*, 2d ed. (New York: Harper & Row, 1948), 50–70; cf. his article in the *IDB*, s.v. "Canon of the OT."

4. See J. A. Sanders, "Cave 11 Surprises and the Question of Canon" (1969). The real value of the very flaccid references in the Ben Sira prologue, in Philo (*De vita contemplativa* 25), and Luke 24:44, must now be reviewed in the light of present evidence. See the excellent remarks of B. J. Roberts in his review of my *Discoveries in the Judaean Desert*, vol. 4 (Oxford: Clarendon Press, 1965) in *JTS* 18 (1967): 185, in this regard, contra his earlier thesis in "The OT Canon: A Suggestion," *BJRL* 46 (1963): 164–78. Cf. P. R. Ackroyd, "The Open Canon," *Colloquium: The Australian*

and New Zealand Theological Review 3 (1970): 279–91. For an early pre-Christian date of closure and a very conservative reconstruction of the meager available evidence in the light of it, see Roger Beckwith, *The OT Canon of the NT Church* (Grand Rapids: Wm. B. Eerdmans, 1985).

5. I here reaffirm my judgment as stated in "Cave 11 Surprises," 106–9—to dismiss 11QPs^a as the earliest example of a Jewish prayer book is unwarranted: the Psalter itself, in whatever early form, is the earliest example of a Jewish prayer book. To the evidence adduced in "Cave 11 Surprises," 105 n. 10, see now other evidence, especially from 4QIsa^c, adduced by Jonathan P. Siegel, "The Employment of Palaeo-Hebrew Characters for the Divine Name at Qumran in the Light of Tannaitic Sources," *HUCA* 42 (1971): 159–72.

6. On the dating of individual psalms by linguistic criteria see the recent work of Avi Hurvitz of Hebrew University. In regard to the larger question of text transmission see F. M. Cross, Jr., "The History of the Biblical Text in the Light of the Discoveries in the Judaean Desert," *HTR* 57 (1964): 281–99; idem, "The Contribution of the Discoveries at Qumran to the Study of the Biblical Text," *IEJ* 16 (1966): 81–95; S. Talmon, "Aspects of the Textual Transmission of the Bible in the Light of the Qumran Manuscripts," *Textus* 4 (1964): 95–132. What is really needed now, as I tried to point out in my "Text Criticism and the NJV Torah" (*JAAR* 39 [1971]: 193–97), is a critical review of method in text criticism—actually how to make a judgment in "establishing the text." This is sharply indicated now by the work of the Hebrew University Bible Project and the International Old Testament Text Critical Committee of the United Bible Societies as over against the results now emerging in the fascicles of the *BHS*.

7. See Jack P. Lewis, "What Do We Mean by Jabneh?" *JBR* 32 (1964): 125–32.

8. See the work of Jacob Neusner, including *Development of a Legend: Studies on the Traditions Concerning Yohanan ben Zakkai* (Leiden: E. J. Brill, 1970) and *The Rabbinic Traditions about the Pharisees before 70*, 3 parts (Leiden: E. J. Brill, 1971).

9. J. A. Sanders, *The Dead Sea Psalms Scroll* (Ithaca, N.Y.: Cornell Univ. Press, 1967), 157–59.

10. Sanders, *Torah and Canon*, ix–xx.

11. See Dominique Barthélemy, "Les tiqqunê sopherîm et la critique textuelle de l'A.T." VTSup. 9 (1962): 283–304.

12. See the pivotal article by Renée Bloch in *DBSup.*, s.v. "Midrash." Parenthetically, it should be noted that because it is the nature of canonical or authoritative communal traditions that they are adaptable to the needs of the ongoing communities, computer analyses of style are limited in value for determining authorship which do not use for control data literature (1) that is not canonical and (2) of absolutely known single authorship.

13. Pseudepigraphal studies have received a new impetus both in this country and abroad in the past ten years. See A. M. Denis, *Introduction aux pseudépigraphes grece de l'A.T.* (Leiden: E. J. Brill, 1970), ix–xx.

14. *Pace* L. Finkelstein, "The Maxim of the Anshe Keneset ha-Gedolah," *JBL* 59 (1940): 455–69; cf. Sidney B. Hoenig, *The Great Sanhedrin* (New York: Bloch Pub., 1953). This is not to deny the need to explain what Finkelstein cites as his evidence, e.g., *ARNA*, folio 65 n. 23 in S. Schechter's edition of Vienna, 1887; see Judah Goldin, ed., *The Fathers According to Rabbi Nathan*, YJS 10 (New Haven: Yale Univ. Press; London: Oxford Univ. Press, 1955).

15. See the trenchant article on the complex situation with the Enoch materials by J. T. Milik, "Problèmes de la littérature hénochique à la lumière des fragments araméens de Qumrân," *HTR* 64 (1971): 333–78.

16. Otto Eissfeldt, *The OT: An Introduction* (New York: Harper & Row, 1965), 560.

17. Aage Bentzen, *Introduction to the OT*, 2d ed., 2 vols. (Copenhagen, 1952), 24.

18. Gunnar Östborn, *Tōrā in the OT* (Lund: Ohlssons, 1945), and idem, *Cult and Canon*, UUÅ 10 (Uppsala: Lundequistska, 1950).

19. See Albrecht Alt, "The God of the Fathers," in *Essays on OT History and Religion* (Oxford: Basil Blackwell & Mott, 1966); O. Eissfeldt, "El and Yahweh," *JSS* 1 (1956): 35ff.; F. M. Cross, Jr., "Yahweh and the God of the Patriarchs," *HTR* 55 (1962): 225–59; idem, "The Divine Warrior in Israel's Early Cult," in *Biblical Motifs*, ed. A. Altmann (Cambridge: Harvard Univ. Press, 1966); and Wright, *OT and Theology*, 70–150. From a different perspective, see Morton Smith, "The Common Theology of the ANE," *JBL* 71 (1952): 135–47.

20. Sanders, *Torah and Canon*, 31ff.

21. G. von Rad, *Das formgeschichtliche Problem des Hexateuchs* (1938); ET: *The Problem of the Hexateuch and Other Essays* (New York: McGraw-Hill, 1966), 1–78.

22. Wright, *God Who Acts*. Wright has clarified his confessional position vis-à-vis the systematic approach of Eichrodt on the one hand, and the form-critical approach of von Rad on the other, in *OT and Theology;* see my review of the latter in *Int.* 24 (1970): 359–68.

23. Wright and Fuller, *Book of the Acts of God*.

24. Martin Noth, *Überlieferungsgeschichte des Pentateuch* (1948); ET: *A History of Pentateuchal Traditions* (Sheffield: JSOT Press, 1972). The ET is admirably done by B. W. Anderson. He has enhanced the volume with a critical introduction (pp. xiii–xxii) and an analytical outline of the Pentateuch based on the source-critical and tradition-critical methods combined (pp. 261–76).

25. See, e.g., J. P. Hyatt's "Were There an Ancient Historical Credo in Israel and an Independent Sinai Tradition?" in *Translating and Understanding the OT* (H. G. May Festschrift), ed. H. T. Frank and W. W. Reed (Nashville: Abingdon Press, 1970), 152–70. In addition to the criticism of Artur Weiser, C. H. W. Breckelmans, Leonhard Rost, Georg Fohrer (ibid., 156–65), and Calvin Carmichael (ibid., 169–70), see now Lothar Perlitt, *Bundestheologie im AT* (1969), and Norbert Lohfink, "Zum 'kleinen geschichtlichen Credo' Dtn 26, 5–9," *ThPh* 46 (1971): 19–39. Lohfink's is perhaps the most thoroughgoing critique of the lot. Note also Lohfink's felicitous emphasis on the Nachleben, or continuing life, of a tradition. Hyatt's argument ("Ancient Historial Credo," 168) that Judaism "came to consider its confession of faith as embodied in the Shema ˙ . . . and . . . the Shema ˙ in the narrow sense says nothing about a saving act in history; only in Num. 15:14 . . ." is something of a tour de force. It is the same sort of observation as that of Sinai's not being mentioned in the recitals. The centrality to Judaism of the Torah *mythos* can be seen in Nehemiah 9, Daniel 9, and throughout the Jewish prayer book. Is it possible to have a synagogue service without mention of it? Cf. Judah Goldin, *The Song at the Sea* (New Haven: Yale Univ. Press, 1971).

26. On OT catecheses see J. A. Soggin, "Kultätiologische Sagen und Katechese im AT," *VT* 10 (1960): 341–47; P. Laaf, *Die Pascha-Feier Israels* (1970); and J. Loza, "Les Catéchèses étiologiques dans l'AT," *RB* 78 (1971): 481–500.

27. But this means only that the story was adaptable to seventh/sixth-century idiom, not that Deuteronomy created the story.

28. Artur Weiser, *Einleitung in das AT* (1948); ET: *The OT: Its Formation and Development* (New York: Association Press, 1961), 81–99.

29. The term *mythos* is chosen to avoid the problems of other words used to date. But I do not thereby wish to prejudice the question of historicity. So far as I am concerned Israel's *mythos* was at base historical. See Brevard S. Child's *Myth and Reality in the OT* (London: SCM Press, 1960), 101–2, and Wright, *OT and Theology*, 39–69. I should really prefer the word "gospel," but since the form-critical study of "gospel" continues to be in a muddle one simply cannot use it. Dennis McCarthy's suggestion of "commonplace" (from Greek rhetoric, *topos*) in "What Was Israel's Historical Creed?" (*LexTQ* 4 [1969]: 46–53), is a possibility, but not immediately

appealing. I prefer the manner in which Jacob Neusner uses the term "Torah-myth": see Jacob Neusner, *History and Torah* (New York: Schocken Books, 1965); idem, *The Way of Torah: An Introduction to Judaism* (Belmont, Calif.: Dickenson, 1970); and idem, *There We Sat Down* (Nashville: Abingdon Press, 1972). See also the way Amos Wilder uses "story" as the means of God's speaking and the typically biblical medium of man's relating God's actions, in *The Language of the Gospel* (New York: Harper & Row, 1964), 64ff. Martin Buber used the word "myth" in the way I mean it in his *Legend of the Baal-Shem* (New York: Harper & Brothers, 1955), xi: "The Jews are a people that has never ceased to produce myth. . . . The religion of Israel has at all times felt itself endangered by this stream, but it is from it, in fact, that Jewish religiousness has at all times received its inner life." The thesis being advanced by F. M. Cross, Jr., and Paul D. Hanson, that ancient Near Eastern myth was, according to the period and the needs of the community, more or less historicized, is not, I think, contradicted by this use of the word *mythos:* cf. Hanson, "Jewish Apocalyptic Against Its Near Eastern Environment," *RB* 78 (1971): 31–58; idem, "OT Apocalyptic Reexamined," *Int.* 25 (1971): 454–79; idem, "Zechariah 9 and the Recapitulation of an Ancient Ritual Pattern," *JBL* 92 (1973): 37–59.

If Immanuel Kant and Max Weber described Western humanity's maturity as transition from *mythos* to *logos*, and a process of rationalization of thought processes and structures (cf. Thomas O'Dea, *The Sociology of Religion* [Englewood Cliffs, N.J.: Prentice-Hall, 1966], 41–47), then it must be admitted that there are many forces today contradicting the truth or validity of that transition as maturation. One thinks of the sociologists of knowledge (Karl Mannheim, Peter Burger, Thomas Luckmann), on the one hand, and the structural anthropologists on the other, especially the work of Claude Lévi-Strauss, *Structural Anthropology* (New York: Basic Books, 1963), and of his student Francois Lacan; cf. Roland Barthes et al., *Analyse structurale et exégèse biblique* (Neuchâtel: Delachaux et Niestlé, 1972). From another direction there is also the work of Joseph Campbell, as in his *Myths to Live By* (New York: Viking Press, 1972).

30. J. A. Sanders, "Dissenting Deities and Philippians 2:1–11," *JBL* 88 (1969): 279–90 n. 12.

31. Sanders, *Torah and Canon*, 36–53.

32. Extreme caution should be used in treating ancient Near Eastern parallels to biblical material; the one has only in modern times been retrieved from some very ancient and remote moment in antiquity while the other is embodied in a canonical and cultic collection that has survived the "repetition" and handling of many generations, before becoming stabilized in the form we have it. The former might possibly be an autograph; the latter could never be. But more important still, precisely because the biblical material has been passed down through many generations of cultic usage, it has had to pass all sorts of tests (precisely of its adaptability-stability quotient) in that canonical process to which the other may never, or only rarely, have been submitted.

33. The relation of some of these assimilating survivors, the "enemies of Judah" and "the people of the land" (of Ezra 4), to the Samaritans of later date is still problematic.

34. Cf. John S. Holladay, "Assyrian Statecraft and the Prophets of Israel," *HTR* 63 (1970): 29–51.

35. Leonhard Rost, "Sinaibund und Davidsbund," *ThLZ* 72 (1947): cols 129ff.; Gerhard von Rad, *OT Theology*, 2 vols. (New York: Harper & Row, 1962, 1965), 1:308ff.; Murray Newman, *The People of the Covenant* (Nashville: Abingdon Press, 1962).

36. Even Leonhard Rost in his critique of Gerhard von Rad (*Das kleine Credo und andere Studien zum AT* [1965], 11–25) admits the antiquity of some parts of the summary.

37. Amos 2:9–11 is an integral part of Amos's address in 1:3—3:2 (though other parts of the pericope may conceivably be from later hands; Shalom Paul, "Amos 1:3—2:3: A Concatenous Literary Pattern," *JBL* 90 [1971]: 397–403). The argument of the "sermon" is clearly that though Yahweh had taken Israel's head out of the dust of the earth of Egypt and set her in a land of her own, Israel, when established in the land, instead of acting as indicated by Yahweh's acts in Egypt, treated the poor of the land as Pharaoh had treated her. The function of the *mythos* was to provide a basic identity and life-style pattern for Israel in terms of her own responsibility.

38. John 5:39 uses the expression *tas graphas* (the writings). In *OT of the Early Church*, A. C. Sundberg attempts to distinguish between "scriptures" and canon in his cogent thesis that the canons of both the OT and NT were fluid until dates considerably later than generally assigned.

39. Cf. Lewis White Beck, *Philosophic Inquiry* (Englewood Cliffs, N.J.: Prentice-Hall, 1952), and idem, *Six Secular Philosophers* (New York: Harper & Brothers, 1960).

40. Sanders, *Torah and Canon*, xff. and 116ff.

41. This is Wright's major thesis about the canon. Eissfeldt uses the same expression in *Introduction*, 568.

42. Brevard S. Childs, *Biblical Theology in Crisis* (Philadelphia: Westminster Press, 1970). Two very instructive responses to Childs's book are by George M. Landes, "Biblical Exegesis in Crisis: What Is the Exegetical Task in a Theological Context?" *USQR* 26 (1971): 273–98, and B. W. Anderson, "Crisis in Biblical Theology," *TToday* 28 (1971): 321–27.

43. J. A. Sanders's review of Childs's *Biblical Theology in Crisis* in *USQR* 26 (1971): 299–304, and of Wright's *OT and Theology* in *Int.* 24 (1970): 359–68. Childs's position was anticipated in part in my "Habakkuk in Qumran, Paul and the OT" (*JR* 39 [1959]: 232–44). Similar kinds of probing may be seen in James Barr's *Old and New in Interpretation* (New York: Harper & Row, 1966; rev. ed., 1985), 149–200; Norbert Lohfink, "Die historische und christliche Auslegung des AT," in *Bibelauslegung im Wandel* (1967), 185–213; and Peter Stuhlmacher, "Neues Testament und Hermeneutik Versuch einer Bestandsaufnahme," *ZThK* 68 (1971): 121–61.

44. Wright states its adaptability, obliquely, in relativistic terms in his *OT and Theology*, 183–85.

45. George Ernest Wright's criticism of Brevard S. Childs ("Historical Knowledge and Revelation," in *Translating and Understanding the OT,* ed. Frank and Reed, 298) is surely, in part, misunderstanding.

46. See Bloch, "Midrash"; Roger le Déaut, "Apropos a Definition of Midrash," *Int.* 25 (1971): 259–82; and Merrill P. Miller, "Targum, Midrash and the Use of the OT in the NT," *JSJ* 2 (1971): 29–82. See now Geza Vermes, "Bible and Midrash: Early OT Exegesis," in *The Cambridge History of the Bible*, 1:199–231. James Barr ("Le Judaisme postbiblique et la théologie de l'AT," *RThPh* [1968]: 209–17), seems unaware of some of this new thrust.

47. See in this regard the probing study by E. W. Nicholson on the prose material in Jeremiah composed by disciples in *Preaching to the Exiles* (New York: Schocken Books, 1971); see also his *Deuteronomy and Tradition* (Philadelphia: Fortress Press, 1967). Similarly see Gunther Wanke, *Untersuchungen zur sogenannten Baruchschrift* (1971).

48. Vermes, "Bible and Midrash," 199; see also Roberts, "The OT Canon"; but see above, n. 4.

49. This is, of course, the nature of the patriarchal blessings, Gen. 27:27–29 and 39–40; Genesis 49; and Deuteronomy 33. This appears to be the function of Melchizedek's blessing of Abraham in Gen. 14:19–20. And it should be noted that the final or redactional form of the Book of Deuteronomy (hence, the Torah?) is that of a patriarchal blessing.

50. Josephus *Against Apion* 1.38–42.

51. This is a major, axiomatic observation of work in Jewish exegesis clearly datable to the early Jewish period. See the works cited in n. 46, as well as B. J. Roberts, "Bible Exegesis and Fulfillment in Qumran," in *Words and Meanings* (D. W. Thomas Fest-schrift), ed. P. R. Ackroyd and B. Lindars (New York and Cambridge: Cambridge Univ. Press, 1968), 195–207.

52. See the works of S. Talmon, esp. "Aspects of the Textual Transmission of the Bible"; and "The OT Text," in *The Cambridge History of the Bible*, 1:159–99; Dominique Barthélemy, *Les Devanciers d'Aquila* (Leiden: E. J. Brill, 1963); F. M. Cross, Jr., "History of the Biblical Text"; and Sanders, *Dead Sea Psalms Scroll*, 157–59.

53. Smith, *Palestinian Parties and Politics*.

54. Smith's thesis fits well into the situation as we know it in the Persian and Hellenistic periods (those parallel to the Golden and Hellenistic periods in the Greek culture). See his contributions in the *Fischer Weltgeschichte* (1965) I and II. And there were surely religious parties (*Palestinian Parties and Politics*, 15–56) in the preexilic period. But Smith practically ignores the period all-important for the canonical process—the crucible of destitution and exile where the existential factor over-shadowed all factious politics. See Smith's brilliant chapter on Hellenization, ibid., 57–81.

55. The most challenging section of Smith's book is the chapter on Nehemiah (*Palestinian Parties and Politics*, 126–47). I think it will cause a major review of our understanding of the work of Ezra and Nehemiah. Most scholars agree that the Torah Ezra brought with him from Babylonia to Jerusalem was essentially (though still unclosed, or adaptable) the Pentateuch. Smith thinks not. He argues that what is reported in Nehemiah 8 violates pentateuchal regulations on Yom Kippur, and assigns the stabilization of the Torah to the period 330–180 B.C.E. (ibid., 187) to combat the "assimilationists." I would still hold that the Torah received its *shape* in the exilic period due to the existential question there faced and that what Ezra brought from Babylon to Jerusalem was the Torah (though not yet closed) very much as we know it: cf. Sanders, *Torah and Canon;* D. N. Freedman, "The Law and the Prophets," VTSup. 9 (1963): 250–65; and P. R. Ackroyd, *Exile and Restoration* (Philadelphia: Westminster Press, 1968), esp. 201–37.

56. Dynamically, adaptability and stability work hand in hand: it is only a question of which is needed the more in given historical circumstances. D. Barthélemy's thesis that *tiqqunê sopherîm* were halted in the period of Salome Alexandra, when her-meneutics could begin to shift to noncontextual techniques, is a parallel observation; cf. Barthélemy, "Les tiqqunê sopherîm."

57. There is no room or need to list all the passages: cf. von Rad, *Problem of the Hexateuch*, 3ff.; Noth, *History of Pentateuchal Traditions*, 46ff.; Wright, *God Who Acts*, 70ff.; J. A. Sanders, *The OT in the Cross* (New York: Harper & Row, 1961); D. R. Hillers, *Covenant: The History of a Biblical Idea* (Baltimore and London: John Hopkins Press, 1969); Klaus Baltzer, *The Covenant Formulary* (Philadelphia: Fortress Press, 1971). Even criticisms of von Rad (largely from the Georg Fohrer school) confirm the point here made: cf. J. Vollmer, *Geschichtliche Rückblicke und Motive in der Prophetie des Amos, Hosea and Jesaja* (1971).

58. There is a lack of clarity in Smith between the *shaping* of traditions in the postexilic period and the creation of literary materials in the same period. Shades of Wellhausen's reconstruction of the literary history of the OT lie scattered on Smith's otherwise valid thesis about shaping. Cf. J. Wellhausen, *Prologomena to the History of Ancient Israel* (1885).

59. G. E. Mendenhall, "Biblical History in Transition," in *The Bible and the ANE*, ed. G. E. Wright (Garden City, N.Y.: Doubleday & Co., 1965), 27–58.

60. Mendenhall himself rightly stresses the limitations of past scholarship in this regard, ibid., 28. I could not agree more if we, too, in our generation, recognize our

being children of our own time and not pretend to be free of Zeitgeist ourselves: cf. Eccl. 3:11. W. F. Albright in his great wisdom advised his students of archaeology to leave more of a tell intact than dug because the next generation will have a different perspective, and perhaps improved tools. The Reform principle of learning God's truth for any age and situation through Word *and* Spirit is a classical recognition of the canon's adaptability.

61. All these quotations are from ibid., 46–48.

62. The most arresting of recent studies on the false prophets is that of Adam van der Woude, "Micah in Dispute with the Pseudo-prophets," *VT* 19 (1969): 244–60. Earlier valuable studies include G. Quell, *Wahre und falsche Propheten* (Gütersloh: Bertelsmann, 1952); E. Jacob, "Quelques remarques sur les faux prophètes," *ThZ* 23 (1957): 47; Eva Osswald, *Falsche Prophetie im AT* (Tübingen: J. C. B. Mohr [Paul Siebeck], 1962); J. Fichtner, *RGG*³, 5:621–22; Rolf Rendtorff, "Erwägungen aus Frühgeschichte zur Prophetentums in Israel," *ZThK* 59 (1962): 145–67; R. E. Clements, *Prophecy and Covenant* (London: SCM Press, 1965), 11–44, 119–29; Barr, *Old and New in Interpretation*, 149–70; D. N. Freedman, "The Biblical Idea of History," *Int.* 21 (1967): 32–49. A fair review of the problem in terms of cultic prophecy is Jörg Jeremias, *Kultprophetie und Gerichtsverkündigung in der späten Königszeit Israels* (1970), cf. esp. 192–93 on the hermeneutic difference between true and false prophets. T. W. Overholt, *The Threat of Falsehood* (London: SCM Press, 1970), provides a good introduction to the whole problem by concentrating on *sheqer* in Jeremiah.

63. The "true" prophets had two bases or references of authority: (1) their own call and (2) Israel's call (the Torah *mythos*); cf. Sanders, *Torah and Canon*, 73ff. We should assume that the "false" prophets did as well.

64. John Bright's view of this, especially in Isaiah, needs critique. Cf. *A History of Israel* (Philadelphia: Westminster Press, 1959), 271ff. I am convinced that Isaiah interpreted the Davidic covenant as conditional to the sovereign will of Yahweh without combining it with the Mosaic: Isa. 1:21–27 and chaps. 28—31 offer ample evidence of this.

65. A brilliant example of Isaiah's basing his message of judgment squarely on the Davidide tradition is Isa. 28:21. The "providence" or status quo of "false" prophets would have cited the traditions we know from 2 Sam. 5:17–25 and 1 Chron. 14:10–17 to argue that Yahweh would act in their day as he had for David on Mt. Perazim and in the Vale of Gibeon—to prosper Israel. Isaiah agreed that Yahweh would act as he had on Perazim and in Gibeon but this time to judge his own people—a strange deed, and quite alien, as he says, to those who would employ the hermeneutic of false providence. Isaiah referred to the Davidide traditions only precisely to counter the view that all one had to do was believe Yahweh was strong enough to save them, exactly what he himself had earlier thought (Isa. 7:9, etc.). Isaiah 36—39, if studied carefully to determine references of authority, shows itself to be largely alien to Isaiah. (This latter point is apart from the question of whether Isaiah 36—39 reflects historical events.)

66. Second Isaiah is omitted from the list partly because Isaiah 40—55 are so obviously full of references to both the Mosaic and Davidic traditions; for there both the judgment and the salvation must be seen in the light of Israel's history: cf., e.g., Isa. 42:24–25 and 54:7–8; and see J. A. Sanders, *Suffering as Divine Discipline in the OT and Post-Biblical Judaism* (Rochester, N.Y.: Colgate Rochester Divinity School, 1955), idem, *The OT in the Cross*, and idem, *Torah and Canon*.

67. Smith, *Palestinian Parties and Politics*, 46. If the great families who befriended Jeremiah early in his career were like the Whig party of England, Jeremiah must have disappointed them gravely to have been tried twice (Jeremiah 20 and 38) and imprisoned at least three times (Jer. 20:2; 36:26; 37:4, 15, 21; 38:6, 13, 28; 39:15; 40:1). I suggest that the family of Shaphan were pro-Babylonian in political leanings and that

they *thought* Jeremiah was also (Jer. 37:9–10). Nothing could be further from the truth as Jeremiah's attitude and response to Nebuzaradan show when the defenses of the city were finally broken. The Babylonians naturally thought Jeremiah was politically anti-Egyptian and pro-Babylonian, because of his identifying the foe from the north with themselves, and hence offered Jeremiah what he willed as soon as the city was taken (Jer. 39:11–14; 40:2–5). But Jeremiah's allegiances were neither to Egypt nor to Babylonia but to a vision of an Israel free to serve Yahweh by surrendering their enslavement to his gifts: he elected to stay in the destitute land and refused a pension and comfort in Babylon (40:6). Jeremiah's relations to Jehoiakim and Zedekiah were informed by an impolitic theological vision of Israel's identity (chaps. 36—37), not by a politic quest for accommodation to a pro-Babylonian policy. The prose sections of Jeremiah are secondary in importance to the poetic oracles, in chaps. 1—23, for judging the prophet's real alienation from *all* Judaic society (Jer. 5:4–5; 9:1; 15:17; 16; et passim). Smith himself at two points takes so much away from the word "party" that one is not altogether sure how he uses it in all instances; cf. *Palestinian Parties and Politics*, 13, 29.

68. Cf. Jer. 28:9 and Deut. 18:22. Jeremiah's conviction was that God's message through prophecy was a challenge to, and judgmental of, existing structure and customs; only if prophecy sponsored a status quo, *shalom*, was it subject to historical proof.

By exile I mean not only the narrow period of 586 to 520 B.C.E., but the fuller experience of destitution plus the failure of Second Isaiah's vision, the failure of the Zerubbabel pretension, the destructive campaigns of Xerxes I throughout the area in the first quarter of the fifth century, up to the final successes of Ezra and Nehemiah within the apparently severe limitations imposed by Persian statecraft, and especially its rule of its provinces. Above all what must be accounted for is that not only was the final form of the Torah shaped by the Babylonian Diaspora but that it was upon that community that most of the hard decisions fell which shaped Judaism as it eventuated in rabbinic Judaism after 70 C.E. Perhaps the historical way to put it is that what survived as the essence of "normative" (Pharisaic-rabbinic) Judaism was the thinking about survival and identity and practice that went on among Babylonian Jewish communities of the "exilic" period, that is, from the time of Ezekiel until the time of Ezra and Nehemiah. See esp. Jacob Neusner, *A History of the Jews in Babylonia*, part 1: *The Parthian Period* (Leiden: E. J. Brill, 1969).

In this regard it would be well to ponder at great length the observation of Morton Smith at the close of his very challenging chapter on Nehemiah (*Palestinian Parties and Politics*, 147): ". . . the connection between Judaism and the worship of the restored temple was, in the philosophical sense of the word, 'accidental.' It was demanded, indeed, by the traditions and aspirations of the religion, but was not essential *to its nature*. The national, political, territorial side of Judaism, by which it differed from the other hellenistic forms of oriental religions, was, as a practical matter, the work of Nehemiah. He secured to the religion that double character—local as well as universal—which was to endure, in fact, for five hundred years and, in its terrible consequences, yet endures." (italics added).

69. Sanders, *Torah and Canon*, 66–90. This hope is sometimes rendered more explicit by later hands, in typically doxological and comforting closing verses in the prophetic books.

70. See the brilliant article by Harmut Gese, "The Idea of History in the ANE and the OT," *JTC* 1 (1965): 49–64.

71. See Otto Eissfeldt's seminal study, "The Promises of Grace to David in Isaiah 55:1–5," in *Israel's Prophetic Heritage*, ed. B. W. Anderson and W. Harrelson (New York: Harper & Row, 1962), 196–207.

72. These two phrases, in Isa. 46:12 and 51:7, are not only antithetic but chiastic in form, and were surely Isaianic epithets for the two groups, faithful and apostate.

73. The harmonistic efforts, in the recent neo-orthodox period, to see the prophets as moralizing in favor of an ethical cult, are now seen as impertinent from the perspective of canonical criticism.

74. Richard L. Rubenstein, in *After Auschwitz* (Indianapolis: Bobbs-Merrill, 1966), observes, "Death and rebirth are the great moments of religious experience" (p. 138). And with most Jews today, Rubenstein sees the modern state of Israel as the modern "rebirth" experience of Judaism.

75. Sanders, *Torah and Canon*, 45–53.

76. Freedman, "Biblical Idea of History," 41–49.

77. Ezek. 37:1 *wywṣ'ny;* 37:2 *wh'byrny;* 37:5 *mby';* 37:6 *wh'lty* and *wntty bkm rwḥ whyytm;* 37:12 *wh'lyty* and *whb'ty;* 37:14 *wntty* and *whnḥty.*

78. Cf. Geza Vermes, *Scripture and Tradition in Judaism* (Leiden: E. J. Brill, 1961).

79. As Wright often points out. Cf. e.g., *OT and Theology,* 180. This was the early process of "dialogical revelation," of the necessary complementarity: "Word" and "Spirit."

80. This is what is right about Childs's thesis in *Biblical Theology in Crisis.* And it is surely the meaning for today of the old principle of "salvation only through judgment."

81. As Jecheskiel Kaufmann apparently thought all ancient Israel did: cf. *The Religion of Israel* (Chicago: Univ. of Chicago Press, 1960) and the very open critique of Kaufmann's *magnum opus,* from which the work cited is extrapolated, by S. Talmon ("Yehezkel Kaufmann's Approach to Biblical Studies," *Conservative Judaism* 25 [1971]: 20–28). The major thrusts of the canon within its pluralism indicate for the believing communities today, I think, (1) an ever-expanding and syncretizing view of God (he is neither Jew *nor* Christian), and (2) a bias in favor of the powerless.

82. That the force of this historic memory should eventuate in the Pharisaic and Christian belief that God could give life again even after death, *tehiyat ha-metim,* should occasion no surprise: it was a (theo)logical issue of Torah. According to Sir. 45:5, the Torah brings life; according to *Masseket Avot* 2:8, acquiring the words of Torah acquires life in the world to come; *Avot* 6:7, Torah gives life, now and in the world to come to those who practice it; cf. Rom. 7:10, Gal. 3:21, and John 5:39—all indirect witnesses to the same Jewish conviction of the period.

2
Torah and
Christ

For six years, from 1973 to 1978, I was a member of and participated in the theological discussions and planning of the advisory council of the journal *Interpretation*. The first meeting of the council I attended involved developing and planning the October 1975 issue which was to be on "the Bible as canon." I was asked to write a follow-up to *Torah and Canon* focusing on the NT and especially on Christ. The result was "Torah and Christ," *Int.* 29 (1975): 372–90.

The basic hermeneutic of the chapter is the same, in my opinion, as that of most of the NT, especially of Paul, in working out its Christology and its ecclesiology—theocentric. If one focuses on what the OT says God was doing in and through creation and Israel up to the Hellenistic era, taking account of all the various cultural idioms by which that was expressed, then one can far better understand the arguments concerning Christ and the church one finds in the NT. Again, if one thinks of Torah as a narrative with some laws recorded in it rather than as records of laws set in a narrative framework, then one can perceive the continuity the early Christians saw between Scripture (the OT, largely for them in Greek translation) and what they believed God was doing in Christ and the church in the first century. That which is called gospel in the NT is perceived there as having begun in Genesis, in Torah, and coming to climax in God's work in Christ.

The old dichotomy between law (OT) and gospel (NT) is turned on its head, as it were. The Torah-Christ story, or the gospel as a whole, is made up, from beginning to end, of both story and stipulation, or gospel and law. Read in this way, Paul was not presenting a choice between faith and works, but was rather asking in whose works we have faith, God's or ours? If we can learn to recite God's words and works as recorded in Scripture, then we should be able to see that Christ was God's climactic act of righteousness; that is, we should be able to have the hermeneutic eyes to see and recognize God's culminating work in Christ.

"Torah and Christ" was a direct sequel to that part of the argument of *Torah and Canon* that was less concerned with Gerhard von Rad's question of why Sinai (law) is never mentioned in the short recitals or kerygma in the OT (gospel), but was concerned to ask why the story of the entrance into the land (Joshua) did not end up in basic Torah (Pentateuch). The NT, therefore, presents not so much a christocentric theology as a theocentric Christology. It is the same God continuing his own story at work in Christ that was at work in creation, redemption, and so forth, of the OT.

But NT ecclesiology is also presented with a theocentric hermeneutic reading of

Scripture (OT). In Christ God was creating a New Israel. Or, Christ was God's gift to the world whereby Gentiles, too, might enter into God's Israel. While the Christian celebrates the whole of the gospel from Genesis through the NT, the Torah-Christ story, and hopes everybody who listens will share the joy of the celebration, there can be and should be no special mission to the Jews. In fact, the proper attitude of Christians engrafted into Israel through Christ should be to listen for the voice of God through those Jacob Neusner aptly calls God's first love, Judaism.

What is the continuity between the Old Testament and the New? What is the relationship between gospel and law? Why do Jews not accept Christ? These are frequently asked questions in the churches today.

In *Torah and Canon* the time-honored question of the relationship in the biblical story between gospel and law was bypassed in favor of addressing the quite different question of why the story of the conquest of Canaan, the Book of Joshua, was not included in the Torah or Pentateuch. Here we shall revert to the question of the relation of law to gospel and suggest, perhaps, a fresh approach to an old problem.[1]

I

From a canonical perspective the Torah is a balanced intermingling of story and law: they go together; they belong together; and Torah means both. This is so clearly the case that a simple diagram is possible:

Torah
{
mythos—gospel—story—identity—*haggadah*

ethos—laws—ethics—life style—*halachah*
}

Torah may mean simply the Pentateuch; or it may have the extended meaning of divine revelation generally; or it may, in some texts, be a symbol for the identity of Jews (as over against Christ having the symbolic meaning of identity for Christians). But Torah never lost or loses the *mythos-ethos* dual character noted above.[2]

Early Judaism (from the sixth century B.C.E. to 70 C.E.) was not a monolithic religion. By the third century B.C.E. it was a complex, pluralistic phenomenon. To simplify the complexity, for the purposes of this chapter, we need but observe that some denominations in early Judaism emphasized the *mythos* aspect and some the *ethos* aspect of Torah. Jewish pluralism in the period of the Second Temple (early Judaism) is well attested to in the early Jewish literary complex represented by the Apocrypha, Pseudepigrapha, Dead Sea Scrolls, Elephantine Papyri, Tanaitic literature, and others.[3]

But only two of those Jewish denominations survived the second great destruction of Jerusalem and the temple which occurred in 70 C.E.: the Pharisees, who became what we know as rabbinic Judaism; and the Christians of the early church. They may be viewed as two daughters of the mother faith of early Judaism, but each going in quite different directions after 70 C.E.

The thesis of this chapter is that those different directions are best understood in the light of the above diagram. Rabbinic Judaism, following the emphasis of Pharisaism, stressed the *ethos* or *halachah* aspect of Torah, while Christianity emphasized the *mythos* or *haggadah* aspect. Neither, however, emphasized one to the exclusion of the other: the Torah was for both a mix of gospel and law. The answer, therefore, to the question of how Christianity and late Judaism (after 70 C.E.) developed in such disparate ways must primarily be located in this basic observation of the gospel-law mix of Torah, the central and unifying concept of early Judaism.

But there was another very important factor as well. Some of the sects of early Judaism, like the Qumran Essenes, firmly believed that the eschaton was near; others, like the Pharisees, devalued eschatology in large measure. Christianity believed that it was born in the end time of God introduced by Christ himself, and, hence, was even more eschatologically oriented than the Essenes! Eschatologically oriented Jews of the time believed that God was working in their time a mighty act of grace, of the sort recited in the old Torah story, but an even greater one, a sort of final one, that would sort out everything on earth and in history and inaugurate a quite different kind of life. The difference between the Qumran sect and Christianity was a more intensive sense of the eschaton among early Christians than even among the Essenes, because they believed that the new age had been introduced in its first phase by the coming, passion, and resurrection of Christ.[4]

Early Christians stressed the haggadic-story aspect of Torah since it provided such a strong argument for their claim concerning the authority of Christ and his place in the work of God as its eschaton.[5] This is the basic reason that Torah as Heilsgeschichte (salvation history) plays a more prominent role in the NT than does Torah as law.[6] Early Christians, like Paul, could correspondingly devalue Torah as law since *halakot*, which had been developed for obedience in an ongoing life style, might not all be pertinent in the intense atmosphere of anticipation of the end. But Torah as story was important to the early churches as they moved out into the Mediterranean world because of its adaptability to the gentile mentality of Hellenistic culture.[7]

The combination, therefore, of an eschatological faith plus a haggadic view of Torah distinguished early Christianity from surviving rabbinic Judaism. Here were two related but different modes of recapitulating Torah and transcending the cataclysm of 70 C.E. Because early Christians seemed to

Jews to overstress the gospel aspect of Torah (as story of God's deeds), and because they seemed to insist that Christ provided a new identity symbol (over against Torah), and because they seemed to insist that it was necessary to recognize the new act of God in Christ as being like the ones in the Torah story but somehow climaxing them, rabbinic Jews were able to resist Christian claims and in doing so deny the validity of the Christian argument. Torah, which for them had since the second century B.C.E. been principally a divine guide for obedience and life style, became all the more so God's law for their lives in response to Christianity. Even so, Torah for Judaism has never been only law: It has always been a combination of *mythos* and *ethos*.[8]

Paul's conversion may be seen, in these terms, as a move on his part from emphasis on the *ethos* aspect of Torah to the *mythos* aspect. This was so much the case that he seems to dwell considerably on the Torah story of ancient Israel's election (Genesis) and to bypass Moses (Exodus-Deuteronomy).[9]

In an article in the *New York Times Magazine* of December 23, 1973, Andrew M. Greeley, head of the Center for the Study of American Pluralism of the National Opinion Research Center of the University of Chicago, wrote, "While the NT critics probe back toward the basic message and behavior of Jesus, the 'intertestamental'—or 'second temple'—historians have made considerable progress toward understanding the fantastically creative religious era of which Jesus was a part. Judaism during the last century B.C. and the first A.D. was a vigorously heterogeneous, diversified phenomenon."[10] This is a good way of putting the situation today.[11] The NT is being approached from several directions and from the standpoints of several types of expertise. Those of us who approach it from the standpoint of the highly diversified history of early Judaism seem at times to have more confidence in the possibility of reconstructing the historical Jesus than our colleagues who approach the NT from other directions; but we need each other.[12]

II

What was the thinking of Paul (1) about the place of Jesus Christ in the biblical story and (2) about the place the story of Jesus Christ should have in the Christian life? The watershed event of the NT is the resurrection of Christ. It is often said that everything reported of the Christ in the NT is reported in the light of that final and ultimate event, and this is the principal reason that it is so difficult to reach behind that event to get a really clear picture of Jesus the Jew. It is also often said that the Bible, and especially the NT, is the churches' book. It comes to us through the faith of the early church in Christ established by the ultimate event reported in it of the resurrection. Much of it comes to us through the early worship and instructional materials, especially liturgies, didache, catechism, and kerygma of the early churches. The Bible is not *primarily* grist for the historians' mill. It is *primarily* a theological library.

And yet the NT is *about* Jesus Christ. One of the important perspectives on the NT and Christianity that is brought into sharp focus by the Qumran literature of the Dead Sea Scrolls is the central place of Jesus Christ in the Christian faith. The Qumran Essenes also had a great leader whose name we do not know but whose title appears as the Teacher of Righteousness. Many scholars are of the opinion that it was the Teacher of Righteousness who shaped the essential theology of the Qumran sect; many scholars also think that he himself composed the Thanksgiving Hymns contained on a large scroll discovered in the first cave (in 1947). One scholar, André Dupont-Sommer of Paris, went so far as to say in the 1950s that this Teacher could be compared in a number of ways with Jesus Christ. Dupont-Sommer has claimed that this Teacher not only shaped the theological thinking of the sect, and gave the sect the key for interpreting the OT (Law, Prophets, and Psalms) aright in their time, but that he, like Jesus (and only a century before Jesus), was crucified and was believed by the Qumran sect to have been exalted or resurrected. Dupont-Sommer has retreated from some of his more extreme views, but his own research on the life of this Teacher rendered the great service of giving us a new shade of light for viewing the place of Jesus Christ in the NT.

By outside count the Teacher is mentioned some twenty times in the Qumran scrolls. In most of the manuscripts he is not mentioned at all, and it is highly doubtful that he was either crucified or was believed to have been resurrected. By contrast, the whole of the NT is about Jesus Christ; so much so that counting the times he is mentioned would be pointless. Also, by contrast, was it even possible to speak of Christianity in those days, or today, without mention of Jesus Christ, indeed, without putting him precisely in the center of what Christianity means? The pagan writers of the Hellenistic and Roman world, whenever speaking favorably, neutrally, or unfavorably of Christianity, always addressed themselves to what they understood of the central figure of Jesus. As Oscar Cullmann pointed out in 1955, in response to Dupont-Sommer's early work on the Teacher, "Would it be possible to describe primitive Christianity without naming Christ? To ask the question is to have answered it."[13] There are important passages in Philo, Josephus, Pliny, Dio Chrysostom, and Hippolytus on the Essenes; but never once do they mention the Teacher of Righteousness. By contrast, there is no treatment of Christianity by any writer of the Hellenistic or Roman world, pro or con, without mention of the centrality of Jesus Christ in the new faith, even in the earliest such notices in Josephus, Tacitus, and Suetonius.

All this but underscores the point that the NT is about Jesus Christ. But what does that mean? What does it mean that Jesus Christ is central to the NT and the Christian faith? Many Christian commentators and theologians in the two thousand years of our history have taken this observation so seriously as to assert that Christ figures also in the OT. This was affirmed as recently as 1934 by the German OT scholar Wilhelm Vischer, who wrote a book on the witness of the OT to Christ.[14] He suggested even that in Genesis 32 it was not an angel with whom Jacob wrestled but Jesus Christ himself. To make such assertions, of course, is to go about as far as one can to dehistoricize Jesus and to deal with the centrality of his person in an exclusively mythical or theological manner. We cannot do this ourselves, of course, but it is important that at times the church has engaged in just that sort of exegesis of the whole Bible—even if we cannot.

The word "Christ" was originally a title. It is based on the Greek word meaning "anointed," or "Messiah," and it stems from the earliest Christian efforts to relate Jesus to the OT and to show his authority therein.[15] Much of the NT is apologetic in the sense of wanting to demonstrate the authority of Jesus Christ. And the only authority that the NT writers consciously acknowledged as authoritative was the OT, or the Torah, Prophets, and Psalms. It was the conviction of the early church that Jesus was God's long-awaited Messiah, the anointed one to come to bring salvation to his people.

And this brings us to the observation that the name Jesus itself means "salvation." Its OT form is Joshua, meaning "Yahweh [or God] saves." Matthew, in his account of the annunciation to Joseph (1:20–21), reports that the angel said, "Joseph, son of David, do not fear to take Mary your wife, for that which is conceived in her is of the Holy Spirit; she will bear a son, and you shall call his name Jesus, for he [God] will save his people from their sins."

As Frederick Grant has observed, Jesus was a common name in the first century, one which Josephus attributes to nineteen different persons in his writings.[16] For parents to name a son Joshua was an expression of their faith in the saving power of God for his people. And I think we can be confident that Jesus' earthly name was indeed Jesus. But the NT writers found in it a far greater significance; as Matthew asserts, it was not Mary and Joseph who bestowed the name but an angel with authority from the heavenly courts.

James Barr, in a book entitled *The Bible in the Modern World*, claims that the Bible is "soteriologically functional."[17] He means by that a number of important things, but the point he makes for us today is that the whole Bible functions in the believing communities to effect salvation; this is and always has been its job description for synagogue and church in their recitation and interpretation of it through the ages. This is to speak of the nature and function of canon. The Bible as the churches' book is not primarily a historical document (though I am among those who insist that it is full of historical fact; that is not the point). It is primarily a canonical document, functioning in the believing communities as canon to assist the ongoing believing communities to seek answers in their times to the questions: *Who are we?* and *What are we to do?* In dialogue with believers, the Bible as canon addresses itself to the questions of identity and obedience—and in that order—first identity and then life style. To know who we are and to act like it is to experience and engage in salvation.

In Hebrew, and to a limited extent in biblical Greek, the words "salvation" and "righteousness" mean the same thing in certain contexts. Paul claims that Jesus Christ is God's righteousness and God's salvation for humankind, and when he does so he is saying the same thing in each case. In certain contexts in the Bible both salvation and righteousness mean a saving act or a victory of God. And the claim of the NT is that Jesus Christ is God's righteousness or salvation for us all. He is our salvation in that sense. And according to Paul he is our righteousness as well. Paul says both things and means the same thing by each. Jesus is God's victory for us.

But how are we to understand such biblical claims? What do they mean to us? I think we can suggest answers to these questions by looking closely at Rom. 9:30—10:4 and then at Phil. 2:1–13.

III

In Romans 9—11 Paul takes up what surely for him was the most important and delicate question of his theological thought, the work of righteousness or salvation by God in Christ and the response of Jews and Gentiles to that work. As Johannes Munck has shown in his pivotal study of these chapters, Paul accepts the fact that Jews rejected that work by asserting that they would later say yes after Gentiles had responded to Christ; and he does so by showing that even the early rejection of Jesus by the Jews was a part of the story or history of salvation.[18] Unless one is a close student of the Bible one can easily misunderstand Paul here and be gravely offended by him. It was a great frustration for the early church that Judaism, by and large, did not accept the Christ; and Paul in these chapters exhibits that frustration in a glaring light. Paul was, of course, wrong in his schema; for Judaism has not, after two thousand years, acceded to the supersession of Christianity any more than Christianity has acceded to the supersession of Islam.[19] And the reason is not that Jews do not read the NT the way we do, but that they do not read the OT the way Paul and early Christians did. The frustration for Paul did *not* stem so much from a lack of affirmation of Christ by the majority of Jews of his day, but that he could not get them to read the Torah and the Prophets correctly, that is, in the way he read them. For he was certain that if they would review the Torah story with him in the way he viewed it, they would then accept the Christ.

To join Paul at this point in his thinking, it is necessary to read this section of Romans, as I think it is necessary to read most of the NT, in the light of the way the writer engages in midrash of the Torah and the Prophets. Midrash means simply the manner in which one reads passages of the OT, especially to render them relevant or functional. This is not the place to go into the exciting subdiscipline of biblical studies we call comparative midrash; but I cannot imagine a period of greater excitement in biblical studies than the present one because of some of the newer emphases in comparative midrash and canonical criticism.

It was Paul's conviction that if one read the Torah story, emphasizing it as a story of *God's* works of salvation and righteousness for ancient Israel, then one could not escape seeing that God had wrought another salvation, and committed another righteousness, in Christ just like the ones of old but an even greater one!

In order to understand Paul here, one must recall the full concept of Torah. The Torah is primarily a story and not primarily a set of laws. There are indeed several codes of law embedded in the Torah, but they derive their authority from the story—not the story from the law. And that story is of the mighty acts of God, something like a divine odyssey,[20] in creating a people for himself; electing the patriarchs and matriarchs, freeing slaves from Egypt, guiding the refugees through the desert, conducting them across the Jordan and leading them to victory in settling Canaan. If the final shape of the Torah had gone on to include its Davidic aspect, then we can be sure that its climax would have been David's conquest of Jerusalem, perhaps even Solomon's access to the throne: In fact, there is reason to think that a very early nationalist form of the Torah story extended that far (the Yahwist tradition). But, interestingly enough, not only is the Davidic aspect left to the section of the canon called Prophets, but so is the conquest part of the story. The Book of Joshua is in the Prophets, not the Torah.[21]

But whether the word Torah signifies the Pentateuch only or all authoritative tradition, it does not primarily mean law; but, as the rabbis know very well indeed, it means primarily revelation. In fact, it came to mean Judaism—the whole covenant concept of God's relation to his people. When ancient Israel lost their land and their temple, in fact all of their religious and national symbols, to the Assyrians (and then to the Babylonians in the Iron Age) Judaism was born out of those ashes because the concept of Torah was both indestructible and portable. It could be taken either on scrolls or in memory to whatever foreign land where Jews lived in diaspora. Torah means the Jewish gospel which, in dialogue with the ongoing believing communities of Jews wherever they might be, gives Jews both identity and a basic understanding of obedience. Torah alone is responsible for the twenty-five hundred years of survival power Jews and Judaism have. Being indestructible and portable it provides the mythic power for life that a dispersed and beleaguered people have had.

If one studies Jewish midrash long enough, that is, the Jewish insistence that the Torah is relevant to all ages and all situations (for questions of identity and life style), then one comes to appreciate the fact that no other people had anything quite like Torah.[22] In the Gospel of John our Lord said to the Jews that they search the Scriptures because in them they think they find eternal life. Such statements and affirmations can be found elsewhere in rabbinic and apocryphal Jewish literature.[23] The ancient traditions that make up Torah proved their true power and worth in the sixth century B.C.E. destruction of Israel and Jerusalem: It was those traditions that gave the survivors, the remnants all over the Babylonian and Persian empires, the power for life to survive as Jews and not lose their identity to the dominant cultures of the age, that is, not assimilate. And it was in that event of exile and restoration that some of Israel's early such traditions were shaped together and interwoven in the experience of exile to become what we basically call Torah, that is, the Pentateuch, the canon within the canon of Judaism. Torah, as a general term, goes on to mean all the later oral traditions and interpretations of the early Torah including the Talmud, and as we have seen, came to mean Judaism itself.

To put it another way, Torah was by the time of Christ and Paul the symbol par excellence, incomparable, indestructible, and incorruptible, of Judaism. It meant Judaism's identity and way of life. This is still the case today.

Torah is concerned first and foremost with salvation and righteousness, the two words mentioned earlier about Christ. But, and this must be understood aright, it is first about God's righteousness, or better, his righteousnesses, and then about the sort of righteousness of which humankind or Israel might be capable.[24] It is first *mythos*, and then *ethos*. It is gospel and then law—both completely intertwined, inextricable one from the other. There is no such thing in the concept of Torah as law without the story, it simply would not exist; it would have no base of authority or authenticity or even existence. Torah is first and foremost a story about the mighty acts of God in creating a covenant people for himself; it is then, and immediately thereupon, a paradigm for understanding how Israel should live from age to age in varying circumstances and in differing contexts. It is first about God's righteousness and immediately thereupon about humanity's putative righteousness or duty to pursue. When Deuteronomy (16:20) says, "Righteousness, righteousness shalt thou pursue," it does not only mean to obey the laws of the Book of Deuteronomy, it means constantly in all circumstances, in all and varying situations and contexts, to contemplate the Torah story of God's great love for humankind; how he chose a motley crew of slaves in Egypt to escape from there so they could go forth to bless the world. The laws in Deuteronomy, then, are a paradigm for how to arrive at answers to the pursuit of God's righteousness in particular situations and at particular times. It is not that Israel should imitate God. That would be impossible. Rather, the story of what God did *suggests* faithful human action. The Torah story is first and foremost adaptable, like a paradigm, to assist in properly conjugating the verbs of God's continuing presence and activity in the world (Deut. 4:9). If particular answers of a given moment in turn get frozen, then a prophet—prophets precisely like Jeremiah and Jesus—turns up to remind us that the Torah once more must be internalized and contemplated, as on the heart and inside personhood.

Now whether or not Paul was right in his schema about Jewish rejection and then eventual acceptance of God's work in Christ, he shows sheer genius at points in his argument in Romans 9—11 and especially at 10:4 and 10:10.

In 10:4 Paul says the following: "For Christ is the *telos* of the Torah righteousness-wise for all who believe." *Telos* means end in the sense of *finis*, but it also means climax, main point, or purpose.[25] Paul in this statement summarizes the central belief of the early church: God had committed another righteousness in Christ, that the Christ event was like the exodus event, or the wanderings-in-the-desert event, or the conquest event, and like them was a mighty act of God. It was different only in the fact that it was climactic to them; it brought all those chapters of the Torah story to completion, fulfillment, and made sense of them all. Paul in this whole section from the beginning of Romans 9 has been saying that to concentrate on the righteousness, or ethics, of which humankind or Judaism is capable, can be to miss the main point of the Torah story, namely, the righteousness or salvation or mighty acts of God in the Torah story.

Now, marvelously and wonderfully, the words for righteousness both in Hebrew and in Greek can mean either human righteousness or divine righteousness. The Greek word *dikaiosunē* can mean either God's right relation with humanity or humanity's right relation with God. Hebrew *tsedakah* has the same wonderful ambiguity except that the Hebrew has the very concrete connotation of a specific act, either mighty act of God or act of obedience of humankind.

In other words, Paul is here saying if you really have in mind the Torah story and that point of view, then you can discern the righteousness of God. If you really know the Torah and know what righteousness of God is, then you know that Christ is precisely that kind of act of God. And you know also that in Christ God really committed an ultimate kind of righteousness; he came *all the way* this time. The God who had crouched down into the huts and hovels of dispossessed slaves in Egypt and led them across the Reed Sea to freedom is the same God who crouched down into the cradle in Bethlehem. Both acts of God are of the same order; that is, they are both Torah-story kinds of acts of God. Paul says that if all Jews would read the Torah in that way, concentrating on God's mighty acts, then they could clearly see that "Christ is the climax of the Torah for all who believe in the righteousness of God." I think this is one of the things he is saying in Rom. 10:4.

IV

Some people wanted to add to the Torah story back in OT times. Jeremiah twice (16:14–15 and 31:31–34) said he was quite sure that the events of his day, about the destruction of Jerusalem and God's regathering the exiles, would be added like another chapter to the Torah story. Ezekiel was quite sure of it and also the Second Isaiah; and the Chronicler rewrote it, shortly thereafter elevating David above Moses. But the final edition of the basic Torah itself only includes the parts up to Moses' long sermon on the east bank of the Jordan (Genesis to Deuteronomy). That was so that Jews, if they happened to be scattered, would not feel they had to change and become something else just because they were not living in Palestine. And that is one reason, I am sure, Judaism has lasted so long, these twenty-five hundred years, because the basic Torah, the Pentateuch, in effect says that if you happen to be wandering and in dispersion, like Abraham, Jacob, Moses, you do not have to fret about not being Jews. You do not *have* to be on a particular piece of real estate to be identified with the people God chose to bless the whole world.[26]

Nobody succeeded in adding a chapter to the basic Torah story until the

NT; and even then not for most of Judaism. Now what we can see from the point of view of the divine odyssey is that the NT really makes this quite bold and scandalous claim that in Christ God committed another salvation or righteousness and that it should be added to the Torah story as a climax, as the ultimate chapter of the whole story or odyssey. To put it another way: While the arguments and debates in the churches of the second century c.e., spurred by the heretic Marcion, were on the point of whether or not the OT was biblical, the great concern of the whole early church of the first century (including most of the NT writers) was to try to show that the New Testament–Christ story was biblical. Most of Judaism said no.

But the argument of the NT and the early church was that God's divine odyssey did not stop with David in Jerusalem. In rhetorical terms they put it this way: If God could go with Abram from Ur of Chaldees to Palestine, down to Egypt, out of Egypt with a motley crew of refugee slaves, through the desert, conquer Palestine with Joshua and take Jerusalem with David—why not Bethlehem? After all it is only five miles down there out of the Jaffa Gate on the old road that runs by Rachel's tomb! If God could go all the way from Ur to Jerusalem by way of Egypt and the Sinai desert, do you not suppose he could make it another five miles to Bethlehem? And if he was with Joseph in prison, and granted his presence in the huts and hovels of slaves in Egypt with Moses, do you not suppose he could crouch down into the cradle of a Jew baby in Bethlehem?

Paul's point, though he himself never refers to the Bethlehem or birth-infancy traditions, would be that you just do not know what God has already been through if you think he could not get into the cradle and onto the cross, if it was his mind to do so and on his own agenda to bring righteousness and salvation to the world. Paul was so excited by his belief that God had committed a new, mighty act in Christ, that he just could not understand why everybody did not see it the way he did. For Paul, as for Jeremiah, it was a question of how you think.[27]

What we have to undersatand is that in Hellenistic Greek as in biblical Hebrew (and in other Mediterranean languages of antiquity too) the heart was the seat of thinking. The saying, "As a man thinks in his heart, so is he," is the key here. It is a question of identity. That is, whatever story completely captivates you is the way you are going to see life and perceive problems and look for solutions to them. So, as Jeremiah and Deuteronomy and nearly everybody else in the OT insists, the person with the true Torah-identity is one who loves the Lord his or her God with all his or her heart, first and foremost. And to love God in this manner, as Deuteronomy 6:5 and following go on to say, is to fill your heart (we would say head) and surround yourself with this story. This is the most important thing of all. That way you know who you are, no matter where you may be or what problems you face. And the story is one of God's righteousness first, and then one of how, in pursuing his "righteousness," that is, pondering the story of God's passionate love for humankind, one can work out one's own obedience, or the church can work out its program in obedience—in whatever age or in whatever circumstance.

In this view, then, it is a mistake to take the specific legal codes embedded in the Torah story, in Exodus, Leviticus, and Deuteronomy, as absolute laws valid for all time. For Paul, as for Jeremiah and some others in the Bible, they are not the most important point about the Torah at all, precisely because obedience has to be worked out by the believer in God's righteousness who studies the problems he or she faces in the light of the story of *those* righteousnesses and tries to be obedient in that situation. For Paul, the specific points of the law if overstressed or if absolutized were the surest way to overlook the Torah story itself, that is, God's righteousness. So Paul makes a big distinction between concentration on the sort of righteousness of which humankind is capable and the righteousness of God which is the heart of the Torah story. This is precisely what he is saying elsewhere in Romans and Galatians, and when he appears to be antilegalistic. But where the church and Christianity have sadly gone amiss is in thinking that all Judaism was therefore legalistic. This is an immense mistake. Every Pharisee (1) knew that the Torah was about God's righteousness. But it was the special vocation of Pharisaism, the most liberal denomination in the Judaism of the time, to try to find ways, in the light of the specific expression of the will of God on Mount Sinai, in the legal codes of the OT, to discern *through them* the will of God for first-century Judaism.[28] And (2) given that point of view on the Torah and that emphasis, no Pharisee and very few really good Jews knowledgeable in Torah would accept the church's and Paul's essential argument that a cradle in Bethlehem and a cross on Golgotha constituted the same sort of mighty act as the exodus from Egypt. In fact, I dare say that if we had lived then and were good members of the first-century Jewish church to the same measure as we are today, by dynamic analogy we would have felt the same way as did the good Presbyterians, I mean Pharisees, of first-century Palestine: *We* would have looked on the idea of additions to the old Bible very skeptically indeed!

This makes it all the more remarkable that so many people in the Hellenistic world, including not a few Jews out in the eastern and middle Mediterranean lands, accepted the point of view Paul here outlines and did believe with their heart in God's righteousness and did confess with their lips the salvation thereof as he says in Rom. 10:10. Paul believed that if people would look at the Torah story from the standpoint of God's activity and journey, they would believe in and confess Jesus Christ as Lord, or *Kyrios*.

V

Kyrios was an important title for Christ in Paul's mind. And nowhere in his letters does it figure more prominently than in the Song of Christ that Paul recites in his epistle to the church at Philippi. I am of the opinion that nowhere in the Bible (except perhaps Micah 6:1–8) do we find a clearer statement of the crucial relation between *mythos* and *ethos*, or between the

Torah-Christ story and the kind of life of obedience the Christian should try to live—that is, the relation between the Christian identity and the Christian life style or between God's righteousness and humanity's possible righteousness or, again, in Lutheran terms, between faith and works, than the way Paul presents this famous hymn in Phil. 2:1–13.[29]

In this passage not only does Paul provide a very vivid picture of divine righteousness, but he also, I think, suggests what the foil to that righteousness would be. The hymn celebrates the work of Christ as humility. One of the best ways we have of making clear what we mean when we make a point, such as Paul is here trying to make, is to present a foil to that point or to clarify what the opposite of that point would be. And in this passage he uses three words: one intrinsic to the hymn itself in v. 6 and two in his introductory remarks before it, in v. 3, as antonyms of what he means by Christ's humility. He says, "Do nothing from selfishness or conceit" in v. 3 to make clear what is meant in the first strophe of the hymn by Christ's not counting equality with God as a thing to be grasped. The word in the hymn itself is *harpagmos*, translated in the RSV as "a thing to be grasped." It signifies a prize of war or a position to be won, and Paul specifies that equality with God is what the Christ figure never sought. The two words in v. 3 further clarify this negative quality as *'eritheia* and *kenodoxia*, translated as selfishness and conceit or ambition. These express what the motives would be for seeking equality with God. And these are precisely the motives of the fallen angels who, according to Genesis 6 and Jewish literature widespread in the first century C.E., descended from heaven, or from the heavenly council, to set up a kingdom to rival that of God. In other words Paul signals for his readers at Philippi a story they would have known very well indeed about another kind of descent from the heavenly heights, that of the fallen angels, as the opposite of what the hymn he recites indicates as the mind of Christ, or the motive of the Christ when he descended from on high. Christ's motive was humility, pure humility, seeking nothing for himself but to do the will of God. He, like the fallen angels, descended, but for entirely different reasons. We ourselves know of the myth of the fallen angels from the pre-Christian Jewish writings called the *Book of Enoch*, the *Secrets of Enoch*, the *Life of Adam and Eve*, and the Dead Sea Scroll Essene work called *Ages of Creation*. And Paul, in using these words, aptly describes their motivation for descending from the heavenly heights. They fully and consciously intended to set up a government and realm in opposition to God's. We even know from these writings some of the names of the fallen angels: Azazel, Samjaza, Satan, Jeqon, Asbeel, Gadreel, Penemue, Kasdeja, Kasbeel, and others.

Now in the picture that Paul is here painting for the congregation at Philippi, these angels, otherwise called sons of god or sons of heaven, would have originally been, like the Christ figure, members of God's heavenly council. In other words, Paul says, there have been two descents from the heavenly heights to earth, the one by these fallen angels out of selfishness and ambition, and the other by the Christ figure out of humility and obedience to God.

Now, in this section Paul five times uses a form of the verb *phroneo*, to have a mind-set, or have a mentality, a way of thinking, or to use the more biblical expression, to have a certain kind of thinking in the heart. "Have this mind in you," Paul says, think this way. It is not that we can ourselves do what the Christ figure himself did, or even that we can acquire the Christ's mind, I think; but rather, Paul bids us to have the story of the humble descent of the Christ figure as our mentality. That is the kind of thinking in the heart we should do.

The story itself is beautifully simple and simply beautiful. The Christ figure out of humility descended from the heavenly council to earth in an act of self-emptying and servanthood taking on human form. His humility extended all the way to death on the cross, says Paul. In other words not only did he descend to earth to take humanity upon himself, he even descended to the chthonian regions, or the bottom story of the three-story universe, the region where death obtains and Mot and Abaddon reign supreme. That is the heaven-to-earth-and-hell trip described in the first strophe of the hymn (Phil. 2:6–8). The second strophe describes the hell-to-earth-to-heaven return trip. (2:9–11). But this time the active agent is the high God himself. "God has highly exalted him." The picture here is thrilling indeed, for we see the humble Christ figure lifted by God out of the depths of death and set upon a coronation route that wends its way through the three-story universe back up to the heavenly heights. Two things here are important to note: Along the parade route every knee, in heaven, on earth, and under the earth, bends and every tongue confesses that Christ is Lord, or *Kyrios*. And who are those who kneel along the route? Surely not only all humanity; for it clearly says every knee in heaven and under the earth as well. No, here we see all of those fallen angels also on bended knee acknowledging the reign of the humble Christ figure whom they had left behind and whom they surely had totally discounted. Their descent was for nought; his for the glory of God the Father. They who had descended to gain a kingdom now must kneel in homage to him who descended in humility.

What does Paul say then is the relationship between God's righteousness and our obedience or putative righteousness? It is clearly not in imitation of Christ. As Ernst Käsemann has rightly said, that cannot be, for we cannot get up to the heavenly heights in the first place to make any kind of descent, much less a humble descent. Nor do I think it can be simply acquiring the mind or mentality of the Christ figure. Would not that be also a form of *harpagmos?* No, the relation between *mythos* and *ethos* or gospel and law, or the Christian story and our obedience, is rather that of so filling our heart and mind with *this story*, this Torah story completed by the righteousness of God in Christ, that this becomes the way we think. This is surely what the *Shema'* in Deuteronomy 6 means by loving the Lord our God with all our heart, soul, and might, to which the NT adds "all our mind" (meaning the same thing as heart). This Torah story should be upon our heart as Deuteronomy and Jeremiah said. This is our access to the thoughts of God which Isaiah said are as high above our thoughts as the heaven is above the earth (Isa. 55:8–9). We cannot think his thoughts, says Paul, but we can believe in his righteousness. We can tell and retell the words of this story with our children and speak of them when we sit in our houses, when we walk by the way, when we lie down, and when we rise up and make them as a sign upon our hands and as frontlets between our eyes and as mailboxes on our doorposts (Deut. 6:7–9). This story is our *topos* (place) on this earth. It is our identity. And out of that identity, constantly and dynamically told and retold, considered and reconsidered, we go on, as Paul says, to work out our obedience with fear and trembling (Phil. 2:12) in the context of our situation and of the problems we face. To think that way, says Paul, to have eyes to see like that and ears to hear like that, is to have God at work among us both to will and to work his good pleasure. Not our good pleasure, thank God, not our agendas and programs, but to know even in our limited lives and in our circumscribed existence that God can and does use us to work out that plan of salvation and reconciliation he has had in mind since he first called Abraham of Ur in Babylonia.

And this brings us back to the first verse of Philippians 2. There Paul uses four expressions describing the enabling power of God for living lives of obedience and for working out the putative righteousness of which we in our limited and frail condition are capable. "So if there is any encouragement in Christ, any incentive of love, any participation in the Spirit, any affection and sympathy. . . ." All these nouns, encouragement, incentive, participation, and the phrase "affection and sympathy," are divine gifts available to us if we have this mind of the Torah-Christ story in us. All of them signify God's mercy and grace available to us in Christ, in God's agape or love, and in the Spirit. The word participation, among them, stands out as indicative of what Paul is saying. The word in Greek is *koinonia*—participation or fellowship. This is the link, the bridge, the means of drawing upon the power of God to live lives in accord with his will and pursuant to his righteousness. We can participate in that power through having this Torah story, which Christ has brought to its full force, in our heart and mind.

VI

So it is just as important, if we take Paul seriously, to know the righteousness of God prior to Christ as it is to know God's righteousness in Christ.[30] For to know the Torah story aright, says Paul, we can also know that Christ is God's final righteousness. It is not so much that Christ reveals God as it is that God revealed Christ. And it is really not a question of faith and works. Because these still emphasize salvation by humankind's faith or by humankind's work. What the Torah-Christ story says is that God has worked for us in this divine odyssey. Nor is it that Christ was God's last righteousness. Not at all. The canon, this full Christian-Torah story, is the paradigm God has given us so that we too can conjugate the verbs of his activity today and know his participation in our lives now and recognize a righteousness when we see one.

For us Gentiles, Christ is our entryway into membership in God's Israel, says Paul. But Paul makes it abundantly clear that "disobedience" on the part of Israel, or Judaism, or failure to recognize the Christ as the climactic chapter of the Torah story does not excommunicate them. Paul maintains his perspective here quite consistently. Jews are already in Israel, or in the Israel of God as he put it in Galatians (6:16); and since they are, they ought to read the Torah story the way he, also a Jew, reads it so that they can recognize Christ as a true addition, nay, as the true climactic chapter. But even if they do not, God can and does use their "obduracy" or lack of recognition of Christ, says Paul, to work out his overall scheme begun in Abraham without ever cutting them out of the true Israel. It is we Gentiles who must enter Israel by the door Christ has provided, not the Jews.

I would make several comments on this point in closing. (1) There is nothing wrong in continuing to hope, as Paul did, that Jews acknowledge the work of God in Christ so long as we do not go on then to insist that they "become Christian." It is we who have in Christ become Israelites, so to speak, says Paul, not the other way around. (2) If we really want Jews, or anyone, to recognize that God committed a righteousness also in Christ, then we must do two things: (a) as Christians, take the trouble to know who we are; and (b) try to live attractive lives reflective of the passionate love of God for humankind instead of practicing prejudice against Jews or Muslims. This does not mean we all live the same kind of life. It means, in my way of thinking, that we must concentrate on broadening our theology. This is the work that needs doing. It means that God is neither Jew nor Christian nor Muslim. *He is God* and he loves us all passionately and equally well. If he has chosen an Israel (or more than one?) it is to use as instruments of his blessing humankind. This emerging theology is what I call monotheizing pluralism. But names and rubrics are not important. What is important is to regain a sense of what Dietrich Bonhoeffer called the reality of God. The heart of the biblical message is not so much that we should believe in God but that God believes in us.[31]

We have tried to explore Paul's thinking about the place of Jesus Christ in the biblical story and his thinking about the place the story of Jesus Christ should have in our lives today.

What, then, is the relation between the Torah-Christ story of God's righteousnesses and the obligation laid upon us by it to pursue them, or as Paul says, to work out the gift of our salvation with fear and trembling (Phil. 2:12–13)? What is the connection, in other words, between *mythos* and *ethos* in Paul's thinking? We should be careful not to assume that we can have in us the mind of God. As Isaiah says, God's ways are as high above ours as heaven is above earth: his thoughts are not ours (Isa. 55:8–9). They are strangely and wonderfully of another order. What I think Paul suggests, however, is in essence what Deuteronomy had already suggested, that our hearts or minds be crammed full of this story of God's humble condescensions to live and work among us. The Greek *metanoia*, often translated "repentance," means a change of mind, actually, a change of head in modern pop idiom. It indicates a real change of identity, a basic, fundamental shift from one way of thinking to another. Kenneth Boulding put it well when he suggested that to receive the biblical message is to experience a restructuring of our whole mental apparatus.[32] The Bible uses the metaphors of rebirth and conversion to express the radical nature of attaining this Torah-Christ mind in us.

Peter Berger said in an oft-quoted speech, delivered at the September 1971 Tenth Anniversary meeting of the Conference on Church Union (COCU) in Denver, that the churches must remember in their dialogues with other faiths and philosophies that they, too, have something to say: The authority of the churches is that they have a story to tell. That story is the Torah-Christ story.

NOTES

1. The question has usually been posed in terms of why the ancient recitals of Israel's faith in the mighty acts of God (1 Sam. 12:8, Deut. 26:5–9) seem not to mention Sinai and the giving of the law. Two answers have been given: the one by the German form critics, notably Gerhard von Rad and Martin Noth and the other by the archaeologists and traditionalists, notably the so-called Albright school. Walther Eichrodt has associated himself with the latter: see "Covenant and Law," *Int.* 20 (1966): 302–21; and J. A. Sanders, *Torah and Canon* (1972).

2. See "Torah and Paul" (chap. 6 of this book) and n. 6 below. Wisdom should not be seen as a separate or third element of Torah, but as a part of both *mythos* and *ethos*, esp. the latter. See Gerhard von Rad, *Wisdom in Israel* (London: SCM Press, 1972), and Moshe Weinfeld, *Deuteronomy and the Deuteronomic School* (Oxford: Clarendon Press, 1972). For this use of the word *mythos* see Jacob Neusner, *The Way of Torah: An Introduction to Judaism* (Belmont, Calif.: Dickenson, 1970), 7–8. For the possible relation of the pattern here suggested to the "visionary" and "realistic" heritages of Torah, see Paul D. Hanson, "Jewish Apocalyptic Against Its Near Eastern Environment," *RB* 78 (1971): 31–58, esp. 57.

3. The concept of normative (Pharasaic-Tannaitic) Judaism in the pre-70 C.E. period, over against heterodox, aberrant sects, is under steady challenge. The concept received considerable impetus in the arguments formulated by George Foot Moore in his debates with the old history-of-religions school (*Judaism in the First Centuries of the Christian Era, the Age of the Tannaim* [Cambridge: Harvard Univ. Press, 1927–30], 3:17–22). Following the lead of Saul Liebermann, Elias Bickermann, Morton Smith, and others have challenged the Moore synthesis in its oversimplified forms. Opposite Moore, on a spectrum of opinion on the matter, is now Martin Hengel, *Judaism and Hellenism*, 2 vols. (Philadelphia: Fortress Press, 1974; 2 vols. in 1, 1981), who contends that all Judaism from the mid-third century B.C.E. was "Hellenistic" to greater or lesser extent, with stirrings of clear opposition in Ben Sira, Wisdom speculation, the Hasidic movement, and perhaps the Essenes. The work of Neusner (see *From Politics to Piety: The Emergence of Pharisaic Judaism* [Englewood Cliffs, N.J.: Prentice-Hall, 1972] also challenges the synthesis. A fine, succinct statement of the pluralism in Judaism prior to 70 C.E. can be seen in Michael E. Stone, "Judaism at the Time of Christ," *Scientific American* 228 (1973): 80–87. For a mediating point of view, see W. D. Davies, *PCB*, s.v. "Contemporary Jewish Religion."

4. See the introduction to K. Stendahl, ed., *The Scrolls and the NT* (New York: Harper & Brothers, 1957), 1–17; and J. A. Sanders, "Habakkuk in Qumran, Paul and the OT," *JR* 39 (1959): 232–44.

5. Dietrich Rössler in *Gesetz und Geschichte, Untersuchungen zur Theologie der Jüdischen Apokalyptik und der Pharisäischen Orthodoxie*, 2d ed., WMANT 3 (Neukirchen: Neukirchener Verlag, 1962) sketches the Nachleben of the two aspects of Torah in early Judaism; see chap. 6 in this book.

6. This observation is quite congruous with the programmatic scheme proposed by Paul Hanson (see n. 2 above). What he calls the "visionary" may be seen as heir to what we call the *mythos* heritage in early Judaism; and what he calls "realistic" heir to what we call the *ethos* heritage. See "Torah and Paul," (chap. 6 of this book) for Paul's uses of the word *nomos* (Torah). Very important now to that discussion is the monograph by Laurent Monsengwo Pasinya, *La Notion de nomos dans le Pentateuque grec* (Rome: Biblical Institute Press, 1973).

7. See J. A. Sanders, "Adaptable for Life: The Nature and Function of Canon" (chap. 1 of this book).

8. It is in the light of this development that Judaism's resistance to developing a full theology should be seen, as well as the overstated Christian polemics about Jewish "legalism."

9. See, e.g., Richard N. Longenecker, *Biblical Exegesis in the Apostolic Period* (Grand Rapids: Wm. B. Eerdmans, 1975), an inadequate treatment that is nonetheless on the right track.

10. Andrew M. Greeley, "A Christmas Biography," *New York Times Magazine* (Dec. 23, 1971): 8, 28–30. See also n. 3, above.

11. See also J. A. Sanders, "Dead Sea Scrolls—A Quarter Century of Study," *BA* 36 (1973): 109–48.

12. J. A. Sanders, "The Vitality of the OT: Three Theses," *USQR* 21 (1966): 161–84.

13. Oscar Cullmann, "The Significance of the Qumran Texts for Research into the Beginnings of Christianity," *JBL* 74 (1955): 213–26, esp. 225.

14. Wilhelm Vischer, *The Witness of the OT to Christ* (London: Lutterworth Press, 1949).

15. Geza Vermes, *Jesus the Jew: A Historian's Reading of the Gospels* (London: William Collins Sons, 1973; Philadelphia: Fortress Press, 1981).

16. Frederick Grant, *IDB*, s.v. "Jesus Christ."

17. James Barr, *The Bible in the Modern World* (New York: Harper & Row, 1973), 30–34.

18. J. Munck, *Christ and Israel: An Interpretation of Romans 9—11* (Philadelphia: Fortress Press, 1967). Munck's work, which first appeared in German in 1956, influenced Krister Stendahl who wrote "The Apostle Paul and the Introspective Conscience of the West," *HTR* 56 (1963): 199–215 (also in *Paul Among Jews and Gentiles* [Philadelphia: Fortress Press, 1976], 78–96). A vigorous rejoinder to Stendahl is in Ernst Käsemann, *Perspectives on Paul* (Philadelphia: Fortress Press, 1971), 60–78. Stendahl tries to move away from Lutheran tradition in understanding Romans 9—11 while Käsemann insists that the issue is indeed justification by faith and that Stendahl has not succeeded. (See Stendahl's counterresponse, *Paul Among Jews and Gentiles*, 129–32.) I prefer not to enter that debate nor the older one about whether "righteousness" in Paul means "right relation" or "act of God." See J. A. Ziesler, *The Meaning of Righteousness in Paul* (Cambridge: Cambridge Univ. Press, 1972), for an emphasis on the first meaning. In the NT, and in Paul, it can have both meanings, especially in this section in Romans. Käsemann says (*Perspectives*, 63): "I would even say it is impossible to understand the Bible in general or Paul in particular without the perspective of salvation history." See W. D. Davies's comments on Munck in *Christian Origins and Judaism* (Philadelphia: Westminster Press, 1962), 179–98.

19. This observation I owe to an oral presentation by the late Thomas O'Dea in Jerusalem at the Ecumenical Institute, Tantur, in 1973.

20. The suggestion of the divine odyssey is based on the actual canonical shape of the biblical story. It is close to another suggestion by Barr (*Bible in the Modern World*, 179 n. 11) who speaks of God's own history. Since a major characteristic of the OT is its monotheizing tendency, Yahwism was highly adaptable (syncretistic) and Yahweh, himself, a growing God. See Otto Eissfeldt, "El and Yahweh," *JSS* 1 (1956): 35ff.; F. M. Cross, Jr., *Canaanite Myth and Hebrew Epic: Essays in the History of the Religion of Israel* (Cambridge: Harvard Univ. Press, 1973), 3–75; and esp. G. E. Mendenhall, *The Tenth Generation: The Origins of the Biblical Tradition* (Baltimore: Johns Hopkins Press, 1973), 198–214.

21. Sanders, *Torah and Canon*, 36–45. In 1 and 2 Chronicles the Torah story is retold from a Davidic point of view in what was apparently an effort to counter the thoroughly "Mosaic" Torah (Pentateuch): see Robert North, S.J. in the *JBC* 1:403.

22. This is the opinion of such classicists and students of Hellenistic rhetoric as Henry A. Fischel. See his *Rabbinic Literature and Greco-Roman Philosophy* (Leiden: E. J. Brill, 1973).

23. John 5:39. See also Sir. 45:5; *Sayings of the Fathers* (Abot) 2:8 and 6:7; Rom. 7:10; Gal. 3:21; and Sanders, "Adaptable for Life" (chap. 1 in this book).

24. The mighty or gracious acts of God in creating Israel are called "righteousness of God" in 1 Sam. 12:7; Micah 6:5; Dan. 9:16; cf. Acts 2:11. See Sanders, *Torah and Canon*, 15–27; and Neusner, *Way of Torah*, 9–26.

25. The position taken here is close to that of W. D. Davies in *Paul and Rabbinic Judaism*, 4th ed. (Philadelphia: Fortress Press, 1980), 147–76; for a more precise statement of my own position, as well as for a review of scholarship on the question of Paul and the law, see Sanders, "Torah and Paul" (chap. 6 of this book).

26. Sanders, *Torah and Canon*, 45–53.

27. J. Munck has shown how Paul's OT model for his own vocation was Jeremiah: *Paul and the Salvation of Mankind* (Richmond: John Knox Press, 1959).

28. So Pharisaism in developing the so-called oral tradition or Mishneh-Torah understood the later *halakot* to take precedence over the biblical stipulations. Another way Pharisaism had of rendering the specific laws adaptable was by a shift in hermeneutics, between 70 B.C.E. and 70 C.E., from *peshat* (contextual meaning) to the rapidly developing rules, from those of Hillel in the first century B.C.E. to those of Ishmael at the end of the first century C.E., following the rise of the concept of verbal or literal inspiration. Once the concept of verbal or literal inspiration became accepted the (often irrevelant or impossible) plain meaning of a law could be bypassed by focusing on a single word or letter within the law or sentence. Once the sentence structure of Torah was thus broken down, it received new life in its adaptability to the problems Judaism faced in the Hellenistic world, the greatest challenge she had ever faced. (See chap. 7 in this book.)

29. See J. A. Sanders, "Dissenting Deities and Philippians 2:1–11," *JBL* 88 (1969): 279–90, where what follows was argued in technical terms.

30. See Sanders, "Torah and Paul" (chap. 6 in this book) for an understanding of Paul's apparently ambiguous attitude toward Torah.

31. See H. W. Robinson, *The Cross in the OT* (Philadelphia: Westminster Press, 1955), 47.

32. Kenneth E. Boulding, *The Image: Knowledge in Life and Society* (Ann Arbor: Univ. of Michigan Press, 1956), esp. the introduction.

3
Canonical Hermeneutics

Chapter 1 in this book was an attempt to look at the Bible as canon in terms of how canon functioned and how it continues to function in believing communities. It explored the concept of canon, for the first time perhaps, in terms of function rather than in terms of closure or of an enclosure of ancient literature. In doing so we made several salient observations about that function: it did not begin at some late point of deciding what was in or out of that enclosure; that same type function could be observed much earlier—even before written literature became in any manner stabilized in the communities—and that same type function continued even after closure. What was there, early and late, was both relatively stable and relatively adaptable, even after closure. The difference was largely in the hermeneutics applied to render it adaptable or relevant. But another difference was in the historical and cultural context in which the resignification took place.

Chapter 2 pressed those observations on into the NT to explore in the terms of early Judaism and early Christianity how to understand the place of the NT, and especially Christ, in Scripture, but in ways different from the way that exercise is generally pursued. A theocentric hermeneutic emerges from such an approach to the NT: God is the unity of Scripture.

The word "hermeneutics" is being used to mean different things these days. Most people mean by it the philosophical mode whereby one "translates" biblical concepts into contemporary ones. Brevard S. Childs means by it the theological movement discernible within a defined text. My work had led me to a real appreciation of the hermeneutics whereby the ancient biblical tradents themselves read and re-presented authoritative traditions whether oral or written. Enlightenment scholarship has exhibited some fear that the hermeneutics of the ancients who contributed to the Bible might not be very respectable or hold up under Enlightenment scrutiny. A great deal of NT scholarship still looks upon most of the citations and allusions to Scripture in the NT as probably some form of *dicta probantia*, proof texts. My work had led me to value the unrecorded hermeneutics that lie between most of the lines of OT and NT as a precious legacy. In fact, so precious that I have sometimes thought that perhaps those canonical hermeneutics might be as canonical as the literature itself. Might not Christ's major contribution to the Gospels, and to the gospel, have been the way he understood and applied Scripture—his hermeneutics? The apostles and evangelists may not have gotten the details right, but they could never forget the way the prophetic wisdom teacher seemed to be able to turn Scripture inside out and speak in such stunning ways to life as they knew it.

Concurrent with that revaluation of biblical hermeneutics, which is explained in the following, was a steadily growing realization that Enlightenment study of the Bible involved a hermeneutical stance and that it seemed to change according to the general characteristics of Western intellectual thought over some 250 years of such study. Not only so, it had become clear that the periodic shifts in the "assured results" of Enlightenment study of the Bible exhibited, dynamically perceived, just about the same kinds of fluidity of understanding of a biblical literary unit or passage as had obtained before the Enlightenment. One need only do a diachronic study of a given passage in the successive scholarly commentaries in modern times to see the same kinds of resignification that had gone on before the Enlightenment. The "original meaning" of such a passage kept changing as time marched on.

Some of the changes, on the other hand, came about because of new discoveries and development of sharper tools for probing into the meanings of a passage, and many of those represent major advances that are still pertinent. I repeat here what I have often said and written: Enlightenment study of the Bible is a gift of God in due season if its proper limitations are carefully observed, and especially if the consciousness of such scholars is kept aware of their own view of authority as they work. Denial of having such a view—claims to "objectivity"—and failure to recognize those limitations tarnish the gift. Enlightenment study of the Bible is one of the most precious gifts for understanding these texts God has granted us humans. But scholarship needs always to remain aware of its humanity.

What follows is a basic and initial statement about canonical hermeneutics. It was originally titled simply, "Hermeneutics" (*IDBSup.*). Along with "the triangle" (see p. 89) it stresses the importance of the three interrelating variables: text, context, and hermeneutics.

The Communities' Book

The believing communities engage in dialogue with the Bible as canon, out of their own ever-changing contexts, asking two questions: Who are we and what are we to do? The fact that the biblical canon functions in this way issues in three basic observations. (1) In a lengthy process of canonization the Bible emerged out of the experiences of ancient Israel, early Judaism, and the early church, when they asked those two questions of their own authoritative traditions. (2) It was shaped in and by those communities in their common life, cultic and cultural. (3) Its proper function continues to be that of being in dialogue with the heirs of those same communities as they continue to seek answers to those two questions (identity and life style, faith and obedience). Essential to that dialogue is hermeneutics, and the hermeneutics most valid is that which can be discerned in the Bible's own history (i.e., canonical hermeneutics), through the tools of biblical research.

Canonical hermeneutics has two basic tasks: determining valid modes of seeking the meaning of a biblical text in its own setting, and then determining a valid mode of expression of that meaning in contemporary settings. It addresses the problem of how to bridge the gap between biblical meanings and contemporary cultural categories of thought. For Western Christians this has meant translating biblical meanings into modern, Western philosophical thought patterns.

Recent Discussions

In the nineteenth century Friedrich Schleiermacher and others based their work in hermeneutics on the common humanity of author and interpreter: the latter could have confidence in an intuitive grasp of what the author intended. Modern categories of understanding were considered fully capable of seizing biblical meanings.

Rudolf Bultmann followed directly in Schleiermacher's wake; but he sought to define more precisely the pre-understanding or presupposition asserted by Schleiermacher. Reacting against what he viewed as simplistic historicism in the early twentieth century, Bultmann stressed an existentialist position informed by the early work of the philosopher Martin Heidegger. Bultmann attempted to discount theological presuppositions by resting his case for pre-understanding solely on technical biblical criticism and the then-regnant existentialist philosophy. Criticisms of his work have been lodged principally on two grounds: that he indeed had theological suppositions and that his method was not adequate for the whole Bible, especially not for the OT.

Over against Bultmann was Karl Barth, who worked out a church dogmatics wherein his pre-understandings were an imposing neo-Reformationist dogmatic of the Word of God derivable from the words of the Bible. Whereas Bultmann's work has seemed to many as anthropological, even non-theological, Barth's has seemed to others as mythic and traditionalist. One of Barth's late essays, "The Humanity of God," seemed to stress the human more than the divine and has given rise to attempts to build bridges between Barth and Bultmann. While Barth's theology was christocentric, much of his dogmatic theology focused on the OT. This was also the case with Dietrich Bonhoeffer, whose hermeneutic issued in a nonreligious interpretation of biblical faith. A criticism of both Bultmann and Bonhoeffer is that their hermeneutics have led to a kind of humanism. One result of the confluence of the work of Bultmann and Bonhoeffer and the essay cited by Barth was the so-called death-of-God movement.

Students of Bultmann continued to read Heidegger as the latter moved from existentialism to ontology. In that move Heidegger revalued the import of language for humanity's understanding of itself, elevating language from a secondary position to primal authority. Language became the home of human being. The importance of this move for proclamation of the Word, that is, for biblical and theological hermeneutics, was recognized by Ernst Fuchs and Gerhard Ebeling. In their view the Christ event was, indeed is, a language event. James M. Robinson focused their work into *A New Quest of the Historical Jesus* (1959). This involves not just translation of words from one linguistic idiom (the biblical languages, Greek and Hebrew) to another (modern tongues), but a transculturation of the Word, as perceived in the text, to new words.

Criticism of the "new quest" centered in questioning language as a valid vehicle of biblical revelation. Barth, with others, had been acclaiming history, or time, as the vehicle of revelation. Wolfhart Pannenberg then attempted to meet this criticism by focusing on hermeneutics that can read both the Bible and human experience in the world. Sensitive to the criticisms of OT scholars and of Jews toward the Bultmannians and the post-Bultmannians, Pannenberg shifted attention to a theology of world history, in which the historical process was sought in a continuum connecting past and present. Reality could thus be viewed as a unity grounded in the biblical affirmation of the oneness or unity of God. The gap between biblical past and human present is spanned by a view of continuing history or story of God's unfolding plan not only for the ongoing communities of believers but for the world. Jürgen Moltmann pressed Pannenberg's case into a "theology of hope" wherein the future aspect of universal history was stressed and stated as God's future continually invading the human present. Thus Moltmann recognized the eschatological aspect of biblical thought.

The Task Today

The task of biblical hermeneutics today is to seek a midpoint between the hermeneutical task of the historical-critical method, which seeks original biblical meanings, and the hermeneutical task of spanning the gap between those recovered meanings and modern cultural systems of meaning. And that task is called canonical hermeneutics: the means whereby Israel, Judaism, and the church spanned the gaps between inherited faith and new cultural settings.

The canon includes the process whereby early authoritative traditions encountered ancient cultural challenges, were rendered adaptable to those challenges, and thus themselves were formed and re-formed according to the needs of the believing communities. (It was in this process, e.g., that ancient Near Eastern wisdom was adapted into biblical literature.) That process itself is as canonical as the traditions that emerged out of it.

Therefore, the Bible may be read as a paradigm not only of God's truth but of how those who find their identity in it should pursue the integrity of reality in their own later contexts. *Canonical* hermeneutics is the means whereby early believing communities pursued, and later believing communities may yet pursue, the integrity (oneness) of God, both ontological and ethical. It is in this sense that the Bible is, canonically viewed, a monotheizing literature.

Hermeneutics, therefore, is as much concerned with the contexts in which biblical texts were and are read or recited as with the texts themselves. It is in this sense that one must insist that the Bible is not the Word of God. The Word is the point that is made in the conjunction of text and context, whether in antiquity or at any subsequent time. Discernment of context, whether then or now, is thus crucial to biblical interpretation. The greater the knowledge we have of the ancient contexts, the clearer becomes the impact the (words of the) text had; and the greater the discernment of current contexts, the clearer one's choice of hermeneutics for transmitting the point originally made.

The Bible as Canon

It is the nature of canon to be both stable and adaptable. It is stable in the sense that once its structure was set and its contents determined, nothing was to be added to it or subtracted from it (Deut. 4:2; 12:32 [Hebrew text 13:1]; Rev. 22:18–19). (The OT canon was closed for Judaism sometime near the end of the first century C.E. and the NT canon sometime in the fourth century C.E.). But it is also the nature of canon to be adaptable, that is, it is believed to speak to the communities generation after generation (see "Adaptable for Life," chap. 1 of this book).

Hermeneutics is the midpoint between the Bible's stability and adaptability as canon. In this sense hermeneutics is the art of interpreting the Bible for the ongoing believing communities. It is the means whereby the professional interpreters within those communities demonstrate the Bible's relevance and help the faithful (and the doubting) to hear its message for their time and situation.

But hermeneutics is also the science whereby the trained interpreter attempts to understand a text in terms of its ancient, original contexts; this is the prior task of biblical hermeneutics. The believing communities have always been interested in what Moses or Jesus "really meant" in their time, as well as in the implications for later believers of what they said. The uncritical reader assumes the earlier and later meanings to be the same, with the conviction that the plain meaning discernible in the text "now" was what it meant then. One result of the Enlightenment has been the development of tools and techniques for probing carefully back to the original meanings. This has resulted in what has been called lower and higher criticism.

Canonical Hermeneutics

The history of "biblical interpretation" begins early in the history of the formation of the Bible itself. The biblical thinkers often cited earlier authoritative traditions in order to validate what they themselves had to say. Most commonly the traditions cited were those that told Israel's epic history; and the most common reason they were recited was (1) to remind Israel who she was and what was expected of her because of that identity, or (2) to remind Israel who God was and what might be expected of him in the covenantal relationship. Where the ancient contexts in which these traditions were recited are available, we are able to discern what the hermeneutics of the biblical author were. The most common hermeneutic rule employed was that of historical analogy or typology, sometimes accompanied by another, the *qal vahomer* argument, or *argumentum a fortiori*.

One obvious example of this is found in Ezekiel 33. The shocked and despondent exilic community is quoted as consoling itself over the recently received news that Jerusalem had fallen. Psalm 137 records, in another form, their shock and despair at the same news: they hung their harps upon the trees of the camps where they were interned and refused to sing the old authoritative Torah traditions that reminded them of God's gracious acts in history in creating an Israel for himself. They undoubtedly felt that God had abandoned them and let them down. But others, trying to take heart, cited an old tradition about the call of Abraham: "Abraham was only one man, yet he got possession of the land; but we are many; the land is surely given us to possess" (Ezek. 33:24). Their ancestors had apparently engaged in the same sort of consolation when Samaria fell to the Assyrians in 722 B.C.E. (Isa.

9:10). Ezekiel here records an excellent example of the hermeneutic rules of typology and *qal vahomer*, but Ezekiel himself disagreed with the argument.

A little later, after it had become clear that Persia was to be the new international power in the Middle East, Second Isaiah consoled the descendants of those same exiled Jews with exactly the same argument that Ezekiel had rejected: "Look to Abraham your father and to Sarah who bore you: for when he was but one I called him, and I blessed him and made him many. For the Lord will comfort Zion" (Isa. 51:2–3). The argument Ezekiel disputed and the argument Second Isaiah supported were exactly the same, indeed employing the same hermeneutic rules. The difference was context.

Second Isaiah lived in the same sort of exiled, dispossessed community as Ezekiel had, but he lived some forty years later, and that made an immense difference. In Ezekiel's time it was still possible to deceive the people into thinking that the fall of Jerusalem had been an insignificant event. In Ezekiel's thinking, it was still necessary for the shock to be absorbed and accepted as part of God's agenda and purpose. Not until that point had been made and accepted, without any false hopes remaining, could Isaiah's subsequent message of restoration be heard properly.

The argument advanced by Ezekiel's contemporaries, which he disputed, had been advanced a few years earlier by a prophetic colleague of Jeremiah's, Hananiah of Gibeon. He argued, in a fully prophetic manner and apparently on the basis of Israel's legitimate authoritative traditions, that God would bring the deportees back home "within two years" (Jer. 28:2–4). As a member of the same covenant community as Hananiah, Jeremiah much preferred Hananiah's message to his own (28:6–9); but he sharply disputed Hananiah's message in the same terms with which Ezekiel disputed the same sort of message only ten years later.

Eva Osswald, following Martin Buber, has put it succinctly: "The true prophet must be able to distinguish whether a historical hour stands under the wrath or the love of God." The selfsame message, based on the same authoritative traditions about what Israel can expect of God (because of what he has done in the past), in the one context was false while in the later was true. In other words, to derive consolation from the Torah story of God's gracious acts, without also discerning the challenges of the covenant relationship, is falsehood (see esp. pp. 99–103). Conversely, the "true" prophets, with the possible exception of Amos, when declaiming their messages of God's challenges and judgments (always based on the Torah story), went on to state how the impending adversity would also have the purpose of purging, refining, disciplining, or healing them (cf. Jer 30:12–17; Ezek. 36:26–31).

Hermeneutic Modes

Behind whatever hermeneutic rules the biblical thinkers employed there were two basic modes: the constitutive and the prophetic, and both were valid. Recent scholarship has shown that in the ambiguity existing at the time a prophecy is made, one cannot so easily distinguish a true from a false prophet as one can by hindsight, after reality has taken shape (Jer. 28:9; see chap. 5, esp. pp. 95ff.). Both used the prophetic-messenger formulas, both cited the authoritative Torah-story traditions, both had great faith, both came out of the people and identified with them; but they had quite opposing messages because their basic hermeneutic modes were different. The one tended to read the tradition in a constitutive or supportive way, while the other caused the tradition to be read in a challenging way.

At those historical moments when Israel was weak and needed reconstituting, the Bible in its canonical shape seems to indicate that the constitutive mode was proper: our father Jacob was a wandering Aramaean (Deut. 26:5); we are lost and wandering like him in exile; maybe like him we mark another beginning and not the end of Israel. But if that same mode of rereading the tradition about Jacob, or Abraham, was read at a time when Israel had power, and had somehow confused it with God's power, then Jeremiah and Ezekiel, as well as the other prophets, called it false prophecy. To continue to draw strength from the tradition would only harden the heart into further irresponsibility. At that historical moment the prophetic mode is indicated: it may be we must wander, once more, like Jacob, long enough to rediscover our true identity.

Theology of Canonical Hermeneutics

The debates between the so-called true and so-called false prophets always seem to have reached a crucial theological juncture. The so-called false prophet apparently believed that the God who had freed Israel from Egypt, guided her in the wilderness, and brought her into Canaan was strong enough and faithful enough to keep her there. The theology was one familiar in the Bible: that of emphasizing the grace of God in the midst of human sin. Even if we are not faithful, God is. He will keep us here. The so-called true prophet went a long way with that theology. But he or she apparently believed that the God who had freed Israel from Egypt, guided her in the wilderness and brought her into Canaan was powerful enough to take her out again and into exile! He recited the same Torah story, but in the prophetic mode.

Not by any means abandoning the doctrine of God's redemptive grace, he instead put it in the larger framework of the doctrine of God the Creator. "It is I who by my great power and my outstretched arm have made the earth, with the men and animals that are on the earth, and I give it to whomever it seems right to me. Now I have given all these lands into the hand of Nebuchadnezzar, the king of Babylon, my servant" (Jer. 27:5–6). God still loved his people, and later would restore them handsomely, but some clear demonstration of God's integrity (unity) and freedom to reject as well as to elect was sometimes indicated by the historical moment. The prophetic indictments of the people were not only that they did not act like Israel, or live up to their true identity, but also that they presumed on God.

These same hermeneutic modes, as well as the same hermeneutic rules, persist into the NT, where the evidence is mounting that Jesus, as a Jew among Jews in the first third of the first century, interpreted scriptural (OT) traditions in the prophetic mode, stressing both the integrity and freedom of God in the coming eschaton.

Principles and Rules

Context

As already stressed, the interpreter must be able to discern the contemporary context so as to know which message is needed, that of constitutive support or that of prophetic challenge. The challenge may vary in intensity from challenge of life style to threat to identity (canceling of election), just as the support may vary from the blessed assurance of divine presence to exhortation to believe in God's plans and power in a very evil situation.

Covenant Identity

In either case, the ancient interpreter had the same essential covenantal identity as the people he addressed. Even Amos, who prophesied in the northern kingdom rather than in his homeland of Judah, nonetheless addressed people of the same basic covenantal identity as his own. Whether the biblical interpreter used the constitutive mode or the prophetic mode, he or she did so as a member of the group.

Memory

A distinctive characteristic of canonical hermeneutics was that of reading or reciting Israel's Torah story *in memory*. To recite the Torah story, in whatever form or in whatever circumstance, was to remember Yahweh's mighty acts in creating the world and Israel. To put God in remembrance of those same mighty acts was to petition or induce him to do the same sort of act again. But the retelling of that epic story of Israel's origins entailed such intensive identification with those in the past who benefited from God's mighty acts in the story that, in cultic terms, time and space were in that moment of recital transcended. Those recalling or remembering the story understood themselves *actually* to be the slaves freed from Egypt, guided in the desert, and brought into the promised land; that is, the holy story became present reality in them.

When the evangelist recounted the command of Jesus to his disciples to engage in the Eucharist "in remembrance of me," the evangelist fully meant that in the moment of that cultic act, accompanied by some form of recital of the Torah-gospel story, the whole scene of the passion account would be actualized, made present, in the believers so "remembering." The Word or message received, however, will depend directly upon whether one identifies with Jesus, the Romans, the Jews, or with the disciples in actualizing the story.

Dynamic Analogy

To attempt to make the same points again today one must employ the basic rule of dynamic analogy. If a prophet challenged ancient Israel, or if Jesus challenged his own Jewish, responsible contemporaries, then a prophetic reading of the Bible today should challenge those dynamically equivalent to those challenged in the text: if the priests and prophets of Hosea's day or the Pharisees in Jesus' day, then the church establishment today, since priests, prophets, and Pharisees represented the responsible church leaders and groups of their time. Dynamic analogy also means that one reads the text for oneself and not only for others. It should not be read to identify false prophets and Pharisees with another group or someone else, but with one's own group and with oneself, in order to perceive the right text in the right context. In fact, there would have to be real humility on the part of modern Christians to identify with the Pharisees, since we hardly ever measure up to Pharisaic devotion and piety, much less their intense desire to please God. But to read the text as though Jesus were condemning either those Jews in their time or condemning some other group than one's own today is to read the text by static analogy. Put another way, to identify with Joseph, Jeremiah, and Jesus in the biblical accounts, without careful discernment of one's present-day context, is to miss what Joseph, Jeremiah, and Jesus have to say to believers today. Conceivably a new movement (one that feels it needs the strength to aid and to forgive those who had earlier sold them into slavery?) might identify with Joseph; but when that movement has become established, such a reading would only induce self-righteousness. The challenge then needed could come only from identifying with the brothers. The climactic point of Amos's address recorded in Amos 1:3—3:2 is that whereas autochthonous Israel should have treated the poor and weak and dispossessed in their own land the way Yahweh had treated Israel when they had been dispossessed slaves in Egypt, they were actually treating them the way Pharaoh had dealt with the Hebrew slaves in the Torah (Exodus) story.

Ambiguity of Reality

Dynamic analogy means also that one must breathe the ambiguity of reality into the ancient situation or context. To read Amos as though what he said was "right" because, after all, he ended up being included in the canon, and as if those he addressed were "wrong" in some absolute sense, would be to miss the realism of the Bible as canon. Good, responsible folk in ancient times held another viewpoint on God's promises and expectations and in all sincerity and good faith considered Amos, Jeremiah, and Jesus to have been wrong. "The tradition works . . . not only to illuminate and to identify the Christ, but also to reject and resist the Christ" (James Barr). We must read biblical texts in terms of the ambiguity of reality that any situation has; this means that we must be able to discern present contexts dynamically, and then read the biblical text in the same dynamic way.

Mirrors for Identity

Most biblical texts must be read, not by looking in them for models for morality, but by looking in them for mirrors for identity. To look for models for morality in the Bible is very nearly a futile task, since a basic emphasis of the canon is on the grace and faithfulness of God and on the sin and faithlessness of Israel as well as of the disciples in the NT. There are hardly any moral models in the Bible as it is canonically shaped, except for a few characters viewed principally through ancient Wisdom thought, for example, Joseph after he gets to Egypt. Abraham and Sarah lied out of fear for their lives and both snickered at the annunciation of Isaac's birth (Genesis 17—18); Jacob was a deceiver and supplanter and yet became Israel (Genesis 27); Moses was a murderer and fugitive from justice and yet became our savior from slavery and our lawgiver (Exodus 2); the disciples forsook Jesus (Matt. 26:56) and denied him (Mark 14:66–71); etc. The point is not that we should be liars, cheats, and murderers in order to be elect; on the contrary, to read the Bible in that way is to moralize statically on the basis of the text.

Theologizing and Moralizing

One must read the Bible theologically before reading it morally. The primary meaning of redemption is that God has caught up human sinfulness into his plans and made it a part of those plans. This theologem pervades the Bible, OT and NT, and so all texts must be understood theologically (in the light of that theologem) before any indication for obedience be drawn from it.

The tendency to moralize first has resulted in dishonest readings of the Bible. Not to accept the clear biblical signal that Abraham feared for his own existence and lied about Sarah is to engage in cleaning up the story. Not to accept what the Bible so clearly says about Jacob's devious character is to concentrate on how bad Esau was to sell his birthright (Heb. 12:16), which is to miss the point of Genesis altogether. But to seek to find the proper place of a passage in full canonical context by theologizing first (God's grace in the midst of human sin; God's free act in electing "sinners") permits the reader then to ask in a fully canonical sense what the passage might indicate for current programs of obedience or life style, without doing violence to the Bible, and without being misled by a false reading of it.

One should read the Bible not only with honesty but also with humility and humor. Humility means one identifies in the stories and episodes not with Joseph, Jeremiah, and Jesus, but with those who heard their challenging messages and learned from them. Whenever our reading of a biblical passage makes us feel self-righteous, we can be confident we have misread it. Humor means that in reading the biblical texts we take God a little more seriously than usual and ourselves a little less so.

The Bible as Paradigm

If the story of Jesus' sermon at Nazareth (Luke 4:16–30) is read constitutively, that is, if one identifies with Jesus, then almost certainly one will read the passage anti-Semitically, get angry with the mob for trying to stone Jesus, and then wonder, missing the point entirely, how Jesus was able to walk through the midst of them unharmed. But if one identifies with the good, responsible folk of Nazareth who attended the service, listens to Jesus' sermon from their standpoint, hears the terrible offense of it, and gets the feelings that the congregation got because of it, then one may want to lynch Jesus also. The question, What did Jesus say that made them so angry? He said that when the great herald, or Elijah, would come finally, he would do the same sort of thing he and Elisha did in ancient Israel (1 Kings 17; 2 Kings 5); he would take his blessings, not to our community, but to foreigners, even to our enemies. That is not the sort of message any congregation wants to hear, especially today, whether conservative or liberal. What is the use of being a member of the in-group if, when God intervenes to sort everything out, he takes his blessings to sinners, or outsiders? There is a deep injustice in paying those who work only one hour the same wages as those who have borne the burden and heat of a full day's work. But the Bible is full of the insistence on God's freedom and generosity (Matt. 20:1–15). Such a reading of Luke 4 (or of almost any passage in the Bible) would bring the church today to ask who it really is and what its self-understanding, or essential identity, ought truly to be. To read the Bible in this way is to engage in biblical "memory."

Even a passage like John 14:6, "No one comes to the Father, but by me," can be read either constitutively or prophetically. Reading in the constitutive mode one assumes one to be "by" or "in" Christ. For young, struggling churches who are not at all sure of survival, such a reading can be a correct one and a genuine encouragement not to assimilate or defect. But for established churches that have confused their identity with the dominant culture (so that, e.g., they think, because of the Puritan heritage, that to be a good Christian is to be a good American, and maybe even vice versa!), to read the verse in that way is to sponsor self-righteousness and pride and to encourage confusion of identity. To read it prophetically would be to hear in it the challenge that indeed the churches are not coming to the Father, and this is precisely because they are not, despite all their confessions and lessons learned by rote, coming "by me." Read in that way, the passage somehow no longer seems to sponsor notions of exclusivity at all, but rather sponsors a further step into understanding what the freedom of God means. Minimally it means that God is not a Christian in the sense that the churches habitually co-opt him to be. "A judge who is the God of all" (Heb. 12:23) read constitutively seems to say, "Our god is the judge of all them" (and the Book of Revelation seems to say something like that to persecuted Christians under the Roman heel). But read prophetically the passage challenges all tribal, sectarian, and denominational ideas of God, especially one's own.

Conclusion

The Bible itself gives indications of how to make again today the points originally made and then to move on in our contexts to further theological horizons (views of truth). The two basic modes are the constitutive and the prophetic, according to context. The crucial distinction between them is theological: the freedom of God on the one hand, and his generosity and grace on the other; and his apparent bias for the powerless, those who have not yet confused his power with theirs. The Bible, read as a paradigm of the verbs of God's activity, permits us to conjugate in our own contexts the verbs of God's continuing activity and how we may pursue, in our time, the integrity of truth, that is, God's oneness both ontological and ethical.

BIBLIOGRAPHY

Paul J. Achtemeier, *An Introduction to the New Hermeneutic* (Philadelphia: Westminster Press, 1969); James Barr, *Old and New in Interpretation* (New York: Harper & Row, 1966; rev. ed., 1985), 149–200; idem, *The Bible in the Modern World* (New York: Harper & Row, 1973), 75–181; Carl Braaten, *History and Hermeneutics* (Philadelphia: Westminster Press, 1966), 130–59; Raymond E. Brown, "Hermeneutics," *JBC*, 2:605–23; Brevard S. Childs, *Memory and Tradition in Israel* (London: SCM Press, 1962); idem, *Biblical Theology in Crisis* (Philadelphia: Westminster Press, 1970); James L. Crenshaw, *Prophetic Conflict: Its Effect Upon Israelite Religion*, BZAW 124 (New York and Berlin: Walter de Gruyter, 1971); J. W. Doeve, *Jewish Hermeneutics in the Synoptic Gospels and Acts* (Assen: Royal Van Gorcum, 1954); Robert W. Funk, *Language, Hermeneutic and Word of God* (New York: Harper & Row, 1966), 1–122; Jürgen Moltmann et al., *The Future of Hope: Theology as Eschatology* (New York: Herder & Herder, 1970); Eva Osswald, *Falsche Prophetie im AT* (Tübingen: J. C. B. Mohr [Paul Siebeck], 1962); Wolfhart Pannenberg et al., *History and Hermeneutic* (New York: Harper & Row, 1967); James M. Robinson, *A New Quest of the Historical Jesus* (London: SCM Press, 1959); James M. Robinson and John B. Cobb, Jr., *The New Hermeneutic* (New York: Harper & Row, 1964); idem, *Theology as History* (New York: Harper & Row, 1967), 1–133; J. A. Sanders, *Torah and Canon* (1972); idem, "The Ethic of Election in Luke's Great Banquet Parable" (1974); idem, "Reopening Old Questions about Scripture" (1974); Claus Westermann, ed., *Essays on OT Hermeneutics* (Richmond: John Knox Press, 1963), 160–99, 314–55. For examples of application of the above hermeneutic principles, see these works of J. A. Sanders: "The Banquet of the Dispossessed," *USQR* 20 (1965): 355–63; "Promise and Providence," *USQR* 21 (1966): 295–303; "In the Same Night," *USQR* 25 (1970): 333–41; *The New History: Joseph, Our Brother* (New York: Baptist Ministers and Missionaries Board, 1968). (The three references from *USQR* have been reprinted in *God Has a Story Too* [Philadelphia: Fortress Press, 1979].)

4

Biblical Criticism
and the Bible
as Canon

During my last year on the faculty of Union Theological Seminary in New York the editors of the *Union Seminary Quarterly Review* asked me to write a valedictory for the spring-summer issue of 1977. It was to form an *inclusio* with my inaugural address on the vitality of OT studies (*USQR* 21 [1966]: 161–84). I wrote about canonical criticism, its inception and development, from the viewpoint of what was happening to biblical criticism generally, especially in view of the increasing voices of detraction about it and its overall impact in the churches. Some of those voices were present in other departments at Union Seminary, and I felt it was time to recognize and respond to them as best I could. The editors of the *USQR* also asked my friend Peter Ackroyd, of the University of London, to contribute to the same issue. His piece, "Original Text and Canonical Text," resonated well with my effort. Some of what is here eventually found its way in another form into the first chapter of *Canon and Community* (1984); but in its original form in what follows it makes crucial points in an overview of how canonical criticism was developing at that juncture (1977).

Biblical criticism began in the seventeenth century with the excitement attaching to new movements and the confidence that ancient biblical wisdom could be unlocked in new ways through Enlightenment methods and then wed with the new sciences to illumine divine revelation in ways never before dreamt of. It bore with it a new meaning of faith that could unleash intellectual honesty within the fold of traditional religious identity.[1]

But as with most other such movements, this one, too, has created some problems: there apparently came a point when its work seemed to produce more negative than positive results for the ongoing believing communities. The charge that biblical scholarship has locked the Bible into the past and rendered it irrelevant has been made with increasing volume since the demise of neo-orthodox theology.[2]

The Great Syntheses

Up to the mid-1960s there had been two great syntheses in Western European theology, both of which attempted to use the results of biblical and historical criticism: first liberalism, then neo-orthodoxy. Each synthesis had so many variations within it that one rightly feels uncomfortable in using the labels to cover such diversities. But there was a hermeneutic *character* or stamp to each that cannot be denied: Liberalism stressed God as Creator of all the world and neo-orthodoxy stressed God as peculiar Redeemer of Israel and in Christ. The one was viewed as capable of adapting and accounting for the humanism and optimism of the eighteenth and nineteenth centuries to basic, abiding Christian principles; the other was viewed as capable of adapting and accounting for the despair, disillusionment, and need for humanity following the First World War and the existentialist mood of the age to the basic (Reformationist) gospel of tradition.

But both used and sponsored biblical criticism. Friedrich Schleiermacher and Adolf von Harnack, using the basic optimist hermeneutic of progressive evolution of the age, could use the tools of biblical criticism to pick and choose in the Bible what spoke across the ages from faith to faith, from biblical author to biblical interpreter. Each, the ancient and the modern, shared a common humanity as creatures of one God of all. Rudolf Bultmann then agreed with their view of humanity but rejected the optimist hermeneutic of evolution for one of existentialism, to suit the new twentieth-century mood after the First World War. Bultmann's main weapon was biblical criticism, and especially form criticism: the NT is a book of post-Easter faith.

All the so-called liberals, whether the nineteenth-century thinkers who had a simple hermeneutic of historicism and progress, or Bultmann with his followers, devalued the importance of the OT. For the earlier group it was superseded; for the late liberals it was at best a functional symbol of what God might have done and might still do, as Creator of all, in any clan or tribe or people anywhere.

Karl Barth's shift to a christocentric hermeneutic of redemption brought the OT considerably back into focus. For him it was neither superseded nor generalized: it was part of God's plan of redemption and essential to the whole. Barth still, however, subscribed to the old supersession tendency of Christianity in insisting on the centrality of Christ: God revealed himself fully in Christ. It was a christocentric theology.

Both the liberals and the neo-orthodox used and exploited biblical criticism. For the liberals it served well to show how truly ancient Near Eastern the OT was and how much of its essential thought and teaching were to be found in other peoples of the ancient world. It was an early product of a history going somewhere beyond it. The OT could thus indicate God's work in any people. Archaeology and philology were especially suited, in addition to the various tools of literary criticism, to support their synthesis. But the same tools were also marshaled to serve neo-orthodoxy. Did not archaeology actually show the amazing accuracy of the Bible? Did not philology show the genius of the Bronze and Iron Age leaders? Did not both show that the first occasion or example in any typology was usually the best?[3] Did they both not provide the answer to the question of the gap between ancient events and the later biblical records thereof? And that answer was simple: it happened that way![4] Hence, the Bible was authoritative. It seemed that biblical criticism and scholarship could serve both camps.

But Barth died in 1968 and W. F. Albright in 1971, and biblical criticism stands exposed with no great synthesis to shield it from the charge that it has locked the Bible into the past. I remember reading a presidential column by John Bennett in an old Union Theological Seminary issue of *Tower* (1966). He wondered if he would live to see what would come after neo-orthodoxy! He has lived, and one of the things he sees is a crisis in biblical criticism.[5] Hans Frei has put it very well: the biblical story has become eclipsed by the work of the very professionals in seminaries and departments of religion who seem to know most about the Bible. In the rhetoric of today, the experts have lost perspective on the very object of their expertise. A colleague calls biblical criticism bankrupt.[6] For some, it has reduced the Bible to grist for the historian's mill, the province of the professor's study. Something like the very opposite of what Albright and George Ernest Wright intended has taken place: often the Bible has been reduced to the status of a tell which only the trained expert with hard-earned tools can dig.

There is clearly a revolt against this situation. What its resolution will be none can say. I have a proposal to offer and am very excited about it.[7] It is the purpose of this chapter. But first it would be only fair to acknowledge the other current solutions being offered.

Recent Proposals

What are the responses now available to the charge that we have locked the Bible into the past and that we respect the Bible only as grist for the historian's mill—whether in seminary or department of religion? The responses may be grouped into eight categories. Most of them had their origins in the 1960s and began somewhat before the deaths mentioned above. I shall simply list them with a few words of explanation about their position on a spectrum of responses. The spectrum moves from left to right, so to speak; from utter rejection of biblical criticism to a plea for extending it further and seeking to make it itself responsive to the charge. I shall give the responses tentative labels hoping to serve clarity.

1. *Pneumatic Appeals.* This solution is perhaps the most historically common of them all. When the doctrine of the Word no longer has seemed to provide grist for theological mills the church often has turned to the doctrine of the Spirit, or focused on the doctrine of creation (for natural theology). Ages of the Word give way to Ages of the Spirit, and vice versa throughout church history: so neo-orthodoxy has given way to secular and sectarian theology in many guises. One of the commotions here is that of turning inward to the individual's private story as ground for theologizing with a concomitant turning away from the Bible, and not just from biblical criticism; another is that of turning outward to nature and creation. One could mention the names of Harvey Cox, Tom Driver, and Sam Keen among those who have tried to be responsible here. Directly related to this liberal tendency is the apparently opposite but concomitant conservative turn to the Spirit, to validate, willy-nilly, the Bible literally or to validate privatistic experiences (not totally unlike those of the liberals) such as glossolalia, healing, and personal trips or journeys in life. Both these groups seem to have a canon within the canon of the Bible, selected passages used as *dicta probantia*.

2. *Structuralism.* Here there are a variety of responses that retain the Bible but, also, like the above, dismiss biblical criticism which seeks points originally scored: it has built a kind of ethos of denigration of biblical scholarship. The final form (any final form) of a biblical text serves the field of semiotics. Claude Lévi-Strauss, A. J. Greimas, and Roland Barthes are the names one

would mention here; in this country there are a growing number of adherents.

3. *Symbolism* shares some ground with structuralism. Here hermeneutics enters the picture in the work of Paul Ricoeur, but the emphasis is largely on the reader's condition and the universal power of symbols and metaphors emerging from the text, no matter original intentions. Historical criticism is employed only reluctantly and apologetically.

4. *Political and Psychological Hermeneutics.* Political hermeneutics such as Marxist modes of reading texts (e.g., Frederick Herzog or Dorothee Soelle) and modern psychological modes (e.g., Walter Wink) are imported to the Bible to order the immediate message of a text in a given contemporary setting. These use the Bible, or certain amenable portions of it, but denigrate or devalue historical criticism.

5. *The New Hermeneutic.* The heir of the old existentialist hermeneutic of Rudolf Bultmann, the so-called new hermeneutic of Ernst Fuchs, Gerhard Ebeling, Robert W. Funk, James M. Robinson, and others has considerable interest in recovering points originally scored and makes full use of biblical criticism. The events that speech created in the first century, or earlier, were viewed as formative for speech events that can take place today in proclamation and witness. If biblical criticism locked the Bible into the past, it stood to reason that modern philosophical hermeneutics would unlock it. There was some willingness to live with the failures of biblical criticism; it was recognized that it simply had not brought the historical assurances anticipated and promised.

6. *History—Holy and Secular.* Combining the neo-orthodox interest in history as a vehicle of revelation with some of the ontological observations of Martin Heidegger, Wolfhart Pannenberg tried to develop hermeneutics that could discern both biblical and current historical truth. Historical process, past and present, was viewed as a fulcrum for divine activity. The Heilsgeschichte of neo-orthodoxy was used as a prism for viewing all history. God's plan continues to unfold in world history not just a peculiar history. Jürgen Moltmann picked up at that point and developed a "theology of hope" in which biblical eschatology was seen as God's future invading the present. Biblical criticism was fully used in these theological efforts.

7. *Functionalism.* Here there is interest in how the Bible has functioned both in the believing communities (e.g., Hans Frei, David Kelsey) and in the culture at large (e.g., James Barr), and how it might continue to function. Criticism is viewed as necessary to recover the early stages of its function. This has some affinity with the following.

8. *The Bible as Canon.* Almost since the inception of biblical criticism, but certainly in the work of Johann Salomo Semler in 1772,[8] the concept of canon was narrowed to include only the final stage of the literary history of the Bible. Prior to that time it had meant authoritative tradition; but since an enlightened study of the Bible, using inductive and scientific tools, was not equipped to handle the questions of biblical authority as they were then

posed—almost completely in transcendent terms—the pioneers in biblical criticism were forced to reduce the concept to problems manageable in their terms. And those terms were literary-historical. Hence, formation of canon was seen as the final stage in biblical literary history; and the fledgling field sought out elements in that history amenable to their developing tools and to the questions they needed to ask: and those elements were councils and lists recorded in the noncanonical literature of synagogue and church.

A major discovery of the time was supposed evidence of a rabbinic council that was thought to have taken place in Jabneh (or Jamnia) in Palestine before the end of the first century C.E. It was argued, and still is in most OT introductions, that the Jabneh council decided, give or take one or two OT books, what was to be in and what excluded from the canon. It was then suggested that there were actually two canons in Judaism stemming from that time—the Palestinian, decided at Jabneh, and the Alexandrian, formed out in the Hellenistic Jewish world, probably in lower Egypt where the *Letter of Aristeas* says the Torah had been translated into Greek. This hypothesis, soon to become dogma, fitted well into another manageable schema of biblical criticism, of Old and New Testament—the unrealistic but absolute distinction between Palestinian Judaism (Hebrew-Aramaic Pharisaic purist) and Hellenistic Judaism (Greek and accommodating).

This view of the matter obtained in biblical criticism until some thirty years ago, and still clings tenaciously to some outposts of scholarship even yet. The first serious challenge to it came from the dissertation by Albert Sundberg, in which, while the dogma of a council at Jabneh was retained, the two-canon theory of the OT was effectively challenged.[9] Sundberg convincingly argued that while surviving Judaism late in the first century had a remarkable consensus about what "soiled the hands" (was canonical), Christianity, which had broken away from Judaism, did not benefit from the Jewish decision. On the contrary, Christianity continued to view as canonical much of the literature that apocalyptic and other Jewish sects had viewed as sacred before those sects disappeared after 70 C.E., such as the Apocrypha (canonical in Eastern churches and deuterocanonical in Latin Christianity) and Pseudepigrapha (canonical in some Orthodox branches of Eastern Christianity).

Sundberg helped the field to break away from and review the Semler synthesis. His work was followed by a review of the literature concerning the Jabneh council, which effectively destroyed that "assured result" of biblical criticism: there had been no such authoritative "council."[10]

The next challenge to the Semler thesis came from study of the Qumran literature, especially the large Psalms Scroll from Cave 11. The Essene Psalter could contain, perhaps alongside a restricted streamlined Psalter of 150 psalms, numerous other psalms and in an order variant to the MT-150 collection. The Qumran open-ended Psalter has the characteristics of an early stage of Psalter development before its curtailment.[11] The case of the Psalter caused a review of the whole question of canon before 100 C.E. Studies in OT text criticism were on a parallel track in indicating that, aside from the

Pentateuch, the period prior to the end of the first century was marked by textual fluidity.[12]

From another direction came another challenge: the ecumenical movement and especially Vatican II. Since the early 1960s the consciousness of everyone in the field has been raised to deal with a plurality of canons in the sense of inclusion-exclusion. It is considerably more difficult now than ever before to think in singularistic modes. Pluralistic thinking is now imperative though considerably more difficult in praxis than in theory.

The next development came in the publication, in rapid succession, of three books: Brevard S. Childs (1970), Morton Smith (1971), and myself (1972).[13] There was no collusion; and yet they all dealt with the question of canon with some areas of agreement despite considerable differences. Childs stressed the canonical and theological context of the final form of the whole biblical text as over against the tendency of biblical criticism to seek the original points intended by biblical authors of earlier, smaller literary units. Smith stressed the role of Jewish political parties in early Judaism (exilic and postexilic) in the actual selection of the literature in the canon: the Yahweh-Only party won out over others (see above, pp. 22ff.). His method was that of political determinism, but even so he thus recognized the important point that what made it into the Bible was the monotheizing literature of old Israel and Judah, as well as of early Judaism. I stressed the role of the early believing communities after the work of the last discreet genuises, the final redactors, was complete; but, in contradistinction to Smith I focused on the existential needs of the communities in the periods of intense canonical process. And in contradistinction to Childs, I focused not on the final forms of the texts revised but on the historical process that yielded the texts.

All three were responding, in some degree, to the conflict that had arisen between the results of form criticism and the results of redaction criticism; and all three moved on beyond them to another stage.

Canonical Criticism

Canonical criticism should be viewed as another subdiscipline of biblical criticism and complementary to the earlier developments. It takes seriously the authoritative function of the traditions that compose the Bible in the believing communities that shaped its various literary units, compiled and arranged its several parts in the conditions received, and continued to adapt its traditions to their ongoing lives. The Bible is the churches' book (in Christian terms) in every sense of the expression. The early believing communities created and shaped it and passed it down to their successors today—hence the term "canonical criticism" and not history of canon. Why? Because those communities found value in these several literary traditions or we would not have them: that is its authority. It gave life, at crucial junctures in its transmission from generation to generation, to the believing communities that read it and sought answers to their existential needs in it. For them it is the Book of Life (sefer ḥayyim).

Its true *Sitz im Leben,* or living context, where it comes alive, so to speak, is those communities, Jewish and Christian—of whatever extent the canon. Its primary *Sitz* is not the historian's study or the archaeologist's dig. It is very helpful to both, so much so that biblical criticism has appeared, as noted above, to lock it in the past. Biblical criticism, however, is but tools; and when the attitudes of those using them ignore the essential nature of the Bible, criticism becomes more than it should be. And that is apparently what has happened.

Canonical criticism corrects those attitudes and brings criticism to its rightful and limited, but very important, relation to the Bible. It puts the Bible back together again by recognizing its nature and function, as well as its literary structure—of whatever length or extent.

Canonization was a historical process that took place in the early believing communities over a period of time between the sixth century B.C.E. and the second century C.E. The process, however, had actually begun with the first occasion, whenever it was, perhaps in the late Bronze Age, that a biblical tradition spanned a generation gap and addressed more than one context. Stabilization of those traditions into their several literary forms was gradual: it was greatly accelerated when traditions became written, especially with the penning of Deuteronomy. Even so, the substance of the traditions attained authority and a sacral dimension—through repetition generation to generation—before the forms were stabilized without variation.

The primary character of canon or authoritative tradition, whatever its quantity or extent, is its adaptability; its secondary character is its stability. This is the reason I hesitate to focus as much on the "final literary text" as does Childs (see below, pp. 166–72). Though the traditions attained stable literary forms at points along the way, they still were rendered adaptable to the needs of the next generation. To focus exclusively on the final full literary form is simply not what either Judaism or Christianity did. As soon as need be, they broke into the frozen text and made it relevant to the next problem faced: and for the most part they fragmented the texts in order to do so—no matter how much we moderns may regret it.

Hermeneutics is the midterm between canon's stability and its adaptability. Discerning the hermeneutics used by the ancient biblical thinkers and authors in adapting the early authoritative traditions to their contexts, for their people, is the essence of canonical criticism. And those hermeneutics cannot be discerned without as much knowledge as possible of the ancient historical (cultural, economic, political, etc.) contexts addressed. Hence, responsible use of all the tools available from biblical criticism is necessary.

Canonical criticism does not assume, as has been tacitly supposed to date, that the canon contains the literature ancient Israel and Judah and the earliest churches had. On the contrary, it is now more cautious to assume that it includes only a portion of what there was.[14] What is there is that which was picked up again and again, generation after generation, and found of value. What did not have value in more than one context simply was set aside to decay—or to be discovered by archaeologists in modern times. What is there passed the tests of the needs of numerous contexts through which the early believing communities passed.

Biblical literature is thus both pluralistic and to some degree ambiguous.[15] It contains messages for many contexts and they sometimes appear contradictory. What was right for one context was not so for another. Isaiah 2:4 and Micah 4:3 say that on some future date all peoples will beat their swords into plowshares and their spears into pruning hooks; but Joel 3:10 (Heb. 4:10) says the opposite, that all peoples will beat their plowshares into swords and their pruning hooks into spears. Differing contexts indicate different messages and programs to follow. John says Jesus gave his disciples his peace (14:27); but Luke says Jesus came to bring not peace but a sword (12:51). The Preacher rather wearily saw that there was a time to kill and a time to heal (Eccl. 3:3). Eva Osswald, following Martin Buber, rightly says, "The true prophet must be able to distinguish whether a historical hour stands under the wrath or the love of God."[16]

Canonical criticism can liberate biblical study from the pervasive tendency to moralize upon reading all biblical texts thus absolutizing ancient Bronze Age or Iron Age or Hellenistic customs and mores.[17] It stresses the ontology of the Bible as a paradigm of God's work from creation through re-creation out of which we may construct paradigms for our own works, rather than as a jewel box of ancient wisdom to be perpetuated. It seeks the biblical hermeneutics whereby we may adapt the new wisdoms of our age just as they back there adapted the wisdom of the ancient Near East from many peoples.

And the hermeneutic it finds in the Bible is its shape: It is a monotheizing literature. Canonically the Bible pursues the integrity (oneness) of God, ontologically and ethically. Truth is an integer; reality is whole—whether any one generation or any one denomination (Jewish or Christian) can see it or not. Evil is a symbol of the freedom of God;[18] and it, too, can be redeemed and woven into God's tapestry of truth.[19] To fail to monotheize, in prophetic terms, was to risk falsehood (see below, p. 103). The Bible celebrates the theme: God's grace works in and through human sins ("Errore hominum providentia divina"). Shall we sin more, then, that grace may the more abound? asked Paul. No! he replied.

Finally, a shape of the canon is the divine bias for the weak and powerless. Israel was so often the vassal or client state throughout her history that there is little wonder at this. But it pervades the whole.

Reviving a sense of the Bible as canon, but at the same time using the valid tools of biblical criticism to discern the hermeneutics of the Bible itself, to recover ancient points originally scored in ancient contexts, can liberate the churches to read it dynamically to learn in our contexts who we truly are, beyond our limited biographies and visions, and what we can do today that would reflect God's righteousness and inject the integrity of reality into contemporary life.[20]

NOTES

1. See R. W. Funk, "The Watershed of the American Biblical Tradition: The Chicago School, First Phase, 1892–1920," *JBL* 15 (1976): 4–22.

2. A judicious and careful statement of the charge is Hans Frei's *Eclipse of Biblical Narrative: A Study in Eighteenth and Nineteenth Century Hermeneutics* (New Haven: Yale Univ. Press, 1974).

3. Cf. W. F. Albright, *From Stone Age to Christianity* (Baltimore: Johns Hopkins Press, 1940).

4. See G. E. Wright, *The OT and Theology* (New York: Harper & Row, 1969).

5. See Brevard S. Childs, *Biblical Theology in Crisis* (Philadelphia: Westminster Press, 1970). Childs's heaviest fire was directed at the confidence of the neo-orthodox biblical theologians in biblical criticism and archaeology. See my review of his book in *USQR* 26 (1971): 299–304.

6. Walter Wink, *The Bible in Human Transformation: Toward a New Paradigm for Biblical Study* (Philadelphia: Fortress Press, 1973).

7. I am sorry it could not be developed at Union Seminary: see my inaugural address, "The Vitality of the OT: Three Theses" (*USQR* 21 [1966]: 161–84).

8. The Union Seminary library has the 1776 edition of Johann Salomo Semler's *Abhandlung von freier Untersuchung des Canon.*

9. Albert C. Sundberg, Jr., *The OT of the Early Church*, HTS 20 (Cambridge: Harvard Univ. Press, 1964).

10. J. P. Lewis, "What Do We Mean by Jabneh?" *JBR* 32 (1964): 124–32.

11. See J. A. Sanders, "Cave 11 Surprises and the Question of Canon" (1969); and idem, "The Qumran Psalms Scroll (11QPsª) Reviewed," in *On Language, Culture, and Religion: In Honor of Eugene A. Nida*, ed. M. Black and W. Smalley (The Hague: Mouton Press, 1974), 79–99. In support of this see, among others, the essay by Peter R. Ackroyd, "The Open Canon," *Colloquium: The Australian and New Zealand Theological Review* 3 (1970): 279–91; see also his "Original Text and Canonical Text," *USQR* 32 (1977): 166–73. For a differing view see P. W. Skehan, "A Liturgical Complex in 11QPsª," *CBQ* 35 (1973): 195–205.

12. See F. M. Cross and S. Talmon, eds., *Qumran and the History of the Biblical Text* (Cambridge: Harvard Univ. Press, 1975); and the article by D. Barthélemy, *IDBSup.*, s.v. "Text, Hebrew, history of."

13. Childs, *Biblical Theology;* Morton Smith, *Palestinian Parties and Politics that Shaped the OT* (New York: Columbia Univ. Press, 1971); and J. A. Sanders, *Torah and Canon* (1972).

14. See the list of references within the Bible itself to other ancient works cited and alluded to, in Sid Z. Leiman, *The Canonization of Hebrew Scripture* (Hamden, Conn.: Archon, 1976), 16–26.

15. See the statement by James Barr, *Old and New in Interpretation* (New York: Harper & Row, 1966), 27; and J. A. Sanders, "Reopening Old Questions About Scripture" (1974).

16. Cf. James L. Crenshaw, *Prophetic Conflict: Its Effect Upon Israelite Religion*, BZAW 124 (New York and Berlin: Walter de Gruyter, 1971), 54; J. A. Sanders, "Canonical Hermeneutics: True and False Prophecy" (chap. 5 of this book).

17. For a clear statement of this point in the context of liberation from sexist interpretation of the Bible, see Sharon Ringe's contribution to *The Liberating Word*, ed. L. M. Russell (Philadelphia: Westminster Press, 1976), 23–38.

18. This phrase I owe to my former colleague Samuel Terrien, in *Job* (Neuchâtel: Delachaux et Niestlé, 1963), 46.

19. See J. A. Sanders, "Adaptable for Life: The Nature and Function of Canon" (chap. 1 of this book).

20. See J. A. Sanders, *IDBSup.*, s.v. "Hermeneutics" (= chap. 3 of this book, "Canonical Hermeneutics"). See also my more popular article on "The Bible as Canon," *CCen* 98 (December 2, 1981): 1250–55.

5

Canonical Hermeneutics: True and False Prophecy

As stated in chapter 4, my thinking about the so-called shape of the canon had been moving more and more toward the Bible's own internal or canonical hermeneutics—the means whereby the ancient tradents themselves resignified and re-presented what was already considered authoritative by their communities in their time. The terms "canonical" and "authoritative" clearly have shared meanings, though not entirely coterminous. I was moving more and more to the view that the unrecorded hermeneutics of the ancient tradents, the authors and contributors to the Bible, were as canonical as the actual literature itself. These provided the paradigms whereby they struggled to monotheize in their time.

Starting with the observation made in *Torah and Canon* (1972) that the great, judgmental prophets of the mid-eighth to mid-sixth centuries B.C.E. were best understood under the general rubric of the covenant-lawsuit metaphor, I broached the time-honored problem of criteria of distinction between the so-called true and so-called false prophets as presented in the prophetic corpus. The field had arrived by the early 1970s, culminating in the work of James L. Crenshaw, at the point of asserting that there were no sure criteria in the ambiguity of reality for making such a distinction when prophetic disputations were or are joined. Later, perhaps, but not on the spot. I had been working for some time on how references to community authoritative traditions, alongside references to the "call" of the individual prophet, functioned in prophetic literature (*Torah and Canon*, 73–90).

Adam van der Woude's work on prophetic disputations had caught my imagination, but I disagreed that the difference between truth and falsehood lay in actual theological tenets or doctrines themselves. He had seemed to arrive at a conclusion that indicated that the tenets of ancient Zionism were being presented in the prophetic corpus as wrong or false. That left too many questions unanswered, not the least of which was what to do with the relation of hope to judgment (see "Prologue," esp. p. 3, above) in the prophets generally or the whole thrust of Deutero-Isaiah. Nonetheless, his method of work was innovative and interesting.

I then set about doing as close research as possible on the question of the hermeneutics implicit in citations of community authoritative traditions in conjunction with the disputation passages. Since it had become clear, as stated in *Torah and Canon*, that the great preexilic prophets had applied the hermeneutic of prophetic critique, that is, of understanding God as the Creator God of all peoples as well as Israel's Redeemer God when citing the community (whether Mosaic or Davidic) traditions, I examined each disputation passage with the question in mind of whether those passages exhibited a similar hermeneutic on the part of the so-called true prophet. In some instances the reference to God as Creator was a bit removed from the narrowly defined disputation passage, but never very far. The hypothesis proved itself with startling impact.

Out of that work I conceived of the triangle as a tool for work on such matters throughout the Bible. Wherever an authoritative community tradition is cited, in OT or NT, one should then study as closely as possible the historical and sociological context in which it was cited (to discern carefully the need of the community as perceived by the prophet—not as perceived by the people or their leaders) and the hermeneutics by which that tradition was brought to bear on the tradition, to relate it and apply it to that situation.

The following chapter starts with an explanation of the triangle specifically applied to the problem of discerning the differing hermeneutics of two prophets addressing the same context. It then explains how it also applies to the case of having the same hermeneutics applied to the same tradition but in quite different historical contexts. That seemed to me to prove the case of the validity of the triangle as a critical tool in working on canonical hermeneutics generally. And it indeed has proved its worth in all cases applied.

The danger of falsehood enters into any debate that appeals to Scripture, or its antecedent traditions, whenever there is failure to understand God as the universal Creator God of all peoples as well as the Redeemer God in Israel and in Christ.

The problem of true and false prophecy in the OT has become a focal point for study of canonical hermeneutics. The thesis of the present study is that prophecy in biblical antiquity, whether "true" or false," can be more fully understood when studied in the light of three major factors where available: ancient traditions (texts), situations (contexts), and hermeneutics. The following diagram may indicate their interdependence and interrelationship.

hermeneutics

texts/ - contexts/
traditions   situations

By texts is meant the common authoritative traditions employed and brought forward (re-presented) by the prophet to bear upon the situation to which he or she spoke in antiquity. Such traditions included both the authoritative forms of speech expected of prophets and the authoritative epic-historic traditions to which they appealed to legitimate their messages.[1]

By contexts is meant the historical, cultural, social, political, economic, national, and international situations to which prophets applied the "texts." Context here, then, is not solely or even principally a literary reference (though often the literary context is determinative for meaning), but refers primarily to the full, three-dimensional situation in antiquity necessary to understand the significance of the literary record or unit under study.[2]

By hermeneutics is meant the ancient theological mode, as well as literary technique, by which that application was made by the prophet, true or false—that is, how he or she read the "texts" and "contexts" *and* how he or she related them.

I

A review of work done to date on true and false prophecy indicates the importance of attempting to discern the hermeneutics of prophecy, especially in those instances where two or more prophets spoke to the same context, notably the disputations. Focus on these may yield indications for discernment between true and false prophecy not yet fully recognized.

Jeremiah 28, with Deuteronomy 13 and 18, is the *locus classicus* of the problem. G. Quell, in a study published in 1952, is often given credit for liberating study of true and false prophecy from a priori assumptions about Jeremiah's colleague Hananiah (Jeremiah 28), who had been thought of largely as a cultic, nationalistic pseudoprophet, a fanatic demagogue, a libertine in morals, illiterate of spirit, and, indeed, an offender against the Holy Spirit.[3] He showed, by contrast, that Hananiah subscribed to the same traditions as Jeremiah, employing the same expected forms of both speech and symbolic action as the latter. It was the LXX that introduced the term "pseudoprophet"; the Hebrew Bible does not have it. Since Quell, intentionality is no longer a criterion for discernment of distinction between Hananiah and Jeremiah, and hence between so-called false and true prophets generally. Not only did Hananiah feel that he was right and Jeremiah wrong, Jeremiah was constrained after their initial encounter to identify with him and his message: "Amen! May the Lord do so!" (Jer. 28:6). It is simply not possible to impugn the so-called false prophets with conscious, evil intention. Recognition of this fact in modern study has received broader support from the acknowledgment of pluralism as a factor in research. Unresolved debate at any juncture of history and recognition of the ambiguity of reality are stressed also in the sociology of knowledge.

Gerhard von Rad in 1933 could with some confidence find in his study of Jeremiah 28, and Deuteronomy 13 and 18, confirmation of what he already knew, that history was the vehicle of revelation.[4] And Sigmund Mowinckel in 1934 found that prophecies based on the Word of Yahweh had greater likelihood of being true than those based on the Spirit of Yahweh.[5] Martin Buber in 1947 anticipated Quell's so-called defense of Hananiah in calling him "ein prinzipientreuer Mann," a man true to his principles.[6] But Buber went on to use quite negative epithets: Hananiah was a political ideologue, blind in comparison to Jeremiah, and a successful politician. Although Buber's study of the crucial debate in Jeremiah 28 contains valuable observations for discussion of prophetic hermeneutics, he leaves us with the impression that the passage offers at least functional criteria for distinguishing true and false prophets. All such discussions and suggestions were well received in the neo-orthodox atmosphere of his time.

Since Quell, however, a healthy measure of the ambiguity of reality, and of the thinking of pluralism, has entered into discussions of the problem with sobering effect: so much so, indeed, that skepticism concerning criteria of distinction has been the salient mark of serious work done since 1952. There is no clearly defined criterion to distinguish true and false prophecy, or to identify the true prophet in a debate.[7] Although Eva Osswald summarized the thinking of von Rad in her 1962 study, she did so only after careful, critical consideration of all criteria that had been advanced.[8]

James L. Crenshaw's study (1971) goes the furthest in the direction of skepticism, even to the point of judging that the inevitability of false prophecy, stemming from the lack of criteria to discern it in any given situation, caused the failure and demise of prophecy in the early Exilic Age.[9] His pressing the matter to its logical and realistic conclusion has drawn considerable criticism.[10] And yet Crenshaw himself, following Edmond Jacob,[11] seems to leave us, if not with a criterion of discernment, at least with a clear warning that all true prophets (whoever they might have been) were in constant danger of succumbing to the temptation of confusing the voice of the people with the voice of God. Indeed, Cranshaw claims, because true prophecy was such a fragile affair and false prophecy so realistically inevitable, that prophecy as a biblical phenomenon failed and wisdom and apocalyptic took their place in early Judaism.

L. Ramlot has revived the criterion of the voice of the people as a positive factor of discernment by suggesting its role in the later canonical process.[12] It was the voice of the later remnant, or surviving Judaism, in reviewing the preexilic and exilic messages of the prophets, true and false, that found value for survival in those messages that it went on to preserve for us in the canon. My own work would underscore such an observation.[13] But that remnant found itself in a totally different situation or "context" from that of their predecessors who had actually heard the canonical prophets and had formed the earlier voice of the people. It is in the canonical process that the so-called criterion of "history" (Jer. 28:9; Deut. 18:22) or fulfillment of prophecy should be understood, rather than in the simpler sense of specific prediction coming to pass or not; and it is in this sense that the emphases of von Rad, Buber, and Osswald on "history" as the vehicle of true revelation can be retained.

Such an observation does not, however, actually contradict Crenshaw's quite valid view that in their time the voice of the people was a negative and powerful pressure on the prophets whose interpretations of their current history and expectations of their immediate future ran counter to those of the vast majority of their people, who were well represented by the so-called false prophets. Numerous passages in the prophets indicate that they were constrained to indict the people and the so-called false prophets often in the same manner and with the same words (Isa. 30:8–14; Micah 2:6; 3:5, 11; Jer. 26:8; Ezekiel 13—14). Their messages simply were not popular in their time: even the exilic Isaiah challenged his people in Babylonia (1) not to assimilate to the dominant culture but to retain their Jewish identity, and (2) to believe that the God who was in his time redeeming and liberating them was the same who had delivered Jacob to the despoilers (Isa. 42:24 et passim). There is no evidence at all that the great prophet of the exile was the voice of the people of his day; quite the contrary.

Hence, Osswald designated the criterion of judgment (Jer. 28:8) as primary; and it was this aspect that Sheldon Blank and A. Heschel elaborated in their different but equally moving descriptions of prophetic suffering and pathos. Their messages were charges (*maśśā*'; Jer. 23:33) that challenged their people's understanding of themselves and their God.[14] Their love for their people was so deep, and their identity with them so complete, that their messages hurt the prophets before and while they delivered them to their people.[15] My own work also affirms such observations as these, and they touch directly on the question of prophetic hermeneutics.

Apparently following G. Wanke and E. Jacob, A. van der Woude stresses ancient Zionism or nationalism as a criterion of false prophecy in the preexilic situation. In recent work on Micah 4, van der Woude broaches the old problems of so-called postexilic additions to Micah in a fresh way by the method of identifying *Disputationswörter* (prophetic conflict passages).[16] Micah 4 would appear to be a locus of record of debates Micah might have had with contemporary prophetic colleagues who challenged his message of divine judgment in the situation of the eighth century B.C.E. Instead of seeing those passages that appear to contradict Micah's message of chapters 1—3 as later additions, one might view them as quotations of colleagues who held a different theology—that of God as the Holy Warrior who sometimes allows Israel's enemies to encamp at Zion's gates to besiege Jerusalem in order that Israel may the more easily thresh them and destroy them. The enemies outside the gates say, "Let her [daughter of Zion] be profaned, and let our eyes gaze upon Zion" (Micah 4:11). "But they do not know the thoughts of the Lord, they do not understand his plan, that he has gathered them as sheaves to the threshing floor," say Micah's prophetic opponents (4:12). Israel's enemies, if they knew the truth, said the latter, ought better to say, "Come, let us go up to the mountain of the Lord . . . that he may teach us his ways" (4:2).

These are valuable findings. A review of what earlier scholarship has called secondary passages or exilic additions might indeed yield considerable recovery of such debates between the canonical prophets and their contemporary colleagues. Scholars have struggled with the observation that the judgmental prophets appear to have opposed static application of royalist theology in their day (Jacob) or a simple "parroting of Isaiah" (Buber).

Buber's essay on the encounter between Jeremiah and Hananiah was seminal and is worthy of review. He sought to understand why and how Jeremiah, after saying Amen to Hananiah's message of consolation, could upon reflection return with the strength of his original conviction reinforced, "Geschichte geschicht" (time marches on).[17] Time marches on and no one moment can be totally equal to another. The living God is not an automatic machine. God's truth cannot be systematized. Humankind endowed with free will changes to the point that historical reality and the divine will may become quite different in one moment from what they had been in another. Hananiah was the person who had real knowledge but was a prisoner of that knowledge. Parroting Isaiah, he was satisfied to repeat a solution of the past; for with all his knowledge of history he did not know how to listen. He was truly a man of principle who was convinced that God too was a man true to his principles, bound by the promises he had made to Isaiah. Hananiah did not know how to recognize history "becoming." He knew only the eternal return of the wheel, but not the scales of history that tremble like a human heart. He was the typical fanatic patriot who accused Jeremiah of treason. Jeremiah, however, did not think of his homeland as a political ideology but as a colony of people, an assemblage of human living and mortal beings whom the Lord did not want to see perish. In counseling them to submission to Nebuchadnezzar he wished to preserve their life. Despite his grand ideology Hananiah was but a blind man while Jeremiah was a realist. The one, concluded Buber, was but a politican with dazzling illusions, the successful man; the other, in his suffering silence, in the pit, and in failure, did not know the intoxication of success.

Ramlot reports that J. Ngally has extrapolated from Buber's essay an affirmation of the sovereign freedom of God and of the politics of the true prophet, which were opposed to the timeless political ideology of the false prophet and which sought the concrete salvation of flesh and blood people.[18]

II

It would be easy, in using without caution the prism of Buber's moving essay, to draw from it false criteria for discernment of prophecy. Surely one cannot always denounce those who appear to be fanatically patriotic or who strive to live by historically learned principles; that would be but to turn Hananiah, as Buber perceived him, around the other way. But one who has read the Bible in all its pluralism of expression can but affirm Buber's basic observation of the dynamic nature of the divine will, as the Bible expresses it, in ever-changing historical and cultural contexts or situations. Within biblical-historical typology there is movement.[19] Although typology appears to be the most fundamental of intrabiblical hermeneutic techniques, especially in the prophets, notably Deutero-Isaiah and the NT, it would be difficult to find a passage where it is applied statically.[20] Although the canonical prophets apparently referred to some form of the Torah story, by citation or subtle allusion, they also stressed listening to the voice of God in their own day.[21]

Crenshaw is right to relate Buber with Osswald's statement: "The true prophet must be able to distinguish whether a historical hour stands under the wrath or the love of God."[22] Such discernment requires both intimate knowledge of the traditions or "texts" of the ways of God in Israel's past (its *mythos* or Torah story) and a dynamic ability to perceive the salient facts of one's own moment in time as they move through the fluidity of history. With apparently no one around after the exile to offer such discernment, history indeed appeared to be static, or worse, to be but some alternating cadence between birth and death, planting and plucking up, breaking down and building up . . . (Eccl. 3:2–3).

The student of the history of interpretation well knows how a single text, when stabilized in form and content, scores different points when read in different contexts. Deuteronomy in its original context of seventh century B.C.E. Judah was a challenge to a royalist theology based on unconditioned promises (no matter how much Manasseh had needed the flexibility of domestic policy it offered in the face of Assyrian foreign policy) and the blessed assurance of God's faithfulness. But a stabilized, inflexible text of Deuteronomy (Deut. 4:2; 12:32), read unchanged a few decades later in a totally different context, apparently scored a quite different point from that intended by its authors, or heard by Josiah; and the Deuteronomic admonition that disobedience would bring abrogation of the covenant was sometimes read to say that if an individual suffered deprivation and hardship he or she must have sinned. Deuteronomy did not say that, but Job was surely written in part to record a resounding no to such inversions of the Deuteronomic ethic of election.[23] No one need have changed the text of Deuteronomy for the inverted reading to occur. On the contrary, if one did *not* alter the reading of Deuteronomy dynamically, to adjust its "text" to the new "context," then the inversion was almost bound to occur. Such an observation is common to the student of canonical criticism; it is the nether side of the "stable" aspect of canon.[24]

But it is the very nature of "canon" to be adaptable as well as stable. On this all segments of both Judaism and Christianity—the full spectrum from liberal to conservative—agree: the Bible as canon is relevant to the ongoing believing communities as they pass it on from one generation to the other. They may disagree on its stability, what books are in the canon and in what order (whether the Jewish, the Catholic, or the Ethiopic canon), but they all agree on its adaptability. Before the triumph of Deuteronomy[25] those authoritative traditions that later came to make up part of the Bible had been quite fluid, largely in oral transmission and subject to many different oral forms, and hence supposedly less subject to the dangers of stability or static application. And yet, as Jacob and Buber stress, the so-called false prophets seemed to tend to employ typology statically.

Hence all scholars since Buber and Quell, as is well attested in the works of Osswald, Crenshaw, and F. L. Hossfeld and I. Meyer, agree that changes in historical-cultural situations indicated that hearing afresh the Word of God and its dynamic message was a mark of the so-called true prophet, although they do not put it quite this way. Probably the Reformers had a similar message when, in devaluing the magisterium of the Roman Church and its extended traditions, they said that the Bible became the Word of God in new contexts only when interpreted dynamically by the Holy Spirit.

Few would wish to debate the fact that a stable tradition or text may say something different to different situations. What is difficult for modern heirs of the Enlightenment is determination or definition of what the canonical prophets meant by listening to the voice of God (Jer. 7:23, 26), or what the Reformers meant by interpretation by or through the Holy Spirit. What can be said today about such a factor in the adaptability of the prophetic message to changing historical moments? What can be said of the prophet's ability to distinguish whether a historical hour stands under the wrath or the love of God?

III

Scholarship seems now to be generally in agreement that nothing really critical can be said. Von Rad and Quell deny that we can establish with clarity or objectivity what the *exousia* (power or authority) of the true prophet at any point was: it simply is not subject to scientific analysis.[26] Ramlot uses the phrase "mystique en un sens large" (mystery in a broad sense).[27] But one wonders if we are reduced entirely to such a judgment. Partly in response Crenshaw points to what he calls the failure of prophecy and its yielding in the exilic period to wisdom and apocalyptic.

The midterm between canon's stability and its adaptability is hermeneutics. The more stabilized a tradition became the more crucial the role hermeneutics played in rendering it relevant to new situations. Even in preexilic times, however, before stabilization of forms had become a dominant feature in the precanonical history of those traditions (the early canonical process), prophets, psalmists, and others frequently made allusion to Israel's *mythos* traditions in order to legitimate their thoughts and messages. Prophetic literature is replete with such references, as von Rad has shown.[28] An interesting aspect of study of tradition criticism today, especially in the Prophets, is prophetic hermeneutics. When the ancient biblical thinkers rendered the old traditions relevant to their day, what hermeneutics did they employ? Such study is keenly advanced when the hermeneutics of contemporaries can be compared, for example, if two ancients apply the same epic tradition to the same contemporary situation but draw quite different conclusions from it.

Studies in true and false prophecy have to date not taken sufficient advantage of such comparative study. In the prophetic corpus recognition of disputations between contemporaries centers, of course, in the encounter between Jeremiah and Hananiah. The work of van der Woude since 1969 has brought the disputations to the fore, as Crenshaw recognized.[29] Every study of true and false prophecy since Quell has attempted, more or less seriously, to discern the theology of the false prophets. But for the most part scholars have so far seemed satisfied to give such theologies labels: royal theology (Jacob), establishment theology (Bright), Zionist theology (van der Woude), *vox populi* (Crenshaw), fanatical patriotism and political ideology (Buber), all somehow voiced at the wrong historical moment. Lacking in the field is a serious attempt to extrapolate from the disputation passages the hermeneutics of the debating colleagues.[30] This chapter is a probe in that direction.

Buber's point, followed by Osswald and others, that the historical context was vastly important in terms of validity of prophetic message, cannot be gainsaid. Careful study of the Bible in search of what the so-called false prophets actually said and preached yields a number of passages where such prophets cannot be dismissed facilely in terms of their theology, or by what little is known of their life style. All scholars of the question agree on this. Such agreement permits us to focus on the form, content, and theology of the "false" prophets. K. Koch's work, because it is so thorough, permits us to move beyond the question of the forms they used: they were the same as those used by the so-called true prophets.[31]

Did they, however, make reference to Israel's ancient epic traditions? The answer all scholars have given to this is yes. But it is apparently at this point that the question of hermeneutics has failed to arise because thus far it has apparently been sufficient to remark, one way and another, on how the false prophets invoked an otherwise decently good theology but at the wrong time, supporting leaders and people when they needed a challenge. And the right theology at the wrong time is variously described, as we have seen, as royalist, Zionist, and the like, while the so-called true prophets were apparently invoking a right theology at the right time, supposedly a Mosaic view of conditional covenant, or, at least, a different tradition.

If, however, both parties invoked the same theology at the same time addressing the same situation, then hermeneutics would have to enter the picture. Such may or may not be the case in the famous debate between Jeremiah and Hananiah, but we cannot know for certain because the immediate record does not state what "text" or tradition each recited. There are other passages in the prophetic corpus, however, which may assist in this regard.

IV

In order to gain further perspective on the importance of "context" or situation, we will compare Ezek. 33:23–29 and Isa. 51:1–3. In the first the situation is 586 B.C.E., or very shortly thereafter, for the pericope is placed just after the report of the message from Palestine to Ezekiel's Babylonian deportee camp that Jerusalem had fallen (Ezek. 33:21; cf. 24:26).[32] The historical moment is very clear. Some of the people on that occasion apparently took heart, in a spirit of hope, and cited an authoritative tradition to apply to their situation: "Abraham was only one man, yet he got possession of the land; but we are many; the land is surely given us to possess" (33:24). The hermeneutical techniques employed were typology and *argumentum a fortiori* (or *qal vaḥomer*). But the central interest of hermeneutics is not in its techniques but in its basic modes and suppositions. In the second passage (Isa. 51:1–3), Deutero-Isaiah advances the same argument, in every respect, which the people presented in Ezekiel 33: "Look to Abraham your father and to Sarah who bore you; for when he was but one I called him, and I blessed him and made him many. For the Lord will comfort Zion . . ." (51:2–3).

And yet in the first passage, Ezekiel rejected the people's argument out of hand. His response to them was as harshly judgmental as any passage in the book: God will continue the judgment upon the land until utter and complete desolation sets in (Ezek. 33:25–29). The time or context was wrong, for the selfsame argument was presented some fifty years later by Deutero-Isaiah as true prophecy. These passages seem not to have figured so far in any discussions of true and false prophecy, one supposes, because the Ezekiel text does not specify that the people who advanced their argument were prophets. And yet, neither does the text say they were not prophets. But it hardly matters since the form of their argument is very close to the form or argument of prophecy when it cites ancient traditions to support its message: it is not, however, in the literary form of *Botspruch* (such a message); hence it has been overlooked. Neither, for that matter, is the form of the passage in Deutero-Isaiah totally conformative!

Both the people in Ezekiel 33 and Deutero-Isaiah use the same hermeneutic techniques of typology and *argumentum a fortiori*. In both arguments the hermeneutic principle is also the same: the God who called Abraham and Sarah out of Babylonia will call the exiles out of Babylonia; he will do the same kind of thing and execute the same kind of mighty act as he had done in the Bronze Age. The assumption is that God will be consistent: "the God who brought Abraham out of Babylonia and brought him into the promised land will bring us out of Babylonia into the promised land—all the more so because we outnumber him by far." Deutero-Isaiah said yes to what Ezekiel fifty years earlier had said no. The hermeneutic principle of the "false prophecy" in Ezekiel and of the true in Isaiah was the same: they both cited the tradition *constitutively*, as a support to what the people felt they needed. Those early moments just after the temple had fallen were not right for such a message: it would have but increased the people's deception (Ezek. 33:30–33). First Isaiah had had to say no to a similar argument in a similar situation just after 722 B.C.E. The good folk of Samaria, with the buoyancy of the human spirit of hope, said: "The bricks have fallen, but we will build with dressed stones; the sycamores have been cut down, but we will put cedars in their place" (Isa. 9:10). Such undaunted spirit all admire and applaud. Who can say it is by principle wrong? But First Isaiah, like Ezekiel later, denounced it in as harsh, judgmental terms as may be found in the prophetic corpus. It was apparently the wrong time.

When Jeremiah used the Rechabites as an object lesson for obedience, he did not approve of their static view of it (Jeremiah 35). The Rechabites practiced obedience by attempting to retain earlier nomadic contexts of living: Jeremiah, in contrast, stressed continually listening (Jer. 35:14).

When Nebuzaradan had taken Jerusalem and offered Jeremiah a pension in Babylon, the prophet elected to stay in the desolate land (Jer. 40:1–6), despite the fact that up to the moment of defeat he had counseled defection to Babylonia (Jeremiah 37—38; cf. 6:16). Jeremiah remained consistent theologically by changing his message when the context changed (cf. Jer. 42:10). Context is an important factor. In point of fact, the messages of Hananiah in Jeremiah 28, that of the people in Ezekiel 33, and of Deutero-Isaiah in Isaiah 51 were all similar in announcing restoration. Isaiah 51 is distinct from them only in contextual timing. If restoration had occurred immediately upon destruction, the transformation of the covenantal relation between Israel and God that both Jeremiah and Ezekiel sought could certainly not have taken place (Jeremiah 24; 30—31; Ezek. 36:26–28). They both used the great physician metaphor, among others, to speak of that transformation. Divinely inflicted wounds for the purpose of transformation take time to heal properly; otherwise they are but soothed with the ineffectual balm of Gilead (Jer. 8:22) or, to use another metaphor, are daubed with whitewash (Ezek. 13:10). It would appear that forty to fifty years were needed to let the message sink into the *lēb* (heart) of the people: God can abrogate the covenant and act very strangely indeed, all the while pursuing his own agenda that no one generation can verify or falsify.

Actually Deutero-Isaiah faced the opposite problem, it would appear. After a period of time the people would be gravely tempted to abandon their Jewish identity and assimilate to the dominant culture—join the First Church of Marduk, or of Ahura Mazda, so to speak. The challenge they apparently needed to retain their Jewish identity amounted to a symphony of consolation, which Deutero-Isaiah nonetheless intimately related to God's judgments of fifty years earlier.

The importance of context or historical situation can also be seen in tracing in the Bible its most common theologoumenon: "Errore hominum providentia divina"—God's grace works through human sinfulness. This "theology" of prevenient grace can be said to underlie some three-quarters of biblical literature. Von Rad has brilliantly shown that it is the foundation of the final form of the Genesis text.[33] It is indeed the foundation of Torah. Deuteronomy indicates, however, that Manasseh exploited it and abused it; Jeremiah and Ezekiel agreed, finding abuse of it right up to the destruction of 586. The priestly theologians who shaped the Genesis traditions in the form we have them, as well as the final form of Torah, however, clearly saw that the old theologoumenon was an idea whose time had come once more. Hosea and Jeremiah reflect a minority view that there had been a golden age of obedience and devotion on the part of Israel in the early days before entrance into the land (Hosea 2:16–17 [= RSV 2:14–15]; 9:10, 15; 11:1–3; Jer. 2:2–3). But the Torah, as well as the other prophets, knows of no such tradition. According to them, although Israel had always been disobedient and recalcitrant, God's grace was not thwarted. Whatever evil Joseph's brothers, Jacob's eponymous sons, "intended" against him, God could and did "intend" it for good to the benefit of all (Gen. 50:20). Insistence on the faithfulness of the promiser (Heb. 10:23) in some contexts was apparently crucial to survival and continuity, but in other contexts (750–586 B.C.E.?) apparently became deception and falsehood.

In the NT the theme is celebrated decisively in the Gospels and Paul. In the former the ineptitude of the disciples is stressed in the teachings, while their failure to support Jesus in the Passion account is woven into the text as integral to his arrest, trial, and crucifixion. In Paul the theme is so central that to comment on it would be to review the Pauline doctrine of grace: God uses human sin and disobedience to effect his plans. Paul celebrates the theme so fully that he had to face the obvious challenge to it: shall we sin the more that grace may the more abound? And his answer was a resounding no (Rom.

6:15). But very clearly the existential age of the delicate birthing of the early churches required an emphasis on the theme, just as the existential age of the birth of Judaism out of the death of old Israel and Judah in the sixth century B.C.E. required equal emphasis on the same theme in Genesis once the message of divine judgment for disobedience and divine expectation of obedience and right understanding of election expounded by the prophets and Deuteronomy had already been fully expressed (750–586).

V

The importance of historical situation and context, therefore, cannot be overstated. In the prophetic disputation, however, the historical situation was always the same for the debating prophets (as ancient biblical theologians): they addressed the same problem but offered totally different suggestions as to what might be expected of God in that context. Even if they simply applied to that situation two different theologoumena, one emphasizing divine grace and faithfulness in and through and despite human sinfulness, and the other stressing divine expectations and obedience of the people in a theology of conditioned grace, the hermeneutical question arises precisely at the point of why they chose the theological theme they did choose.

Did they have a choice, willy-nilly, between a royalist theology of God's unconditioned promises and a Mosaic theology of divine expectation of obedience? Or, more acutely, was the one bound by personal identity to Davidic tradition and the other to the Mosaic, so that they had no such choice?

The case of First Isaiah would indicate otherwise. The central theological complexity of Isaiah 1—33 is that of its seeming to contain both these theological themes—grace and judgment—both based on authoritative Davidic traditions. Isaiah apparently in his early ministry could base a message of blessed assurance to Ahaz (Isa. 7:1–16) on the same Davidic traditions that he later cited in his message of stringent judgment.[34] At some point in his ministry Isaiah perceived that the earlier message had caused deceit and falsehood when carried into the era of the Assyrian threat (7:17—8:8). Upon reflection he perceived that God urged him not to walk any longer in the way of the people in this regard (8:11–15). Such reflection apparently caused him to claim that continuing to rely on the earlier message had caused the people to become deaf, blind, and insensitive to the later message of divine judgment through Assyrian assault upon Judah (6:9–13). God had, in his inscrutable way, poured a spirit of deep sleep upon those prophets who remained true and consistent to the message of divine grace without judgment (29:9–10). Did he include himself in that indictment to the extent that he had been consistent before altering his own hermeneutics?

Isaiah did not change theologies; nor did he shift allegiance from one tradition, the Davidic, to another, the Mosaic. There is simply no textual evidence for such a shift.

Is there, on the other hand, textual indication that he changed hermeneutics, that is, applied Davidic traditions to the new historical context of Assyrian threat *in a different hermeneutic mode?*

Isaiah 28:21 is a crucial passage in this regard. "For the Lord will rise up as on Mount Perazim, he will be wroth as in the valley of Gibeon; to do his deed—strange is his deed! and to work his work—alien is his work!" The historical references in this remarkable statement are to 2 Sam. 5:17–20 (Mount Perazim) and to 2 Sam. 5:25 plus 1 Chron. 14:10–17 (valley of Gibeon). But in those traditions it was claimed that Yahweh arose to *aid* David against the Philistine threat. Such references, on the face of it, would seem more (theo)logically apt if advanced by those prophets who argued that Jerusalem would be saved from the Assyrian siege, just as David had been saved by Yahweh. And yet Isaiah refers to them to score the opposite point! Yes, indeed, Yahweh *will* act again: he *will* rise up and be wroth as he has done in the past; but this time the Holy Warrior will direct his wrath toward his own people. He will indeed execute another "mighty act" as in the tradition, but this time it will seem strange and alien. Thus, Isa. 28:21 seems to be another biblical record of but one side of an ancient debate: in this case, that of Isaiah.

If the selfsame authoritative "text" (the tradition in 2 Samuel 5) can be appealed to with such opposing conclusions the difference lies not in theological tradition (Mosaic or Davidic) but in the hermeneutics applied to that tradition. They both referred to the same "gospel" text (of God's past activity) but derived from it totally different messages.

Isaiah 29:1–8 seems to demonstrate the same point. Again the same historical context or situation is addressed with both parties apparently appealing to the same Davidic tradition. David did indeed encamp in Jerusalem; it is Ariel, the city of the Lion of God. But Ariel is also God's altar where sacrifices are made to him, and Jerusalem will burn like an altar. God will encamp against it and besiege it through the agency of the invader; and the multitude of the foes doing so will be as numerous as the small dust particles Jerusalem experiences in its seasonal *hamsin* (desert wind) when heat currents are inverted and the air is polluted so thickly that the city is enveloped in them. It will be like the nightmare of a hungry, thirsty man who awakens to find no relief from his misery. (The metaphor is comparable to that of the Assyrian flood reaching Judah's neck in Isa. 8:8.)

Isaiah agrees again that Yahweh is a Holy Warrior, but this time he will be at the head of the enemy forces (cf. Isa. 1:24). Again each appeals to the same tradition in the same context, but with radically different hermeneutics. And the difference is indicated in Isa. 29:15–16. Those who hide deep their counsel and their deeds are those who turn things upside down, that is, those who regard the potter as the clay—those who deny God as Creator.

And therein lies the clue to the hermeneutics of those who from 750 to 586 could apply the ancient traditions of either the Davidic story or the so-called Mosaic Torah story to their contexts or situations and prophesy salvation in and through judgment.[35] To stress the tradition of Yahweh as Redeemer,

Provider, and Sustainer and deny Yahweh as Creator would be, in that historical context, to engage in "false prophecy." The so-called true prophets never *denied* that God was the God of Israel who had elected Israel and redeemed them from slavery in Egypt, guided them in the desert, and given them a home, *and/or* had chosen David and established his throne and city. They referred to those authoritative traditions sufficiently and often enough to be convincing. But in addition to affirming God as Redeemer and Sustainer, the true prophets stressed that God was also Creator of all peoples of all the earth. This would have made a radical difference in hermeneutics.

Amos seems to have been quite clear on this point, but in a different way. " 'Are you not like the Ethiopians to me, O people of Israel?' says the Lord. 'Did I not bring up Israel from the land of Egypt, and the Philistines from Caphtor and the Syrians from Kir?' " (Amos 9:7). If this sequel of rhetorical questions is viewed in the context of a colleague continually stressing the tradition, or "text," of the exodus as authority for a message of assurance that the God who brought Israel out of Egypt would not abandon it but would sustain it, it takes on considerable significance. The God who thus redeems and creates Israel also sustains; he is not a whimsical deity who cannot be trusted. His grace would be constant and would indeed function even in the midst of Israel's sinfulness. Amos's reply would indicate that he agreed with the "text." Indeed Yahweh *did* bring Israel out of Egypt. But did Israel think it was the only folk who ever had a migration? By no means. If the Philistines and Syrians migrated, as indeed those archenemies of Israel had done (in their own traditions), then Yahweh as Creator of *all* peoples had been their guide *(mōlîk)* as well. But, it was protested, he made a covenant only with us! Yes, indeed, Amos said, but being the Creator of all, as well as your Redeemer, he is free to "punish you for all your iniquities" (Amos 3:2). Just as being Creator of all he was free to judge Israel's neighbors (Amos 1:3—2:3), so he is free as well to judge Israel itself!

The assurance, "disgrace will not overtake us" (Micah 2:6), can indeed be drawn from the Torah story when the hermeneutics of divine grace is applied without reference to divine freedom. "Is not the Lord in the midst of us? No evil shall come upon us" (Micah 3:11; 4:9) is excellent theology in certain situations (Rom. 8:31).[36] Deutero-Isaiah could magnificently combine belief in God the Creator with belief in God the Redeemer[37] when the challenge indicated was Israel's need to maintain its identity, sustain a remnant, and resist assimilation to Babylonian and/or Persian cult and culture. Historical moment, or context, as stressed above, is a crucial factor in determining which hermeneutic to apply.

But that alone would be insufficient, for the factor of hermeneutic is equally crucial. *Whenever the freedom of God as Creator is forgotten or denied in adapting traditional "text" to a given context, there is the threat of falsehood.* In Deutero-Isaiah's situation, the conjoining of emphasis on God as Creator of all the earth with emphasis on God as Israel's particular Redeemer in the exodus issued in a powerful *message of retention of identity in the regathering of the people*. He who had used Nebuchadnezzar as instrument of judgment could use Cyrus as instrument of blessing: his was the world and all that was in it.

In Jeremiah's situation, the conjoining of emphasis on God as Creator of all the earth with emphasis on God as Israel's particular Redeemer in the exodus had issued, on the contrary, in a powerful *message of retention of identity in the scattering of the people*.

If the message of Hananiah as prophet can be viewed also as applying authoritative tradition to the context that he and Jeremiah both faced, the debate takes on a dimension beyond what has so far been suggested in studies on it. If he used the traditions of "form" in delivering his message, as has often been noted, might he not also have used the traditions of "text"? Those who transmitted the record of the debate to the literary form we inherit in Jeremiah 28 do not suggest reference to authoritative "text" tradition. But with the constitutive hermeneutic of God as Redeemer and Sustainer with emphasis on his grace, he might well have preached in the following manner: "Thus says the Lord of hosts, the God of Israel [who brought Israel up out of Egypt, guided it in the wilderness, and brought it into this land]: I have broken the yoke of the king of Babylon. Within two years I will bring back to this place all the . . ." (Jer. 28:2–3 with insertion). He might have said, in the debate, "Jeremiah, it is a question of having faith in God that he is powerful enough to keep his promises. He is not whimsical. He who brought us out of Egypt and into this land is strong enough to keep us here. It is a matter of firm belief in his providence and sustaining power." And Jeremiah, upon returning with the iron yoke, might have said, "Hananiah, he who brought us out of Egypt and into this land is strong enough *and free enough* to take us out of here. It is a matter of belief in God not only as redeemer and sustainer, but also as creator of all." As Jeremiah says in 28:14 in reference to Nebuchadnezzar, ". . . I have given to him even the beasts of the field." This is a clear reference to the same God the Creator that Jeremiah portrays in 27:5–7:

> It is I who by my great power and my outstretched arm have made the earth, with the men and animals that are on the earth, and I give it to whomever it seems right to me. Now I have given all these lands into the hand of Nebuchadnezzar, the king of Babylon, my servant, and I have given him and his son and his grandson, until the time of his own land comes; then many nations and great kings shall make him their slave.

There is considerable debate about whether Jeremiah said all that or others later attributed it to him. But as H. Weippert has indicated with regard to the so-called C or Deuteronomistic source in Jeremiah, much of it is in congruity with what the prophet says elsewhere.[38] And certainly Jeremiah frequently refers to the freedom of God the Creator. "Am I a God at hand, says the Lord, and not a God afar off? Can a person hide himself in secret places so that I cannot see him? [This is a direct reflection of Isa. 29:15–16.] Do I not fill heaven and earth? says the Lord" (Jer. 23:23–24).

VI

What seems quite clear is that the so-called false prophet did not refer, in times of threat, to God as God also of the enemy. Such an affirmation of God the Creator of all peoples is a part of the canonical monotheizing process.[39] It is at one with those struggles elsewhere in the Bible to monotheize in the face of evil, to affirm the oneness or (ontological and ethical) integrity of God in the face of an almost irresistible temptation to polytheize or particularize, and attribute evil to some other god or gods. Because he wanted his people to fall and stumble, or be tested, as a part supposedly of a much larger plan,[40] from the hardening of the heart of Pharaoh all the way to attributing to God the message of false prophets (1 Kings 22; Deut. 13:1–5), all was a part of a monotheizing process to which, apparently, the so-called false prophets did not, like the true prophets, consciously contribute.

Within and through the pluralism in the Bible a basic feature of the canon is its tendency to monotheize. It may be doubted if any large literary unit of the Bible, even Deutero-Isaiah, is thoroughly monotheistic. But there seems to be no literary unit of any size that contradicts the observation that the fundamental canonical thrust of the Bible is its struggle to monotheize.[41] Can it be affirmed that wherever the struggle to monotheize failed "false prophecy" threatened?

Study has indicated that no single criterion of distinction between true and false prophecy can be emphasized, whether judgment (Jer. 28:8), "fulfillment" (Jer. 28:9; Deut. 18:22; cf. Deut. 12:2), or any other criterion or combination of such. But surely to polytheize (Deut. 13:2; 18:20) in any form whatever (including particularizing God without affirming his ontological *and* ethical integrity) is in canonical terms falsehood. Conversely, to adapt any "text" or tradition to any "context" without employing the fundamental hermeneutic of monotheizing within the dynamics of that situation is in canonical terms falsehood.

Under that fundamental hermeneutic rubric, a given context or situation may indicate adapting the "text" in a constitutive mode—to organize and lead a program of obedience by seeking supportive guidance in the "texts," in the manner of Deutero-Isaiah; or in a prophetic mode—to challenge an established program of obedience by seeking corrective guidance in the "texts," in the manner of Jeremiah. The impulse to monotheize must affirm the possibility that the Creator was fashioning a new thing, a new heart, a new spirit in his people, indeed was transforming his people, by wounding and healing, into a new Israel.

NOTES

1. J. A. Sanders, *Torah and Canon* (1972), 54–90.
2. See the critical discussion of "situation" by M. Buss in "The Idea of *Sitz im Leben*—History and Critique," *ZAW* 90 (1978): 157–70.

3. G. Quell, *Wahre und falsche Propheten* (Gütersloh: Bertelsmann, 1952), 65.

4. Gerhard von Rad, "Die falschen Propheten," *ZAW* 51 (1933): 119–20.

5. S. Mowinckel, "The 'Spirit' and the 'Word' in the Pre-Exilic Reforming Prophets," *JBL* 53 (1934): 206.

6. M. Buber, "Falsche Propheten," *Die Wandlung* 2 (1947): 279.

7. F. L. Hossfeld and I. Meyer, *Prophet gegen Prophet*, BibB 9 (Freiburg: Schweizerisches Katholisches Bibelwerk, 1973), 161.

8. Eva Osswald, *Falsche Prophetie im AT* (Tübingen: J.C.B. Mohr [Paul Siebeck], 1962).

9. James L. Crenshaw, *Prophetic Conflict: Its Effect Upon Israelite Religion*, BZAW 124 (New York and Berlin: Walter de Gruyter, 1971).

10. See the reviews of Crenshaw by G. Fohrer, *ZAW* 83 (1961): 419; J. G. Williams, *JBL* 91 (1972): 402–4; W. Brueggemann, *Int.* 27 (1973): 220–21; M. Bic, *ThLZ* 97 (1972): 653–56; F. Dreyfus, *RB* 80 (1973): 443–44; E. Jacob, *Bib* 54 (1973): 135–38.

11. E. Jacob, "Quelques remarques sur les faux prophètes," *ThZ* 23 (1957): 47.

12. L. Ramlot, "Les faux prophètes," *DBSup.* 8 (fasc. 47, 1971), cols. 1047–48.

13. J. A. Sanders, *Identité de la Bible* (Paris: Cerf, 1975), 153–67; "Adaptable for Life: The Nature and Function of Canon" (chap. 1 of this book).

14. S. Blank, *Of a Truth the Lord Hath Sent Me: An Inquiry Into the Source of the Prophet's Authority* (Cincinnati: Hebrew Union College, 1955).

15. A. Heschel, *The Prophets* (New York: Harper & Row, 1962), 103–39.

16. A. van der Woude, "Micah in Dispute with the Pseudo-Prophets," *VT* 19 (1969): 244–60; idem, "Micah IV 1–5: An Instance of the Pseudo-Prophets Quoting Isaiah," in *Symbolae Biblicae et Mesopotamicae Francisco Mario Theodoro de Liagre Böhl Dedicatae*, ed. M. A. Beek et al. (Leiden: E. J. Brill, 1973), 396–402.

17. Buber, "Falsche Propheten," 277.

18. Ramlot, "Faux prophètes," col. 1042.

19. Cf. Harmut Gese, "The Idea of History in the ANE and the OT," *JTC* 1 (1965): 49–64.

20. Cf. H. W. Wolff, "The Hermeneutics of the OT," and "The Understanding of History in the OT Prophets," in *Essays on OT Hermeneutics*, ed. C. Westermann (Richmond: John Knox Press, 1963), 160–99, 336–55.

21. See Sanders, *Torah and Canon*, 87–90.

22. Crenshaw, *Prophetic Conflict*, 54.

23. J. A. Sanders, "The Ethic of Election in Luke's Great Banquet Parable" (1974).

24. See Sanders, "Adaptable for Life," and below, pp. 180ff.

25. See Sanders, *Torah and Canon*, 36–53.

26. See also Hossfeld and Meyer, *Prophet gegen Prophet*, 160–62.

27. Ramlot, "Faux prophètes," col. 1044.

28. G. von Rad, *OT Theology*, 2 vols. (New York: Harper & Row, 1962, 1965).

29. Crenshaw, *Prophetic Conflict*, 23ff.

30. See J. A. Sanders, "Jeremiah and the Future of Theological Scholarship," *ANQ* 13 (1972): 133–45, for a preliminary effort; idem, "Canonical Hermeneutics" (chap. 3 of this book).

31. K. Koch, *The Growth of the Biblical Tradition* (New York: Charles Scribner's Sons, 1969), 200–210.

32. See W. Zimmerli's excellent discussion of Ezek. 33:23–29 in *Ezekiel 2*, Hermeneia (Philadelphia: Fortress Press, 1983), 195–202; also *Ezechiel: Gestalt und Botschaft*, BibST 62 (Neukirchen: Neukirchener Verlag, 1972), 35–37.

33. Gerhard von Rad, *Genesis* (Philadelphia: Westminster Press, 1961), 13–42.

34. Cf. T. C. Vriezen, "Essentials of the Theology of Isaiah," in *Israel's Prophetic Heritage*, ed. B. W. Anderson and W. Harrelson (New York: Harper & Row, 1962), 138–46.

35. Cf. W. D. Davies, *The Gospel and the Land* (Berkeley and Los Angeles: Univ. of California Press, 1974), 46 n. 23.

36. Van der Woude (see above, n. 16) does not seem to recognize this.

37. B. W. Anderson, "Exodus Typology in Second Isaiah," in *Israel's Prophetic Heritage*, 177–95.

38. H. Weippert, *Die Prosareden des Jeremiahbuches*, BZAW 132 (New York and Berlin: Walter de Gruyter, 1973); cf. W. L. Holladay, "A Fresh Look at 'Source B' and 'Source C' in Jeremiah," *VT* 25 (1975): 394–412.

39. See above, nn. 13 and 30, as well as chap. 3.

40. Crenshaw here is especially perceptive; see *Prophetic Conflict*, 77–90.

41. Morton Smith (*Palestinian Parties and Politics that Shaped the OT* [New York: Columbia Univ. Press, 1971]) confirms this observation by a quite different method of approach to the canonization of the OT.

6
Torah and Paul

The question of the meaning of the Greek word *nomos* among Greek-speaking Jews in early Judaism and in Paul's correspondence with his congregations—including and especially perhaps with one he loved but had not founded, the one at Rome—heats up at times to a boiling point. It is an important question but also a very difficult one for moderns who like to think we have orderly minds. It is exacerbated, however, when we insist that Paul was like us in such matters! The history of efforts to address the problem would indicate that we should not make such an assumption when attempting to make sense of a concept like "law" over the whole of the Pauline corpus.

This chapter includes two modest efforts to look at the problem from the standpoint of one who approaches it from viewing Scripture in canonical perspective, moving toward Paul's letters from study of the OT (MT and LXX) and from study of early Judaism—not by perceiving the problem then going back to the earlier literature. The first part of this chapter is a statement in short compass about the very concept of Torah from its inceptions in the Iron Age into early Judaism, with particular attention to its translation into the Greek term, *nomos*. The second is a bold suggestion, on that basis, for understanding that Paul used the term in his writings with the same sort of latitude perceived earlier.

A person such as Paul, like other Jewish writers of the era and since, would think of Torah as made up of both story and stipulation. Abraham Heschel stated clearly in one of the last articles written before his untimely death that Torah, and indeed Judaism, is made up of equal parts of haggadah (story) and halachah (law).[1] Its two basic ingredients remain forever essential to its nature.

Nils Dahl's understanding of Paul had always interested me and seemed to make a great deal of sense to one who had learned as much from rabbinic instruction as from Christian, and as much from Catholic scholarship as from Protestant. Thus it was a timely opportunity for me to contribute what I felt I had to say about Torah and Paul (the second part of this chapter) to the Festschrift being prepared in his honor.

Everyone recognizes that most words have several meanings. The needs of Christian apologetics seemed to me to have colored scholarship to some extent from reading Paul in a fully canonical way: Paul certainly knew Scripture and tradition very well indeed. How could he say here in his writing that *nomos* was abrogated and there that it was holy, eternal, and good? What if it was not a real contradiction in the context of early Jewish literature?

What if *nomos* was a word well chosen by the Septuagint translators to reflect the multivalency of the word "Torah" as understood in Judaism? What if Paul was also addressing the same problem that proto-Pharisaic Judaism had already confronted in the Hellenistic crisis of the third and second centuries B.C.E.? How could Judaism make the old Bronze and Iron Age laws frozen in a stabilized Pentateuch apply to the totally new problems arising out of the Hellenization of the whole Mediterranean world—and beyond? Judaism had found two important ways to tackle the problem, as argued in chaps. 7 and 9. Paul's was a third! The old Bronze and Iron Age laws, as well as those worked out during the Persian period, were abrogated while the Torah story was eternal, holy, and good, precisely the beginnings, from creation onward, of the gospel, God's story. Those laws had a role as pedagogue for the non-Jewish Christian, and indeed for the world perhaps as a whole, if one was convinced of the great value of the Septuagint in general culture; and certain of the ethical laws, and perhaps others, were still authoritative for the nascent church, or at least instructive.

But in God's barely introduced Jubilee or kingdom, they were basically *overridden* precisely because the new age or Jubilee had begun. Paul would have known very well of the practice in Pharisaic parlance and debate: if two different sets of laws in Judaism were in conflict, largely because of a calendar accident such as when the eve of Passover fell on a Sabbath, then the decision had to be made as to which laws were *overridden* and which operative. But when the arrival of the eschaton in Christ meant that the big Sabbath, the Jubilee, had been introduced then it took precedence over all laws up to that point.[2] Essentially it was a third solution to the very problem already faced in Judaism earlier because of its new Hellenistic context. But the Jew who could not believe the prior and basic Christian point that in Christ God had indeed introduced the eschaton, or new age, then this third solution had to be rejected. The rejection by those Jews of the Christianity that survived the destruction of the temple would follow perforce. On the other hand, Christianity thereafter became even more Hellenized. The solution, therefore, proved decisive and effective.

After review of some of the current discussion about Paul and the law (as it is still being put) over the intervening years, I feel that reaffirmation of these points is indicated.[3] Like other Jews of the time Paul sometimes meant *ethos* or stipulation by his use of Torah-*nomos*, at other times he meant *mythos* or gospel—God's story. The fact that he used the term to mean stipulation in a third way[4] is quite understandable. One might think of Calvin's expression "third use of the law," not only as pedagogue to faith, but also as guide for obedience. Such multivalency of crucial and important terms was and is common.

NOTES

1. Abraham Heschel, "A Time for Renewal," *Midstream* 18, no. 5 (1972): 46–51. See above, p. 43.

2. A crucial point I failed to make in "The Ethic of Election in Luke's Great Banquet Parable" (1974) was the reason for the "wrath" of the householder in Luke 14:21. One notes that Joseph Fitzmyer fails also to address the issue (see Preface above, n. 6). The reason for the "wrath" was that those who had sent in the excuses submitted for exemption from service in the war did not yet believe that the battle, indeed the eschatological battle, had been won. What they were invited to was the victory banquet; the old laws, such as those in Deuteronomy 20, were now indeed *overridden* and had to be read in quite a different way, that is, with a hermeneutic that was based on the belief that in Christ the victory was won. This is clearly a Lukan restatement of whatever had been received of such a parable. This work of mine is not included in this volume because the parable will be reconsidered in my work on Luke, noted in the Preface.

3. See Heikki Räisänen, "Paul's Theological Difficulties with the Law" in *Studia*

Biblica 1978, Vol. 3: *Papers on Paul and Other NT Authors,* ed. E. A. Livingstone, JSNTSup. 3 (Sheffield: JSOT Press, 1980), 301–20; idem, *Paul and the Law* (Philadelphia: Fortress Press, 1986); Hans Hübner, *Law in Paul's Thought: Studies in the NT and Its World* (Edinburgh: T. & T. Clark, 1983); E. P. Sanders, *Paul, the Law, and the Jewish People* (Philadelphia: Fortress Press, 1983).

   4. See Sanders, *Paul, the Law, and the Jewish People,* 161.

Torah: A Definition

Torah (perhaps from "to throw," "to point the way," or "to cast lots"; perhaps related to Akkadian *tērtu,* "oracle") is a word in the Hebrew Bible meaning "instruction, guidance, oracle"; in Deuteronomy and postexilic literature it also means "law" or "law code." In early Judaism it had a wide range of connotations, from Pentateuch, Torah par excellence, to all divine revelation in biblical and postbiblical literature; in some contexts it is a designation for Judaism itself.

In the OT, Torah can mean a priestly or prophetic oracle, a divine response to a particular question, a directive sign; it can also mean instruction by a parent or wise person. In Isaiah, it seems to designate the prophet's system of teaching. Generally in prophetic speech, it is used as a synonym for Yahweh's Word or Way. In the broadest sense, it designates the divine will for Israel in the covenant relationship—both specific directive and the entire body of tradition that relates God's gracious acts and anticipates Israel's obedient response.

The entire range of meanings is retained in postbiblical Judaism. Torah includes not only halachah (the rules of conduct: commandments, statutes, and ordinances) but also haggadah (religious teaching in a more general sense). It thus includes the whole of revelation, preserved in writing or orally—all that God has made known of his character, purpose, and expectation. "Talmud Torah" (study of Torah) includes reading a postbiblical midrash or a medieval commentary. "In a word, Torah in one aspect is the vehicle, in another and deeper view it is the whole content of revelation" (Moore). Whether in the Bible or in Judaism, Torah was clearly viewed as a mixture of two equally essential elements: story and stipulation, haggadah and halachah, *mythos* and *ethos,* gospel and law.

How and when was this balance misperceived, so that Torah came to be viewed largely and in essence as halachah (or "law")? One point of view places the blame upon the translators of the LXX: too consistently they rendered the word *torah* by the Greek *nomos* instead of varying the translation according to the contextual demand (e.g., as *didache, didaskalia, dogma,* etc.). In any case, there has been consistent agreement that their rigidity in the use of *nomos* has been misleading, since it conveys only the narrower sense of the word *torah*. But more recent study suggests that they chose precisely the word that they should have chosen. In the Hellenistic world which early Judaism inhabited, *nomos* had at least the same breadth of meaning that *torah* had for Judaism. "*Nomos* in the Pentateuch . . . means divine revelation, considered as a whole, composed of a doctrinal part and of a legislative part" (Pasinya).

However, there is a general recognition that Judaism, in some aspects and expressions, had tended to stress halachah (and the necessity for obedience) as a condition for survival. This would have been a major lesson of history for those who experienced the exile of the sixth century B.C.E. One view is that it was the priestly writers and editors of the exilic period who began to equate Torah with law and to use the word interchangeably with statute, commandment, and so forth (Östborn). A more recent view would place the narrowing of meaning in the Book of Deuteronomy, especially in its exilic redaction (Lindars). In any case, it would be a mistake to think that Judaism as a whole concentrated on halachah to the neglect of haggadah. In Pharisaic-rabbinic Judaism, as in all Jewish denominations, Torah has always retained the meaning of revelation in a general sense. This observation has led to the view that it was in Hellenistic Judaism that Torah came to be understood primarily as law (Dodd). This view cannot be maintained.

It is becoming increasingly clear that sharp distinctions along such lines between Palestinian and Hellenistic Judaism (or between so-called normative and heterodox Judaism) did not exist. Early Judaism (i.e., that of the period before 70 C.E., when Jerusalem fell to the Romans) was remarkably diverse, not only in Palestine but also in the Diaspora communities.

An intense struggle took place in Palestine ca. 175–164 B.C.E. as the result of efforts to accommodate Jewish cult and life to "modernization" (Hellenization). The zeal of the reformers was matched and countered by reactionary forces who feared the loss of Jewish identity. The reaction was marked by a distinct zeal for Torah as a countermeasure to assimilation. Out of this crisis arose such traditionalist adherents as the Hasidim and Essenes, who, Hippolytus noted, were characterized by zeal for Torah. The reaction led to a successful armed revolt against the Seleucid domination of Palestine (see 1 and 2 Maccabees). Thereafter, the fortunes of such traditionalists waxed and waned under the political and cultural ambitions of the Hasmoneans and Romans.

The destruction of the first temple (sixth century B.C.E.) had already necessitated the study of the ancient authoritative traditions for answers to the questions of identity and life style in that destitute situation. While many exiled Judeans assimilated to the dominant Babylonian and Persian culture, others turned to the old stories for reaffirmation of their ancient identity, and drew from them survival power. This quest resulted, not only in a singling out of the Pentateuch for special emphasis (a Torah within the Torah, a status that it has had ever since) and its final shaping, but also in its receiving the enduring designation, the "Book of Life" *(sefer ḥayyim)*. Torah became stable textually and adaptable canonically. It could be taken anywhere (Palestine or the Diaspora) and made relevant to changing contexts by whatever hermeneutics were necessary to make it so. Of secondary authority were other traditions (Prophets and Writings) that were part of Torah in its wider sense.

Such Torah zealotry gave rise to the oral Torah (as with the Pharisees, the Mishnah, and the Talmud). When the written Torah no longer seemed relevant to some aspects of the new situation under the challenges of Hellenism, oral traditions were collected and expanded in order to address the question of identity. Emphasis was placed upon recognizable practices in personal and communal life, that is, upon halachah. An enduring attitude of self-examination and correction arose that sought not only to maintain identity but also to prevent a repetition of past and present catastrophes. The lessons of the past must not go unheeded. No detail of the Torah was so insignificant as to warrant neglect. Out of such desire for obedience and dedication to righteousness arose what, from another point of view, came to be viewed as the pursuit of righteousness based upon works of the law (Rom. 9:31–32). There is no basis, however, for thinking that the more the Pharisees emphasized halachah the more they neglected haggadah. On the contrary, Torah for them always meant both the story of God's gracious acts in creating and preserving a people for himself and also God's will for the way that people should shape their lives in the light of those acts.

The wide spectrum of Jewish belief and practice prior to 70 c.e. included groups who were preoccupied with scenarios of how God would act in their own time. Just as he had acted at the exodus or at other times in the Torah story, perhaps he would act now for a final settlement of the struggle between right and wrong, between the forces of light and the forces of darkness. Belief that he could and would do so took precedence for some over the other rightful Jewish concern to reflect God's righteousness in daily life.

Concentration on the traditions of God's free acts to effect righteousness resulted in an apparent emphasis on Torah as precisely that type of story; concentration on the traditions of Israel's proper response to those acts resulted in an emphasis on Torah as precisely a call to response. But Torah itself was always a balance between the two.

In order to understand Paul's attitude toward the "law" *(nomos)*, it is necessary to remember that this term, after all, is used in the LXX to express the full range of meanings that the word *torah* expressed in Hebrew. In some NT passages, and especially in Paul, *nomos* is used in the sense of Torah story as well as Torah stipulations. Paul possibly does not set faith over against works (as is commonly thought), but asks in whose works one should have faith—those of God, or those that humans perform in obedient response to God's works. If the former, argues Paul, then one could recognize in Jesus another climactic work of God (Rom. 10:4). If the latter, then one might fail to recognize the work of God in Christ for what Paul was sure that it was.

Thus the early church should be seen as an heir of those denominations in early Judaism that focused on Torah as the story of the free acts of God that he performed in order to establish righteousness on the human scene. Rabbinic Judaism should be seen as an heir of those denominations that focused on Torah as indicative of how one should live in obedient response to those free acts of God. In either case, Torah was the way, the truth, and the life for Israel.

BIBLIOGRAPHY

W. D. Davies, *Paul and Rabbinic Judaism*, 4th ed. (Philadelphia: Fortress Press, 1980 [1948]), 147–76; idem, *Torah in the Messianic Age and/or the Age to Come*, JBLMS (Lancaster, Pa.: Society of Biblical Literature, 1952); C. H. Dodd, *The Bible and the Greeks* (London: Hodder & Stoughton, 1935), 25–41; I. Engnell, *Israel and the Law* (1946), 1–16, a review of Östborn; W. Gutbrod and H. Kleinknecht, "Law," in *TDNT*, 4:1022–85; Martin Hengel, *Judaism and Hellenism*, 2 vols. (Philadelphia: Fortress Press, 1974), 1:58–254; B. Lindars, "Torah in Deuteronomy," in *Words and Meanings* (D. W. Thomas Festschrift), ed. P. R. Ackroyd and B. Lindars (New York and Cambridge: Cambridge Univ. Press, 1968), 117–36; George Foot Moore, *Judaism in the First Centuries of the Christian Era, the Age of the Tannaim* (Cambridge: Harvard Univ. Press, 1927–30), 1:235–80; Laurent Monsengwo Pasinya, *La Notion de nomos dans le Pentateuque grec* (Rome: Biblical Institute Press, 1973); Jacob Neusner, *The Way of Torah: An Introduction to Judaism* (Belmont, Calif.: Dickenson, 1970), 1–52; Gunnar Östborn, *Tōrā in the OT* (Lund: Ohlssons, 1945); D. Rössler, *Gesetz und Geschichte, Untersuchungen zur Theologie der Jüdischen Apokalyptik und der Pharäischen Orthodoxie*, 2d ed., WMANT 3 (Neukirchen: Neukirchener Verlag, 1962); J. A. Sanders, *Torah and Canon* (1972); idem, "Torah and Paul" (the second part of this chapter); idem, "Torah and Christ," (chap. 2 of this book); Morton Smith, "Palestinian Judaism from Alexander to Pompey," in *Hellenism and the Rise of Rome*, ed. P. Grimal (London: Weidenfeld & Nicolson, 1968), 250–66; Michael E. Stone, "Judaism at the Time of Christ," *Scientific American* 228 (1973): 80–87; V. Tcherikover, *Hellenistic Civilization and the Jews* (New York: Atheneum, 1970), 1–265; E. Würthwein, "Der Sinn des Gesetzes im AT," *ZThK* 55 (1958): 255–70; Paul D. Hanson, "Jewish Apocalyptic Against Its Near Eastern Environment," *RB* 78 (1971): 31–58. (See also pp. 108–9 n. 3, above.)

Paul and the Law

Paul's attitude toward the law has been one of the most puzzling and seemingly insoluble in biblical study. Statement of the problem is considerably easier than suggestion of a solution to it.

I

On the one hand are a number of passages in the epistles that seem clearly to say that the law has been abrogated or abolished: Rom. 7:1–10; Gal. 2:19; 2 Cor. 3:4–17; Eph. 2:14–16. Paul uses in this regard a verb, *katargeō*, which is rather unequivocal in meaning. It can, according to context, range in connotation from "abolish" to "fade away": but there seems no way to alter its basic denotation.[1] Along with these assertions one must align Gal. 3:19—4:5 where Paul apparently says that the law had been valid from Moses only until Christ.

On the other hand are a number of other passages that apparently contradict such assertions. While in Rom. 7:6 Paul says, "We are discharged from the law . . . ," in the same epistle at 3:31 he asks, "Do we then abolish the law by this faith? By no means! On the contrary, we affirm the law." The words "discharged" and "abolish" are both forms of *katargeō*. The apparent contradiction is lodged in one and the same epistle so that solutions sought by means of audience criticism would not seem valid. At Rom. 7:22 Paul claims that he delights in God's law in his inner self; and in Rom. 13:8–10 he seems to say that stipulations of the law must still be obeyed, and are indeed obeyable through agape.

At the heart of the problem stands Rom. 10:4 which seems to belong to the first group of passages: "Christ is the end of the law . . ." And yet the word translated "end," *telos,* can also mean "purpose, goal, accomplishment, or climax."

The problem, therefore, is that Paul apparently contradicts himself in the attitudes he expresses toward the law. Solutions have been sought for the dilemma in a number of directions: to deny the dilemma by rejecting the OT entirely; to attenuate it by putting the two testaments on different levels of authority; to distinguish between the oral and the written Torah; to see the death sentence of the law as abrogated; to shift the emphasis from the troublesome word *katargeō* to the more pliable *telos*, and to see Christ as the New Torah in an eschatological age; to see idolatrous abuses of Torah as abrogated; to see Christ as displacing an older, invalid hermeneutic; to see the function of Torah in isolating and separating Jews from Gentiles as ended; and to understand that all Paul meant was that the curses of Deuteronomy 28 were suspended for the gentile Christian only.

After cataloguing the solutions proposed to date (as of 1977 and insofar as I have been able to identify them) I will suggest that a fruitful approach to the dilemma might be to focus, not on *katargeō* or on *telos*, but on the binary nature of Torah that research on *nomos* also indicates.

II

Perhaps the earliest solution, after the apostolic age, was that of Marcion. Marcion took Paul's use of the verb *katargeō* in its strictest sense and decided that it meant that the OT itself should be eliminated from the Christian canon. To cling to one horn of a dilemma, however, does not eliminate the problem it poses. Marcion's "solution" found expression again in the liberal period of the late nineteenth century in Adolf von Harnack, who also concluded that the OT should be removed from the Christian canon. While Luther would by no means have abrogated the OT from the Bible he apparently distinguished in some of his writings between the two rather sharply by saying that we have law in the OT and gospel in the NT. In his commentaries on the OT, however, he looked upon the OT as promise and the NT as fulfillment agreeing with Augustine that the law demands what the gospel gives. In Lutheran tradition the OT is valid for the Christian as a guide for morality.[2]

Another early solution to the problem, in part prompted by Marcion's severe surgery on the canon, was that of Origen, more or less followed in later times by Jerome, Calvin, W. Bousset, and G. Bornkamm among others. In this view only a limited number of OT commandments were abolished in the work of Christ, such as circumcision, kashrut, and the laws about festivals, while the ethical and moral laws were "elevated and raised to their proper glory and place."[3]

A third solution has been to distinguish between the written law of Moses, in the Bible, and the oral law developed thereafter. The latter, also called Mishneh Torah (*Torah she-bĕ-'al-peh*), should be regarded as "commandments of men learned by rote" (Isa. 29:13) and "the false pen of the scribes" (Jer. 8:8), and accordingly be abrogated. It would, however, be very difficult to attribute such a distinction to Paul.[4]

A fourth possible solution is to view the sentence of death issuing from the law as that which was abrogated in the work of Christ. Its role in bringing knowledge and an increase of sin, and in inflicting curse and death upon humanity has been abrogated.[5] Related to this would be the suggestion that Paul, in this case, meant something like fate, in speaking of the law, and that it was this evil fate in general that was abrogated.[6]

A fifth solution is that advanced and developed over the past thirty-five years by W. D. Davies.[7] Centering his thesis in Rom. 10:4 Davies understands Christ, for Paul, to have been the New Torah. Out of a depth of knowledge of rabbinic literature Davies brings to bear on Paul's view of salvation history discussions by the rabbis of the fate of Torah in the messianic age. There were three dispensations in some rabbinic thinking of world history: the age of chaos (Gen. 1:2); the age of Torah; and the age of Messiah. And in Paul there were three similar periods: that from Adam to Moses; that from Moses to Christ; and that from Christ to the Parousia (Rom. 4:15; 5:13; 10:4). In the first the world was lawless (Torahless); in the second Torah reigned; and the third had begun in Christ. Christ, for Paul, was not only the Second Adam, accounting for the first period (typologically); but he was also the New Torah.

The Torah did its noble work in its time leading history right up to the age of Christ (Gal. 3:24; Rom. 10:4). Paul lived in that moment when the second and third ages met (1 Cor. 10:11). In Rom. 10:4 Christ is the *telos* (end) of the law; in 1 Cor. 10:11 the *telē* (ends) of the ages meet. Davies picks up on earlier work done on wisdom in the Christ figure in Paul and suggests that this had been the wisdom already seen in Judaism incarnate, if that is the right word, in Torah. At any rate, it is now incarnate (admittedly a non-Pauline word, says Davies) in Christ. Davies's position is the most developed of those viable today and in it he is followed by many current scholars, at least in certain aspects.[8]

Very close to Davies's position as it centers in Rom. 10:4 is one that understands *telos* in that passage to mean "goal" or "purpose," so that Christ for Paul was the exponent of the Torah's fulfillment in unifying all humanity.[9]

A sixth suggestion has come recently from Ragnar Bring, who nowhere mentions Davies; nor does he attempt to review the literature at all.[10] "For Paul faith in Christ is faith in the Torah, God's revelation in the Scriptures." Bring centers much of his thought in Gal. 3:24–25. The law leads to Christ in that it clearly shows right from wrong, but it did not give righteousness. God does that; and he did so in Christ. Following Odeberg he views the *telos* in 2 Cor. 3:13 as important as that in Rom. 10:4. This passage speaks not only of the end of the fading splendor of Moses' shining face on the mountain but also of the end of Torah—precisely that which the Israelites could not see at that point. The law is good in that it leads to Christ, but becomes idolatrous when the election of which it speaks is taken as privilege. This idolatry of Torah is what God has abrogated in the coming and work of Christ. The law itself is still valid, however, in that it reveals the extent of humanity's fall and sin, and liability to judgment.

There is much in Bring's position to commend it, especially his seeing that law means not only legislation but includes also the story of Israel's election.

He does not carry through on the idea, however, as does G. E. Howard. His work is considerably less valuable than it otherwise would be had he attempted to locate his own thoughts in relation to those of others, especially Davies.

Rather close to Bring's position is the view that what Paul considered abrogated were misinterpretations and misuse of Torah. And the reason these have now been ruled out is that Christ has brought a new, the true hermeneutic whereby to read Scripture and understand Torah.[11]

A seventh solution is that of Markus Barth in his work on Ephesians, especially Eph. 2:15, which has commanded his attention for some years. That aspect of Torah which created a separation of Jews from Gentiles is now abrogated or set aside. What Paul viewed as annulled was the middle wall of partition indicated by such central passages as Exod. 33:16; 1 Kings 8:53; and Exod. 19:5–6. Insofar as God's gift of Torah rendered Israel separate or distinct, or a priestly and holy folk, to that extent is Torah set aside.[12]

An eighth solution has been advanced by Michael Wyschogrod, an Orthodox Jewish scholar, who openly approaches the problem Paul poses from an Orthodox point of view. Dismissing earlier Jewish (scholarly) attempts to address the problem Wyschogrod disarmingly states, ". . . I would like to confess that it is difficult for me to see how a thinking Orthodox Jew can avoid coping with the Paul-Luther criticism of the law. For me it has been the only criticism that I have found really interesting."[13] Wyschogrod, in a paper as yet unpublished, centers his argument in Gal. 3:13; 5:2; and especially in Acts 15.[14] His argument is that Paul was an Orthodox Jew and remained one. Hence Paul knew that the Gentile was not subject to the laws of Torah but only to the Noachide Laws, just as the Ger Toshav (resident alien) was not subject to the same stipulations as the Ger Tsaddik (full convert). For Paul, then, Christ had taken on himself the curses for disobedience to the law, of Deuteronomy 28 (cf. Gal. 3:13), thus eliminating the threat thereof, or God's Measure of Justice (*middat ha-Din*), for gentile converts to Judaism through Christ, who remain subject only to the Noachide Laws, like the Ger Toshav. What has been abrogated, then, is simply the effect of Deuteronomy 28 in the case of Gentiles who have been engrafted onto the stock of Israel through the agency of Christ. The conciliar decision at Jerusalem, reported in Acts 15:20 and 29, proves this because there it is clearly stated first by James and then by message from the apostles and elders that "Gentiles who turn to God" are obligated only to the Noachide Laws. All Paul was trying to do was to provide access for Gentiles to membership in Israel in good, Orthodox mode. In no way did he really depart from Orthodox practice.

This is not the place for a full critique of Professor Wyschogrod's position. There will be time for that when he will have published his intriguing paper.[15] Interestingly enough, it is not as *hors cours* as might first appear: for it is not very distant from Markus Barth's emphasis on Paul's search for a way to tear down the middle wall of partition between Jew and Gentile, noted above.

III

There is a phrase, however, in Professor Wyschogrod's paper that arrests one's attention. "Just as Judaism . . . cannot claim on *a priori* grounds that God could not have become incarnate in a Nazarene carpenter, since to do so would be to make of Judaism a philosophic system rather than the story of the free acts of God, so, it seems to me, Christianity cannot argue on *a priori* grounds that God could have admitted the Gentiles to the house of Israel and suspended the wages of sin only by means of an incarnation and crucifixion." The intriguing questions that such a generous view prompts must be bracketed for the time being. To introduce another view of Paul's position with regard to Torah I want to lift out of Wyschogrod's context the phrase he uses to describe Judaism—"the story of the free acts of God"—and suggest that it can also be used to describe one aspect of Torah. And that is as it should be if Torah is Judaism and Judaism Torah in the broad sense.[16]

All of the above solutions, it seems to me, stress the halachic aspect of what Torah meant to Judaism in the time of Paul almost to the exclusion of its haggadic aspect. Davies, Bring, Howard, and D. E. H. Whiteley recognize broader meanings of Torah, but only Howard perceives this aspect of Paul's thought in the way I think it should be pursued; and yet he has done so only briefly, centering in Rom. 10:4 exclusively. Wyschogrod, save for the one sentence quoted above, consistently uses Torah in the sense of legal stipulations for the faithful; and even there he uses it of Judaism, not of Torah.

I think there is a clue here to our problem in understanding Paul. All scholars agree that the NT rests its case for Christ and the church (as the true and new Israel) on a basically heilsgeschichtlich (salvation-historical) view of Scripture, including Torah.[17] The NT views the OT largely in terms of a story of God's mighty acts of creation, election, and redemption, and within that view Torah also as the expression of God's will for how to live before him. And yet, so-called normative Judaism, that which Professor Wyschogrod assumes in his writings as true Judaism, seems to have stressed Torah largely as the latter, and considerably less as the former.[18] In fact, as one reviews the problem of Paul's attitude to the law one senses, after considerable reading, that though most scholars are prepared to recognize the two basic facets of Torah, the story and the stipulations, greater weight is given the latter than the former where the word *nomos* appears in the NT, especially in Paul.

Since the work of Gunnar Östborn, in modern times, there has been general recognition of the multiple meanings of the word Torah.[19] Östborn's work was seminal in that it showed clearly that the word Torah, as applied to the Pentateuch, already had a long history of bearing the two connotations: message or instruction, and law. A similar service has been rendered the Greek word *nomos*, going considerably beyond the work of C. H. Dodd and H. Kleinknecht.[20] The tendency among scholars working in the field to express regret that the Septuagint overemphasized the legal aspect of Torah can be put into perspective.[21] On the contrary it appears that *nomos* in the

Hellenistic age had at least the full range of meaning that Torah had, perhaps more. It appears that the LXX translators chose precisely the word indicated to translate Torah.

It has long been recognized that Paul used the word *nomos* in several senses. Rudolf Bultmann outlined five: OT law without distinguishing between the legal and nonlegal parts of the Pentateuch; the OT as a whole; the general sense of norm or principle; the sense of constraint or necessity; and finally in the phrase the "Law of Christ."[22] To these one must add *nomos* (Torah) in the sense of Judaism itself, the identity symbol, over against *Christos*, for those Jews who maintained their identity "in Torah" rather than changing it to "in Christ." Just as *nomos* apparently meant "religion" in the Hellenistic world, so I think Paul could use *nomos* to mean the Jewish religion, in that sense of the use of Torah, and make himself clear to his Greek-reading correspondents.

IV

What this means is that the problem of Paul's attitude toward the law devolves upon each passage in the problem-dilemma posed above. There is no question but that in many passages he meant by *nomos* specific legal stipulations. But it is becoming increasingly clear that the question of what Jewish laws gentile converts to Christianity had to obey depended on factors other than Paul's view that the *Nomos-Torah* had somehow been abrogated. To this extent I think Wyschogrod is right: Paul could conceivably have been as Orthodox as Wyschogrod himself and have argued that many of the specific laws did not apply to gentile converts to Israel. Where one must differ from Wyschogrod is in his viewing Orthodox Judaism as normative in the first century, and in his viewing Christianity as a kind of Reform Judaism subject only to the Noachide Laws.[23] On the contrary, Paul may have viewed certain laws as abrogated for gentile converts (and for Jewish converts),[24] but still have viewed *Nomos-Torah* as abrogated as well, in the limited sense that the new era had arrived, that Christ was the Torah Incarnate, the New Torah, the new identity symbol that opened God's work of election-redemption to all people who would believe. Christ as the New Torah inaugurated the messianic era and to that extent superseded the Torah era, but also to that extent did not eradicate or annul Torah. Torah was caught up in Christ in a new age.[25]

Paul's argument in this regard is basically a salvation-historical argument in an eschatological mode. As has been shown by Dietrich Rössler, intertestamental Judaism, in its variety of religious expression, emphasized the Torah story on the one hand in some sects or denominations, and the Torah stipulations on the other in others.[26] Of the two Jewish denominations that finally survived the destruction of the second temple in 70 C.E., Christianity fell heir to the emphasis on the history-of-salvation-story aspect of Torah in the broad sense while Pharisaic-rabbinic Judaism fell heir to the emphasis on Torah as the divine will expressed for life style.

Just as the function of canon for the believing communities has always been, in dialogue, to answer, ever anew, the two questions of who we are and what we are to do: so the several meanings of Torah can be ranged under the two rubrics: *mythos* and *ethos*, or story and laws, or haggadah and halachah.[27] Torah is and always was a balance between the two: to emphasize one to the exclusion of the other would be to misunderstand both Christianity and Judaism.[28] But perhaps the best way, now, to broach the problem of Paul and the law is to make the prior observation here indicated, and to acknowledge that Paul, with others in the early church, but especially Paul in facing his mandate (which he strongly felt he had received "from the Lord": Galatians 1—2; 1 Cor. 9:1; 15:5–9; Phil. 3:5–11; 2 Cor. 4:6) to preach the gospel to Gentiles, found it well to emphasize Torah as the story of divine election and redemption, in the eschatological conviction that God's recent work in Christ had made that election and that redemption available to all humankind, while at the same time to deemphasize those specific stipulations that seemed to present stumbling blocks to carrying out the mandate, and which seemed to detract from the Torah-gospel story of God's righteous acts that had found their culmination, goal, and climax in God's eschatological act in Christ. The combination of Torah story and eschaton was adaptable for life wherever it was told to the extent that the story was emphasized and the laws seen as dynamically or spiritually enforced (2 Cor. 3:4–6).[29]

NOTES

1. Cf. M. E. Dahl, *Resurrection of the Body*, SBT 36 (London: SCM Press, 1962), 117–19. He attacks the problem by focusing on *katargeō*. The question of the authorship of Ephesians need not arise for the purpose of this study since a judgment about it would not actually affect the discussion.

2. See W. D. Davies, *IDB*, s.v. "Law in the NT"; Ragnar Bring, "Paul and the OT," *ST* 25 (1971): 21–60; and the full discussion by Hans von Campenhausen, *The Formation of the Christian Bible* (Philadelphia: Fortress Press, 1972), 1–102.

3. See the discussion of the problem in this regard by Markus Barth, *Ephesians 1—3*, AB 34 (Garden City, N.Y.: Doubleday & Co., 1974), 287–91, esp. 287–88. The distinction between ceremonial and moral laws, in the thinking of Paul, has been denied by W. Gutbrod, "Law," in *TDNT*, 4:1063; cf. D. E. H. Whiteley, *The Theology of St. Paul* (Philadelphia: Fortress Press, 1964), 86.

4. Cf. Barth, *Ephesians*, 288.

5. G. Klein, *Studien über Paulus* (Stockholm, 1918), 62–67, cited by H. J. Schoeps, *Paul, the Theology of the Apostle in the Light of Jewish History* (Philadelphia: Westminster Press, 1961), 179; cf. Whiteley, *Theology of St. Paul*, 83–85.

6. Refuted by Barth, *Ephesians*, 290.

7. W. D. Davies, *Torah in the Messianic Age and/or the Age to Come*, JBLMS 7 (Lancaster, Pa.: Society of Biblical Literature, 1952); idem, *Paul and Rabbinic Judaism*, 4th ed. (Philadelphia: Fortress Press, 1980 [1948]), 147–76; idem, *The Setting of the Sermon on the Mount* (New York and Cambridge: Cambridge Univ. Press, 1964), 161–90, 447–50.

8. See, e.g., J. A. Fitzmyer, "Pauline Theology," in *JBC*, 79:41–42, 105–16.

9. G. E. Howard, "Christ the End of the Law," *JBL* 88 (1969): 331–37; cf. C. E. B. Cranfield, "St. Paul and the Law," *SJT* 17 (1964): 43–68.

10. Ragnar Bring, *Christus und das Gesetz* (Leiden: E. J. Brill, 1969), summarized in his "Paul and the OT."

11. Cf. Barth, *Ephesians*, 288, no reference given.

12. Ibid., 290–91.

13. Michael Wyschogrod, "The Law, Jews and Gentiles—A Jewish Perspective," *LQ* 21 (1969): 405–15. Wyschogrod approaches the problem fresh, like Bring, without relating his suggestions to those of others.

14. Michael Wyschogrod, "Paul, Jews and Gentiles," presented to the Columbia University Seminary on Studies in Religion, 11 Nov. 1974.

15. At this point I would simply note that Gal. 4:21–31 is clearly a midrash on Gen. 21:10–12, a passage central to Paul's understanding of Christ, with the curse of Deut. 21:23 seen as devolving upon Christ in the light of his being the New Isaac. Cf. Geza Vermes, *Scripture and Tradition in Judaism* (Leiden: E. J. Brill, 1961), in conjunction with the dissertation of David Bossman, "A Midrashic Approach to a Study of Paul's *'en Christo'"* (St. Louis Univ., 1971).

16. Cf. J. A. Sanders, *Torah and Canon* (1972), 1–8, 117–21.

17. Even Ernst Käsemann in *Perspectives on Paul* (Philadelphia: Fortress Press, 1971), 63, says, "I would even say it is impossible to understand the Bible in general or Paul in particular without the perspective of salvation history." Cf. Campenhausen, *Formation of Christian Bible*.

18. George Foot Moore, *Judaism in the First Centuries of the Christian Era, the Age of the Tannaim* (Cambridge: Harvard Univ. Press, 1927–30) 1:265, clearly states that early Judaism held both aspects of Torah in balance: " 'Law' must, however, not be understood in the restricted sense of legislation, but must be taken to include the whole of revelation—all that God has made known of his nature, character, and purpose, and of what he would have man to do."

19. Gunnar Östborn, *Torā in the OT* (Lund: Ohlssons, 1945), is well reflected in Walter Harrelson, *IDB*, s.v. "Law in the OT."

20. Laurent Monsengwo Pasinya, *La Notion de nomos dans le Pentateuque grec* (Rome: Biblical Institute Press, 1973); cf. C. H. Dodd, *The Bible and the Greeks* (London: Hodder & Stoughton, 1935), 25–41, and H. Kleinknecht, "nomos, ktl," in *TDNT*, 4:1022–35.

21. Cf. e.g., Dodd, *Bible and the Greeks*, 33, followed by Davies, *Paul and Rabbinic Judaism*, 149: "It is unfortunate that its rendering in the LXX by the Greek *nomos* should have over-emphasized its legal connotation." See, too, the misleading statements in W. Gutbrod, "nomos, ktl," *TDNT*, 4:1036–91.

22. Rudolf Bultmann, *Theology of the NT* (New York: Charles Scribner's Sons, 1965), 1:259–60; cf. Cranfield, "St. Paul and the Law," 44–50.

23. Cf. Michael E. Stone, "Judaism at the Time of Christ," *Scientific American* 228 (1973): 80–87. The problem whether the stipulations in Acts 15:20 and 29, incumbent even upon gentile Christians, relate to the Noachide Law or, as usually seen, to the laws for the *ger* in Leviticus 17—18, needs further exploration.

24. Cf. Gal. 5:2–6; 6:15–16; Acts 15:11.

25. The *kaine ktisis* for Paul introduced a new *kanōn* for the Israel of God to walk by (Gal. 6:15–16). One simply cannot avoid the fact, Romans 9—11 notwithstanding, that Paul saw the New Israel of God in some sense superseding the Old.

26. Deitrich Rössler, *Gesetz und Geschichte, Untersuchen zur Theologie der Jüdischen Apokalyptik und der Pharisäischen Orthodoxie*, 2d ed., WMANT 3 (Neukirchen: Neukirchener Verlag, 1962).

27. See "Adaptable for Life: The Nature and Function of Canon" (chap. 1 of this book).

28. W. D. Davies, *The Gospel and the Land* (Berkeley and Los Angeles: Univ. of California Press, 1974), 24 n. 19, asks if I have not stressed the story aspect of Torah too much. I trust that the present study may redress the balance. I find on the

contrary, however, that the Torah problem is dealt with throughout biblical studies with too much stress on the law aspect of Torah.

29. See "Torah and Christ" (chap. 2 of this book). There these observations are carried forward with an exploration in Paul of the relation of *dikaiosynē* to *nomos*, and of the relation of *mythos* to *ethos*, with observations on how Paul indicates the believer, in Christ, can move dynamically from gospel to law, or from identity to ethics, in ever-new and ever-changing contexts. Cf. Nils Dahl, "NT Eschatology and Christian Social Action," *LQ* 22 (1970): 374–79. For Paul it was not a question of faith or works; for Paul it was consistently a matter of faith. The question he posed, if seen in the light of these observations, was rather: in whose works (righteousnesses) should one have faith, those of God in the Torah-Christ story, or those of which the believer is capable when one attempts to respond to that story and reflect it in one's own life? Nils Dahl comes close to saying something similar in "The Social Function and Consequences of the Doctrine of Justification" (in Norwegian), *NorTT* 65 (1966): 284–310, according to the summary of the article in *NTA* (1967), 851.

7

Text and Canon: Concepts and Method

The following chapter was delivered as the presidential address at the annual meeting of the Society of Biblical Literature (SBL) that convened in New Orleans in November 1978. In it I tried to pull together my two major interests in an attempt to describe how I understood them to relate to each other, and how the two disciplines—study of texts and versions and study of the Bible as canon—had changed over the course of the previous twelve years. I turned fifty-one during the conference and was attending my twenty-fourth annual meeting of the society, but I felt as excited about the occasion as I had when, exactly seventeen years earlier, I unrolled the large Psalms Scroll from Qumran Cave 11! The earlier experience opened up a treasure of raw primary material; this one would hopefully provide an evaluation of their value in these two areas.

Both fields, text and canon study of the OT, have changed considerably since the discovery of the Dead Sea Scrolls (see the bibliography at the end of this volume), and I wanted both to explain those changes and to celebrate them. I wanted to share my view that there had come a much earlier change in ontology of canon in the two centuries prior to the Common Era that would explain many phenomena in both Judaism and Christianity.

Study of text and canon of the OT has taken on new life and direction over the past twenty-five years, and especially in the last ten (1968–78). Concept and method for study of text and canon have changed rather dramatically in that time. Manuscript discoveries have contributed to rephrasing of old questions as well as to discovery of new questions. We are now far enough into the history of modern biblical criticism that we are able, with or without the tools of the sociology of knowledge, to see with some clarity why earlier generations of biblical students asked certain questions and viewed the evidence in certain lights, but failed to ask other questions, nor saw even the evidence they already had in ways we now have of looking at it. To make such an observation is not to belittle the work of our predecessors; it is rather to try to account for what is happening to us now. We are in quite a new day in both fields, and I have suggested that they might each be grouped with other biblical disciplines rather than together.[1] I would like instead to argue now that they still belong together in certain aspects of biblical study, and in fact, study of one throws considerable light on the other in ways perhaps not thought of when they were paired in introductory handbooks or lectures as perhaps the most boring class or chapter to endure. Scholarship, in order to meet its own needs, had made of textual criticism a first stage of literary criticism; and had made of study of canon a final stage of literary criticism. Text criticism was either something to settle before getting on with the important business of original source, provenance, and shape of a passage, or was used to reflect the latter; and study of canon was viewed as the last stage in a literary history of how the larger literary units of the Bible (discrete books thereof) got together in a given order.[2]

I

The very ground of concept in OT text criticism, the history of transmission of the text, has recently had to be rewritten,[3] and this has been due in large measure to new viewpoints gained from study of the so-called Dead Sea Scrolls, of provenance from Qumran south to Masada. The first stage of revision of OT text history due to the scrolls came in the mid-1950s with the work of Moshe Greenberg, who argued convincingly from study of the early publications of biblical texts among the scrolls that a process of stabilization of biblical texts took place with increasing intensity between the first centuries B.C.E. and C.E., a process largely complete by the beginning of the second century C.E.[4] The work of M. Goshen-Gottstein, S. Talmon, F. M. Cross, and D. Barthélemy on the same and other texts supported the thesis.[5] But it received its greatest boost in 1963 from the work of Barthélemy on the Greek Dodecapropheton, *Les Devanciers d'Aquila:* the more or less literalist translations of Theodotion and Aquila had apparently had antecedents in a process extending back into the first century B.C.E.[6] The gathering data suggested to Cross a theory of three text families.[7] One was now able to range the newly discovered biblical texts on a spectrum from fluid to fixed, placing the earliest Qumran fragments at one end and the biblical texts from Murraba'at, Hever, and Masada at the other. Whether there were three basic local families of texts or there were numerous types of texts,[8] it became quite clear that up to and including most of the Herodian period the text of the Hebrew-Aramaic Bible was relatively fluid.

Running parallel to and congruous with study of the text in this same period was study of ancient biblical interpretation. Making many of the same observations as the text critics but studying all the various texts available from the scrolls as well as many known previously, some students of biblical interpretation formulated new questions and a new subdiscipline that has come to be called comparative midrash.[9] One of the basic interests of the new students of biblical interpretation in the period was in how the biblical text was adapted to the needs of the context in which it was cited. Observations about the text's adaptability matched what text critics at the same time were calling the text's fluidity. They, too, noticed that the biblical text where it surfaced in documents of biblical interpretation appeared to become more standard, as it were, in literature datable to the end of the period in question. By contrast, interpretive literature from earlier in the period seemed free to remold or reshape a biblical text in light of the need for which it was cited, not only in allusions to a text but even in citation of the text. The common body of relatively new observations between the disciplines, OT text criticism and comparative midrash, was growing. Study of the one in some ways involved study of the other and a few scholars saw how each discipline needed the other.[10]

The next development came about as almost a single-handed achievement. In 1967 Goshen-Gottstein published a pivotal study in which he argued that the medieval manuscripts collated by Kennicott and de Rossi, and so often cited by text critics to support textual emendations, were essentially derivative of the masoretic tradition, oftentimes reflecting late ancient and medieval midrashic interpretations of Scripture, and had little value for reconstructing pre-masoretic text forms.[11] The challenge of Goshen-Gottstein's essay was directed at the very concept of text criticism as understood in biblical criticism until recently.

II

It might be well here to signal the rather radical shift in concept that has taken place in OT text criticism in the twenty years just past, before turning to look at the two major projects currently active in the discipline. It has long been agreed that the task of text criticism is "to establish the text." This means that it is the province of text criticism to determine the best readings of texts and versions of the Bible, whether OT or NT, from which translators render the text into current receptor languages. Such may still be said to be the task of text criticism. In the case of the OT the almost universal practice has been to use a basic single text such as that of Jacob ben Hayyim, Leningradensis (L), or now Aleppensis (A). In the case of the NT the common practice since the eighteenth century has been to establish an eclectic text for printed editions. In the case of the OT the apparatus of a critical edition has had the purpose of considering and evaluating ancient variants in texts and versions and proposing emendations even where variants did not exist. In the case of the NT the apparatus of a critical edition has had the purpose of defending the reading chosen in the eclectic text above, and also offering conjectures proposed by modern scholars. *BHK* stands as the great exemplar of this understanding of text criticism.

In *BHK* there are two apparatus. The first signals interesting variants in ancient manuscripts that are not considered superior to the L text. The second signals variants *and* modern scholarly conjectures that the editor considers more or less preferable to the reading in L. *BHS* differs to no great degree even though it (1) has combined these two into one apparatus, and (2) has eliminated some of the rather private and particular conjectures of scholars of the latter part of the nineteenth and early twentieth centuries. The really significant difference between *BHK* and *BHS* is in the apparatus keyed to the masora magna added in the bottom margin of *BHS* as well as in the masora parva in the lateral margins. All of this is the work of Gérard Weil to which we shall return later.

The essay of Goshen-Gottstein addressed itself to the practice exemplified and most effectively propagated in *BHK*—and not greatly changed in *BHS*—that of citing a medieval Jewish manuscript to support an emendation arrived at by scholarly conjecture based on scholarly disciplines outside the province of text criticism. Because one could felicitously point to one or more manuscripts collated in Kennicott or de Rossi, or lesser-known sources, to support a reading that had actually been arrived at by other means altogether, such as philology, form criticism, poetic analysis (or simply what the ancient author in his or her right mind ought surely to have said), it was felt that scientific confirmation had been offered from another quarter, the medieval manuscripts. It was this practice on which Goshen-Gottstein shone a rather harsh and revealing light.

The light of Goshen-Gottstein's essay shed its broad beams on the larger concept and practice of text criticism, that of the abuse of text criticism for purposes of rewriting the Bible. The scholars cited above, and a few others, were arriving at the same observations as Goshen-Gottstein, but it was he who provided the clear voice of the time. Text criticism was being called upon to do tasks outside its competence to do, nor was it doing well the job it should do: it is a considerably more limited discipline than indicated in practice and capable of being far more precise than most work in it had to that point indicated.

This is the position taken now by the two current, active OT text-critical projects: The Hebrew University Bible Project and the United Bible Societies Hebrew Old Testament Text-Critical Project.[12] The former is the older of the two and was given impetus by the accessibility after 1948 of the Tiberian manuscript recovered from the burning of the synagogue in Aleppo, a magnificent facsimile edition of which was recently published by Magnes Press.[13] The recovery of Aleppensis was only an initial impetus. The discovery of the Judean scrolls and the newer attitudes mentioned above caused the launching of the project that has to its credit not only the beautiful facsimile edition of photographs of A, but also thirteen (to 1986) volumes of the annual *Textus* founded as a forum for the newer work being done as a result of the new finds, as well as sample editions based on the text of Isaiah of what Goshen-Gottstein and Talmon hope to do in a fully critical edition (with four [five?] separate apparatus) of the Hebrew Bible using Aleppensis as text.[14]

The younger of the two projects is that of the UBS committee. This committee was established by Eugene Nida for the same purpose for which the companion NT committee had been formed and from which we now have a fourth edition of the UBS Greek NT in preparation.[15] The OT committee began its work in 1969 and completed in August 1978 its tenth annual session. The scope of its work is less ambitious than that of the HUBP: its principal raison d'être is to offer help to the scores of translation committees sponsored by or affiliated with the UBS. But, nonetheless, to do such a task well the UBS committee has had to work just as much in depth on the questions of concepts and method of text criticism as their colleagues in Jerusalem. The younger committee has benefited considerably from the published work of the members of the HUBP, whether in *Textus* or elsewhere, but it has consistently done its own work forging its own concepts and method in the light of the new developments. To its credit are five volumes of preliminary and interim reports of decisions taken on specific passages. After completion of that preliminary series, it will, under the direction of Barthélemy, publish five volumes of in-depth discussion of all the major aspects of text criticism, as a scholarly and scientific discipline today, as well as detailed reports of the data considered and evaluated in arriving at its decisions (cf. n. 12, above). It plans eventually to publish a successor to *BHK* and *BHS* using L and Weil's work on the masorot but constructing a totally new apparatus otherwise.

The two projects agree completely on three basic concepts in OT text criticism: (1) limitation of its work to textual options actually extant in ancient texts and versions with the concomitant elimination of modern scholarly conjectures from consideration in text criticism; (2) a four-stage history of the transmission of the Hebrew text; and (3) a revised and renewed appreciation of the process of stabilization of the text begun in the first century that culminated in the work of the Tiberian Masoretes. Each of the three areas is very important to understanding what is going on currently in OT text criticism. I shall attempt to signal the importance of each before noting less important areas of disagreement between them. I shall discuss the masoretic phenomenon and its historical antecedents and background, and finally focus on the second period of the history of text transmission and some basic concepts necessary to understand the data available from that period. It is at this last point especially that one must relate basic concepts of text and canon: each illumines the other.

III

The new appreciation of the limits of text criticism goes hand in hand with the need for the discipline to be considerably more thorough and precise in its work. Here the HUBP is very clear. This point perhaps characterizes its purpose and goals better than the others. An apparatus should note only the genuine variants in ancient texts, versions, and citations, and it should be arranged in such a way as to exhibit the genuine variants in the several categories of ancient literature in which they appear. The apparatus should be as neutral as possible and as thorough and as precise as possible. The importance here of working with facsimile and microform publications is stressed. For not only the expert but even a good beginning student who has access to the actual manuscripts, in one form or another, is able to make significant corrections in the apparatus of both *BHK* and *BHS*. John Wevers's recent report in Göttingen on the unreliability of the apparatus in *BHS* to LXX Deuteronomy came as no surprise to critics who work with the manuscripts themselves. HUBP, as can be seen in the facsimile editions of Isaiah already published, plans to be as exhaustive as possible in reporting variants in ancient texts, versions, and citations; and it plans to group the variants according to the ancient literature where found. The apparatus of Biblia Hebraica is not only often inaccurate in terms of what is there but cites only what it deems necessary and does so in such a way as to confuse evaluation of the sources cited. HUBP will consciously refrain from specific evaluation but will provide clear information as to the provenance *and type* of provenance of the ancient variant. The UBS project agrees in concept with this procedure but will, in its final scholarly publications, show how significant variants were evaluated in the terms of the problems treated. HUBP will rest its case simply in the format of the four apparatus projected.

Our base of agreement here is so strong that I shall not elaborate this point further, except to stress the need now to have available, on as wide a base as possible, photographic facsimiles, in one form or another, of the actual ancient manuscripts. This is the reason, in part, that we have founded in Claremont the Ancient Biblical Manuscript Center for Preservation and Research. We plan there eventually to collect and make available, on as wide a base as possible, microforms of all manuscripts pertinent to biblical study, not only actual biblical texts but those texts from the Bronze Age to the close of antiquity necessary for full biblical study. This is admittedly ambitious, and we recognize that; but we hope that with the cooperation of similar centers in this country and in Europe, and of our blue-ribbon board of advisors, we will be able to amass an internationally visible and significant collection. The importance of scholars being able to do comparative work on as many different texts and versions as possible without reliance on prior apparatus and footnotes is gaining wide recognition in view of the whole new situation in text criticism.

The importance of working on the ancient manuscripts themselves need not be belabored. And yet I wish I had the time to tell what I have learned personally in the past year by simply being able now to compare the facsimile editions of L and A, thanks to the Maqor and Magnes presses, the Israeli government, and Goshen-Gottstein. Working on them, and on similar documents, underscores the point that critical editions of texts are filtered through the interests and questions of the editor, no matter how scrupulous or ingenious he or she may have been. If one's work gives rise to new questions one must have the original to turn to, to seek the answers; and turning to them gives rise to more questions. Goshen-Gottstein, Weil, and others had written many important things about A; but it was not until I opened the new facsimile edition of A that I was able to formulate hundreds of questions the manuscript itself gives rise to.

This observation underscores also the absolute need for the scholarly community to reform itself and revise its attitudes about dissemination of photographs of new finds. I thoroughly agree with my colleague James Robinson, in his SBL address in San Francisco, and with Noel Freedman (also a member of the board of trustees of our center in Claremont), who has written in a similar vein in a *Biblical Archaeologist* editorial.[16] We must no longer permit ourselves, for whatever refined reasons, to withhold publication at least of microfilms of new finds. When one thinks of the great minds deprived of working on texts discovered since World War II, who have since died, never to be able to share their observations about the texts, withholding publication of at least photographic reproductions becomes morally questionable.

A final point needs to be made about the focus of text criticism and the limitations of the discipline. Conjectures about what might have been the original text have no place in textual apparatus and only a limited value in a final stage of text-critical method. Conjectures about a nonextant Urtext of any biblical passage have their place elsewhere in biblical study—form criticism, philology, perhaps archaeology, the general domain of "higher criticism"—but not in text criticism in the strict sense. The one area of function of such higher critical method in the work of text criticism is at the final stage, *if* very pragmatically the text critic must come up with a relative evaluation of which ancient reading he or she would recommend to translators. But even there the text critic should be constrained to enter into discussions of literary form of the original, or even philology or geography, only after all the other work is done and only in the most circumspect way using the most widely accepted observations out of those other fields. This is an area of difference between the groups in Jerusalem and in Freudenstadt: the HUBP apparently will not enter this realm at all! But, then, they are not related to a translation project. We in the UBS project have to do so because our basic mandate, when all our other work is said and done, is to provide finally some kind of *Hinweis für die Übersetzer* (suggestion for translators); but we do so only in constraint and circumspection, usually insisting that the other options be left open if the text-critical work properly speaking indicated so.

IV

The work of OT text criticism centers primarily in the second phase of the four-stage history of the Hebrew text. The third and fourth phases receive due attention where need be and in perspective; but the first phase is left to the other disciplines of biblical research. The four phases are: (1) that of the Urtext; (2) the accepted texts; (3) the received text; and (4) the Masoretic Text. This is the second area of basic agreement between Jerusalem and Freudenstadt. While Goshen-Gottstein published his historical schema a short while before we began our own work, we started from scratch, as it were, and arrived at almost an identical view of the history of text transmission.[17]

Reconstruction of the Urtext entails most of the biblical-critical disciplines developed up to about 1960; for biblical criticism since its inception in the seventeenth century has been primarily interested in reconstructing biblical points originally scored. This is especially the case with philology and form criticism as they have been generally practiced, but also to a great extent with source criticism, tradition criticism, and even to some significant degree with redaction criticism. Certainly all those disciplines are properly concerned with what text critics now call the first period. The fact that biblical criticism for some two hundred years has mainly been concerned with the most primitive aspects of biblical study—the so-called *ipsissima verba* (the very words) of authors at the first stages of the Bible's formation and development—interests students of canonical criticism today, as we have tried to state elsewhere in other contexts.[18] Since the late 1950s a few scholars, in increasing numbers, have been turning their attention to the *Nachleben* of biblical passages and the fact that the nature of canonical literature lies in its adaptability as well as its stability, and certainly as much in the later resignification of biblical images, traditions, and textual passages as in their most primitive meanings.

When one turns toward use of a biblical tradition within the Bible, interest is roused by the function of the tradition in the new context and the modes whereby the tradition was conveyed to and applied to the later biblical contexts.[19] And those modes are evident even in the first repetition or copying of a literary unit that later ended up in the Bible. We do not have biblical autographs. Everything we have went through the experience of the need of an early community, Jewish or Christian, to hear or see again what had been heard or seen by the parents or ancestors of that community. There is no early biblical manuscript of which I am aware no matter how "accurate" or faithful it is thought to be to its *Vorlage* (text before it) that does not have some trace in it of its having been adapted to the needs of the community from which we, by archaeology or happenstance, receive it. Such observations are relative and pertain not to method in text criticism, but to the concepts on which method is based. All versions are to some extent relevant to the communities for which translated: it was because the Bible was believed relevant that it was translated. Much of the so-called Septuagint is midrashic or targumic.[20] But even biblical Hebrew texts are to some extent, greater or less, adapted to the needs of the communities for which they were copied. Again I stress that these are relative observations. Their pertinence for text criticism lies in the fact that the earlier the date of biblical manuscripts the greater variety there are in the text types and text characteristics.

One of the salient observations we have to make about the significance of the Dead Sea Scrolls is that though they are approximately a thousand years older than the Hebrew Bible manuscripts we had had before (except the Nash Papyrus?), they have by no means displaced the great masoretic manuscripts from the ninth, tenth, and eleventh centuries. The older the biblical manuscripts are, the more fluidity they seem to exhibit in actual text. Hence, the period from which we actually have the oldest handscripts is characterized by the textual fluidity of the Period of the Accepted Texts (Period 2 in the historical schema arrived at independently by both projects). The standardization process that took place in the first centuries B.C.E. and C.E. was apparently so pervasive and complete for Hebrew texts of the Bible that variants in biblical manuscripts, and even in rabbinic citations after the event, drop dramatically to the point of underscoring this prime characteristic of the second period. The manuscripts deriving from the second period, that of relative textual fluidity, may possibly have readings superior to anything in any Tiberian manuscript: that judgment has to be made ad hoc in each case and cannot be prejudiced by observations dealing with basic concepts, such as historical schema. The matter of method in text criticism has come to the fore quite dramatically in part because of the new sense of how fluid the text of the Bible was in the second period, that of the earliest manuscripts. And it is largely because of having to develop those methods to the fine point that we have now to be very careful in using work in text criticism since the seventeenth century.

The third period in the history of OT text transmission is called the Period of the Received Text. It is not improper to use the singular "text" here, as the stabilization that had begun in the first century B.C.E. seems by 100 C.E. to have been essentially complete. As Goshen-Gottstein puts it, only "a thin trickle continues" of non-proto-masoretic texts.[21] The salient observation here is the amazing uniformity of consonantal text form in the biblical manuscripts dating from the end of the first century C.E. through the Second Jewish Revolt. In contrast to texts datable before 70 they are almost consistently proto-masoretic. The biblical texts from Murabba'at, Hever, Mishmar, Se'elim, and Masada present minimal variants against the great masoretic manuscripts of the fourth period. The process of stabilization that had begun in the first century with the cessation of scribal changes of the sort called *tiqqunê sopherîm* (the errors of the scribes), as indicated in the work of Barthélemy,[22] or of the sort brilliantly studied by Talmon,[23] in the Qumran manuscripts, was essentially complete by the end of the first century C.E. Barthélemy's work on the Dodecapropheton has shown some of the process by which the standardization took place leading to the Greek texts of Theodotion and Aquila.[24] As Goshen-Gottstein puts it, ". . . the period of the Destruction of the Temple—that is, the last third of the 1st century C.E. and the first third of the 2nd century—is the main dividing line in the textual history. . . ."[25] We shall return to further observations about the phenomenon of stabilization after consideration of the fourth period of text transmission and the masoretic phenomenon.

V

The third area of basic and fundamental agreement in concept between the Jerusalem and Freudenstadt projects is appreciation of the process of standardization of text form that finally culminated in the work of the Masoretes. There is an interesting difference between us in the value attached to the masorot parva (mp) and magna (mm). While HUBP dutifully records the corrected mp and mm of A in the proper margins, no coordinating apparatus is provided for the masora.[26] By contrast, the UBS committee makes careful and judicious use of the masora wherever it is pertinent. The great contribution of *BHS* is in Weil's work connected with it. After the facsimile edition of L was published I offered a reward to any student who could discover in the masora parva (mp) of *BHK* any discrepancy between the mp in the lateral margins of L and *BHK*.[27] Even beginning students of the Hebrew Bible often observe how blurred the mp seems in recent printings of *BHK*; but 99 percent of them can tell you that their teachers never refer to the mp any more than they refer to the masoretic *te'amim*. The point in these observations is that throughout the history of *BHK* in the first two-thirds of this century few Western scholars were interested in the masorot of Hebrew manuscripts, even of L, those Aron Dothan calls "keepers of the flame" and Harry Orlinsky calls "Masoretes of our time."[28] As every historian knows, in those periods when there is little interest in a form of literature that literature has a chance of being copied accurately, that is, no one attempts to make it relevant to the needs of those periods. So through most of the history of *BHK*, editions 1 to 3, the mp in Kittel is printed quite accurately, from the margins of L. If one wants to know what is in the mp of L one for the most part has but to check the lateral margins of *BHK* (in contrast to *BHS*). A few like Paul Kahle and his students, among them Weil, now of the University of Nancy II, were interested in the masorot. If one compares the mp as it appears in *BHS* with the mp of any ancient MT manuscript one will find many differences. It is basically the mp of L, but Weil is, in fact, a latter-day Masorete! He has considerably edited the various entries of mp in L in the light of other mp entries and of the mm of L, and of his own study of the discrepancies between the two and the text itself.[29]

Weil well points out that there was no canon of the masora. In fact he has proved that the masora in L was added by a hand (Samuel ben Jacob) later than that of the basic consonantal text. Traditions contributing to the great masorot, especially of L, extended considerably back into masoretic history; but as C. D. Ginsburg frequently reminded S. Baer and H. L. Strack, there was never a process of standardization of the masora as there had been earlier of the consonantal text. There are no two masorot that are the same. Hence Weil composed the mp for the lateral margins of *BHS* in the best and finest tradition of the Masoretes themselves. He did his own basic work in order to render the mp of L in *BHS* really usable.[30] It has a few errors in it,[31] but it is essentially a rich source of information for anyone who will take the little amount of time necessary to learn how to read it. It makes the masora available to students less expert than those who could use Solomon Frensdorff or Christian Ginsburg.[32]

By contrast, as Weil makes clear in the introduction of volume 1 of his *Masorah Gedolah (MG)*, the lists he provides there are essentially the mm lists provided in L in the top and bottom margins of the manuscript.[33] Here his restraint is clear: he omits from the lists only the obvious repetitions, and he does that only because the printed mode employed to publish the lists and key them to the mp makes exact duplication of all the lists costly and useless. No one can fault him in this. Volume 1 of *MG* is a rich mine of information much more accessible to most students of the Bible than ever before, simply because of the mode of keying the lists to the mp in *BHS*. Weil has corrected the errors of the scribe of the mm in L, but made, so far as I have been able to detect, very few of his own. Volume 2 of Weil's *MG* will compare the masoretic marginal commentaries in L with other great manuscripts such as others from Cairo and the Aleppo manuscript and provide a paleographic and philological commentary on the mm lists. As noted above there was no canon of masora, and volume 2 will explore and study the differences among the masorot themselves. Volume 3 will analyze and study the divergences between the mp and mm, and between the masora and the consonantal text. Volume 4 will discuss the final masora (mf) and will include a general introduction and history of the masora.

The debt that we owe Weil for this work is considerable. He has by his mode of presentation and publication made study of the masora available to all students: and he has focused attention on a heritage of biblical study that only a few have heretofore carefully studied. It brings us to appreciation of the real contribution of the Masoretes to textual study. It is often said in the introductions and handbooks that their great contribution was in the system of vocalization that they appended to the consonantal text of the Hebrew Bible. As great as that contribution was, and as great as the contribution of the *te'amim* to understanding how the Masoretes inherited their reading of the text, these pale beside the outstanding fact that the masorot parva and magna stand on all sides of the text, right margin, left margin, top margin, and bottom margin, as sentinels to guard the particularities of the text. They provide not only a fence around the Torah, they constitute an army guarding the integrity of the text. Our appreciation of this fact simply must increase to the point of realizing our immense debt to the whole tradition that began at the end of Period 2 and increased through Period 3 culminating in the masorae in the great Tiberian manuscripts.

A *lamed* in the mp, keyed by the Masoretes to a word in the line indicated, stands like a soldier to remind the next scribe that the word in question must be copied precisely as written or corrected in the *Vorlage*. The text critic who takes the masorot seriously and pursues each case far enough soon realizes that there was often good reason for them. The word in question with a *lamed* in mp is a *hapax* in the detailed form in the text. There is no other quite like it anywhere else in the Bible and it must be guarded in its particularity; it must retain its peculiarity and not be assimilated to another form of the word more common in the Bible or elsewhere. In the Psalter the mp in Weil's *BHS* has a *yod-alef* in each case beside each hallelujah at the end of a psalm. That means that the next scribe had better not start or complete any other psalms with hallelujah than those so marked.[34] This may well illustrate the point someone made that "not a jot or a tittle shall pass away. . . ."

Pursuit of such cases will usually result in the observation that some other manuscript tradition may have had more or fewer hallelujahs—as indeed is the case in the Qumran Psalter and in the LXX—and that the masoretic tradition insists that the next scribe not be seduced by such variant texts or traditions. Often one can find in the LXX or the Syriac a variant that the masora warns the next scribe to be cautious not to emulate. Not infrequently the scrolls will indicate the kind of text the masora wants to insulate the standardized Masoretic Text against, sometimes a later midrash or a targum reading will indicate the kind of reading guarded against. In many cases, of course, we simply do not know what specific problem scribes might have faced, but herein is the invaluable aid of the masora to the text critic. Even the beginning student trained to see the circellus over a word or phrase in the

MT notes how often they appear precisely over words emended in the apparatus of *BHK* or *BHS*!

One day in a class in Deutero-Isaiah I noticed, while a student was translating Isaiah 43, that there was a gimmel in the mp keyed to the expression *'am zu* in v. 21, "this people." I had never before noticed the gimmel. Of course, it means that the expression *'am zu* appears three times in the Bible and the next scribe had best watch carefully that he or she not put four into the Bible, or indeed omit one of the three. I thought to myself: I do not have a masora magna here to see the full list of where the three occurrences are, but I know where one of them is myself. And while the student continued to recite I turned to Exodus 15 and began to compare the text there with the one in Isaiah 43. Not only did I note that the other two occurrences are precisely in Exod. 15:13 and 16, but I began to see, as I had never seen before, that the pericope in Isa. 43:16–21 was a beautiful contemporizing midrash done by the prophet of the exile on the great Song of the Sea. The prophet was resignifying the great anthem of the liturgy of redemption in the exodus tradition for his people in his day. He was claiming in good midrashic fashion that God was doing for *'am zu* another mighty act in their day comparable to the one the people sang about in celebration of the exodus. When the student had finished his laborious translation I gave a lecture on Isaiah's mode of midrash in Isaiah 43 on the Song of the Sea, a lecture I had only that moment perceived—all due to the fact that the Masoretes put a gimmel in the margin of the Isaiah text.[35] The lists in the mm fill out the knowledge of the text as a whole that the mp instigates and signals. The integrity of the text is safeguarded. Why?

What lies back not only of the masorot parva and magna but also of the lists of numbers of letters, words, verses, sedarim, parashot, petuhot, and setumot provided in some MT manuscripts at the ends of the several books, as well as at the ends of the several sections of some manuscripts of the Hebrew Bible? What lies behind all this madness for scrupulous count of words in the masoretic tradition? One of the reasons few modern scholars since the eighteenth century have been interested in the masora is that it seems to run counter to their own interests. Modern scholarship's great interest in the Urtexts of the Bible, in what this or that great thinker-contributor of the Bible actually said, has meant that most of us over the past two hundred years have been doing what the Masoretes themselves feared most: we have been changing the text because of our knowledge of other matters. For instance, our tendency has been to assimilate 2 Samuel 22 and Psalm 18 in our attempts to get back of both to an Urtext:[36] the apparatus in *BHK* and *BHS* attest to the tendency. Because of the criteria we bring to bear upon these texts in search of their common origin, we choose a word or phrase in the one or the other, according to the best lights we have from philology, form criticism, poetic analysis, archaic speech, archaeology, geography, extrabiblical literature, etc., in order to reconstruct a semblance of what might have been the original. The apparatus in each case tends to homogenize the two into one psalm. Translators then use the apparatus and try to present the same psalm in both Samuel and the Psalter.

It is precisely this result that would have horrified the Masoretes—no matter our noble motivation. In antiquity a scribe might assimilate two such passages out of an innocent but intimate knowledge of the one while copying the other. Today we apparently do so out of an innocent but intimate knowledge of what we think an early form of such a poem ought to have been like. The result is much the same. Before we ask the obvious question why the Masoretes were so intent on preserving the integrity of each individual text, nay each individual verse, word, and letter in place, let us first ask why we moderns like to press back to some supposed original.

Such questions almost invariably issue in the question of authority as it is framed and posed by any given generation. The attempts of the secularized mind to devalue the question of authority require perhaps the greatest skill of the sociologist of knowledge; but it is perhaps an attempt to evade looking at what the so-called secular scholar really holds dear. The modern period since the Enlightenment has apparently been as interested in the *ipsissima verba* of the origin of a biblical text as the Masoretes were interested in the *ipsissima verba* of the *received* text. One of the reasons that Johann Salomo Semler's attempt to devalue the concept of canon in the eighteenth century to a kind of final stage in a literary-historical process was so successful was that he was willing to shift ground in precisely the question of authority. He and his Enlightenment colleagues needed what Semler did to continue their then-exciting work viewing the whole process of formation of the Bible in one literary-historical light from beginning to end.[37] Once they had reduced the question of canonization of the Bible to study of lists of books and councils where big decisions would have been made, they had the question of authority reduced to what the historian could cope with. The bottom end of the canonical process could then be bracketed so that focus could continue on the earliest (and hence really authoritative?) biblical forms and content.

A part of this attitude emerges in our use of the words "secondary" and "spurious." To call a passage in Amos or Paul secondary is to diminish its importance in some measure. We tend to think of it as less important, for our purposes—whatever the purposes might be—than passages we call "genuine." Notice the choice of words. It might be one thing to call a passage genuine with regard to reconstructing as historians what we think Amos might actually have said; but it is quite another matter to leave the impression with students that what is "secondary" has no authority otherwise. And yet that is what has been taught, innocently or otherwise, in most seminaries and departments of religion. Until recently even the historian found it less interesting to give so-called spurious passages their just value. This attitude is fortunately being corrected in many ways. Yet still, the legacy of Enlightenment biblical scholarship includes a fairly clear system of values: one of these is that the most primitive is the most authentic.[38] Among the students of W. F. Albright there was a tendency to revalue much of what the liberals had

called secondary and to view as authentic or primary much that had earlier
been devalued. But that tendency only underscored the basic view that the
first or earliest was best. There is a clear line between our modern attitude
toward secondary passages and our attitude toward the masora: we have
tended to ignore both in our concern for the most primitive values in the text.
The basic Enlightenment tenet that "nothing is spurious to the scholar" has
not always been observed.

VI

The answer to the question why the Masoretes were so intent on preserving
the integrity of the text down to the least detail lies in a careful study of what
happened in the history of the transmission of the text during the course of
the second period, that of relative textual fluidity, from the Persian Period till
late in the first century C.E. In 1961 an essay appeared in our journal titled,
"Matthew Twists the Scriptures."[39] The author expressed the consternation
of many excellent OT and NT scholars of the period over how the NT seems
to "distort" the OT texts it cites. But the same can be said of nearly all Jewish
and Christian literature in the NT period. While there was a certain measure
of respect for the constraints inherent in the text,[40] the hermeneutics of the
second period were quite different from those that characterize use of scripture after the first century. The remarkable thing in the NT is the high
respect for the text of the LXX in the Epistle to the Hebrews, not the other
way round. The so-called Apocrypha, Pseudepigrapha, and all sectarian
literature clearly datable to the pre-70 C.E. period may all be seen in the same
light with regard to their attitude to biblical texts. I include in the category of
sectarian also the so-called proto-rabbinic literature of the period: the great
problem is, as Jacob Neusner has brilliantly shown, that there is very little
there that can be dated early enough in the form received to include it in the
second period.[41] Most ancient rabbinic literature, on the contrary, is a prime
example of the attitude toward and use of scripture in the third period, that of
the basically stabilized text after 70 C.E.[42]

Whether it was a matter of copying an actual biblical text, citing a biblical
text for comment, rewriting a whole segment of the biblical story as in the
case of Chronicles, the targumin, Jubilees, or the Genesis Apocryphon, the
inherent constraints of the text were balanced over against another factor that
was apparently equally important—the utter conviction of the time in the
immediate relevance of scripture. What they perceived God was doing in
their time had as great a bearing on their thinking as the text that reported
what God had done in earlier times. They knew how to identify God's
dealings with them because they had scripture, but most of that scripture had
not yet become "sacred text." The colophonic character of the prohibitions
stated in Deuteronomy against adding to or subtracting from the text of that
book was still far from the same as the utter taboo later to arise when the
concept of sacred text became the dominant concept. The period bracketed
by the fall of the first temple and the fall of the second, from the sixth century

B.C.E. to the end of the first C.E., precisely from the time of Deuteronomy to the time of Rabbi Meir and the beginnings of the oral codification of the Mishnah, was marked by a coexistence of two distinct ideas about the Word of God, the idea of the living Word of God ever dynamically new and fresh, and the idea of traditions that were becoming stabilized into certain forms but were generation after generation in need of being adapted to and heard afresh in new historical contexts.

Traditionally the spirit of prophecy ended sometime between the time of Ezra and the men of the Great Synagogue, and the time of the Era of the Contracts, that is, the time of the Seleucids.[43] Such efforts to account for the shift of which we speak in understanding the very concept of the Word of God testify to the ambiguity of attitude held toward scripture in the period. Barthélemy has shown that the phenomenon of the cessation of scribal changes in the early first century C.E., those called *tiqqunê sopherîm*, was a stage in the development of the shift in basic concept of scripture in the period.[44] This is surely correct. Talmon has capably shown that other kinds of scribal activity, actually adding to the biblical text poetic doxologies and other types of biblical literary forms, extended down to approximately the same time frame.[45] Talmon remarks that such scribes considered themselves to be contributing to the biblical process. All of this scribal activity came to a halt sometime in the first century C.E. The shift from understanding scripture as sacred story to sacred text[46] was long and gradual; but it took place precisely in what in text criticism we call Period 2, that of the accepted texts. And we say texts for the time precisely because of the pluralistic character of the texts in the period before the standardization process took place.

I have called these different understandings of the nature of scripture a question of the ontology of canon.[47] It was apparently not until the first century B.C.E. that the concept of the verbal inspiration of scripture either arose or began to take hold in Jewish thinking. Prior to that time there had been various mantic or shamanistic concepts of inspiration of tradition and early scriptures, such as attributed to the words of a dying patriarch (the very form of the Book of Deuteronomy [and hence the Torah?]); but the concepts of verbal, and soon thereafter literal, inspiration did not become operative for the function of scripture in Judaism until the first century B.C.E., and that at about the time of the cessation of the two kinds of scribal activity in changes and alterations in the texts of which Barthélemy and Talmon speak in the first century B.C.E. Phenomenologically, this new view of inspiration was linked to the concurrent conviction of the demise of prophecy. Even so, the older attitudes still held on and did not completely die out until the final period of textual standardization after 70 C.E. Those attitudes were in point of fact the salient and characteristic ones of the second period, that of fluidity and flexibility. For them as seen in Qumran and Christian literature, for example, the greater piety was expressed in moderately reshaping the text within the limits of their view of textual constraints in the light of the greater conviction of what God was doing in their time.

Once the concept of verbal inspiration arose, those adhering to it needed a whole new set of hermeneutic axioms and techniques to render the stable text adaptable to new situations. And it was those very proto-rabbinic circles in which the scribal activity of alteration of text ceased in the first century that the first efforts were made in developing the new rules of the game. And one can see some of the new techniques coming to play to a limited extent in Qumran commentaries (most of which came late in the history of the sect) and in the NT. But it was in the proto-rabbinic denominations and groups that the so-called seven hermeneutic rules of Hillel were developed supposedly by the end of the first century B.C.E. These were extended and developed considerably by the end of the first century C.E. into the thirteen rules of Ishmael and finally into the traditional thirty-two rules by the time of Judah ha-Nasi in the second century C.E.

Such rules could not have arisen and would not have done so except that the very ontology of scripture had changed from sacred story to sacred text as well as the fundamental understanding of its inspiration or authority. What happened and why?

VII

The answer to these questions lies in an understanding of Torah. Increasingly in the exilic and postexilic periods Torah came to have a very special meaning and a very special function in Judaism. There is a manner of speaking in which one may say that Torah was Judaism and Judaism was Torah.[48] The very concept of Torah shifted from that of being the story of God's dealings with the world and with his people Israel (with legal suggestions included within it as to how the people should shape their society and their lives) to being a quite stable and discrete body of literature. But the function of Torah remained the same as it had been in its process of literary formation, the source of the believers' knowledge of who they were and what they should do with their lives. What changed was a shift from highly adaptable living traditions, such as those to which the early biblical writers themselves referred in whatever manner and mode they needed to do so, to a highly stable body of literature. If, however, the function was to remain the same then methods had to be developed to render the stable adaptable, to make it relevant to ever-changing situations, and that at a time when Judaism was becoming more and more pluralistic due to the fact of dispersion and the fact of Jewish communities facing widely differing problems according to where and when they lived.[49]

If nothing now was to be added to or subtracted from the text of Torah—in that colophonic sense to which we referred in looking at Deuteronomy—how could the old Bronze Age and Iron Age legal systems be made relevant to all the new problems? We sophisticated children of the Enlightenment know that those legal systems embedded within the Torah story were actually already adapted much earlier from the codes of Hammurabi and of Shamshi Addad of Eshnunah, and from the Hittite legal system. But how were our friends in the postexilic age to manage if they could not adapt legal systems much closer to their own needs (whether homegrown Jewish laws or the best of their neighbors) right into the text of the Torah as their ancestors had done? As long as Persia was the dominant political and cultural force surrounding them, the problem was not too bad.[50] But once Judaism faced the Hellenistic challenge something had to be done, for here was truly the first really serious threat to the suppositions on which Jewish existence rested—no matter what denomination to which one might adhere or how eschatologically oriented or not one's immediate identity group might be. On the one hand the text of Torah had become stable to a large degree, at least to the point that no major alterations could be made; while on the other hand cultural clash was at every hand.

Torah, which had precisely become Torah because its central traditions had given life in the earlier challenge of the discontinuity of the old cultic and cultural symbols in the Babylonian destruction of temple and city, was still the source of life for Judaism. It had done it before, it could do it again even though the literary form of Torah had become basically stable. But how? The first answer came in the form of *torah she-bě-'al peh*. God had given Moses more laws on Sinai than were contained in the scrolls Ezra brought with him from Babylon to Jerusalem. These had been passed down generation to generation from Moses to Joshua to the prophets to the sages, and could now be called on to continue to render Torah relevant to ongoing life situations. Those new situations had pointed up two shortcomings of a literarily stable Torah in pentateuchal form: (1) there were not only new problems in no way addressed in the laws in Torah, but (2) it was becoming more and more evident that there were an increasing number of laws in written Torah apparently no longer relevant to the new situations. *Mirabile dictu*, the oral law contained all kinds of relevancies to meet the first apparent shortcoming of stabilized Torah.

But what about the other shortcoming? What to do about all the old laws apparently out-dated? Were they simply to lie there unused? Here was where the laws of written Torah had their continuing part to play. Where they were clearly applicable, fine and good. But those that were in danger of falling out of usage also needed attention. And here is where the shift from *peshat* exegesis of laws to other forms of interpretation began to take place. If the obvious syntax of a passage did not render relevant value of an ancient law, then maybe a value needed could be found, not in the plain sense of the verse in question, but in focusing on key words within it. Once this process started, literary context became less and less a restraint inherent in the text: and single words needed could be drawn from verses in different literary contexts.

This process meant not only a moderate diminishing authority attached to the syntax of the ancient text but the ability of the new interpreter to make a new literary context where needed. One could take a verse out of one context and put it with another out of another and thus create an entirely new literary context. This was undoubtedly done at first by the ancient and continuing literary technique of word-tallying or *Stichwörter*. This came to be called *gezerah shavah* (word-tally), after *qal vaḥomer* (argument from lesser to greater) perhaps the most basic of the seven hermeneutic rules of Hillel, and the rule most seriously developed by Aquiba. Clearly once this mode of biblical interpretation was accepted, and ancient syntax and integral literary context were devalued to that extent, there were nearly infinite possibilities of rendering legal Torah relevant to new problems whenever and wherever they might arise.

The two means of assuring the relevance of Torah as law guaranteed the survival of Judaism, and of Torah itself. A third way of handling the problem is exemplified in the NT, which exhibits an attitude toward Torah already clearly manifest in some Jewish eschatological circles, to view the Torah *story* as of continuing value (Rom. 7:12), but to view the Torah *laws* as abrogated.[51] A fourth way of handling the situation was at Qumran in its open-ended attitude toward the canon: to include in its canon whatever was needed to meet the new situations as they perceived them.[52] Witness the canonical dimension of the Temple Scroll, as viewed by Yigael Yadin. This scroll might well be called Tritonomos or Tritonomy.[53] Here were the laws Qumran apparently needed in its self-understanding as the True Israel of its day with a special mission of preparedness for the eschaton. A fifth mode of dealing with the problem was allegory, a spiritualizing hermeneutic that permitted, if need be, a total revaluation of apparently outmoded passages.

In the Judaism that would close its canon by the end of the second period of text transmission, that is, by the end of the period of intense standardization of text and the close-off of normal textual adaptation, in that Judaism, new hermeneutic techniques had been developed for rendering the old stable text adaptable to whatever situation might arise. For them sacred story had yielded to sacred text almost completely. The fact that the Torah itself was basically a story and not basically a legal code was for them no longer in focus. It was now basically sacred text. The ontology of scripture had shifted. And in the process of that shift one can see how scripture interpretation presupposed aspects of the shift. Scripture began to be viewed, Merrill Miller points out, as oracle, sign, and riddle, as well as story.[54] If one reads a passage of scripture as though it were an oracle, one reads it entirely differently from when one views it as a story. Each word of an oracle or a riddle is assumed to have significance whether one understands it right away or not. One needed now a *raz* or *kleis*, some key, to unlock its meaning. Mystery enters in in new ways and the meaning God intends for one's time may depend on external factors such as a denominational secret tradition.[55]

Even so, it was all in the realm of hermeneutics; and hermeneutics depends in part on one's view of the text being rendered relevant. No wonder then that once the new views of verbal inspiration, and soon thereafter literal inspiration, took hold, one could entertain the idea of a closed canon. It already contained all the possibilities ever needed to give value to the communities as they needed it, wherever they might be. As A. C. Sundberg has correctly pointed out, the Christian communities, which split off from Judaism definitely in 70 c.e., did not benefit from closure of canon but could carry on with the older attitudes and the larger OT canon for considerably longer.[56] Christians had already fallen heir to the thinking about Torah of denominations other than the Pharisaic-rabbinic anyway.[57] For them it was basically a story about what God had done in the past with promise of what he would do in future and not basically a set of laws in the first place. But no group or denomination was insulated from the others, and some of the basic concepts in the shift of ontology of scripture became common to all groups. Among these was the new view of verbal inspiration. This gradually took hold also in Christianity so that one sees an increasing difference between how the NT writers adapted scripture and how patristic writers rendered it relevant to their times. The idea was there to stay, and it manifested itself in how texts of scripture were copied and treated and read thereafter.

VIII

Those sentinels standing in the lateral margins of masoretic manuscripts thus have a long prehistory. The whole concept of masora developed directly out of the shift in ontology of scripture that took place in the second period of text transmission, with accelerated pace after 70 c.e. No matter whether one thinks the right text was selected in the late second period to be the standard text,[58] we can only be grateful to the rabbis, the proto-Masoretes, and finally the Masoretes themselves for so zealously guarding the particularities, peculiarities, and anomalies in the text as received in the process. They have preserved for us a pluralistic text that has remarkably resisted assimilations and homogenization of readings.[59] What we, in our sophistication, might call contradictions and discrepancies were, for them, latent possibilities for meaning at some future time that they themselves might not yet have discerned. After all, texts full of oracles and riddles implanted there by God himself by verbal inspiration no one generation could possibly understand. Let future generations have a chance. Parallel to appreciation of the work of the Masoretes and the earlier standardization of the Hebrew text of the Bible is renewed appreciation of the integrity of the LXX. Note that the NEB and the new TOB offer two Esthers, the LXX Esther in its full Greek form as well as Esther in its Hebrew form. Whatever one may decide about the original Esther, from a very early date there were extant side by side two Esthers each having its own integrity. Here was another form of pluralism by which we may benefit, never mind the discrepancies between them. The same may be said, perhaps, of the LXX texts of Samuel, Jeremiah, Proverbs, and Ezekiel 40—48.

The craze of the Masoretes for textual *ipsissima verba* and *ipsissimae litterae* can now be seen for what it was. They had their own reasons for preserving the integrity of the text, but we may have ours for appreciating now their labors. They have richly enhanced the pluralism of the Bible by their care for the text and by their preserving the multiple possibilities thereof not only in the masora but also in the *ketiv-qerē, sebîr, ḥillufîm, teʿamim,* and *tiqqunê sopherîm* traditions. And it is in part the (limited) pluralism of the Bible, rather than its obvious unities, that canonical criticism also celebrates.[60] Though we have benefited by the apparent madness of the Masoretes, beyond even our current ability perhaps to evaluate it, theirs was not a scholarly craze for simple scrupulosity or scientific accuracy. Theirs was a faith in an ontology of scripture (did not some say Torah was even preexistent?)[61] which meant there was always more there than any one person or any one generation could fully understand. We may not be able to share the faith. But can we deny the insight? Are we not ourselves far enough into the history of Enlightenment study of scripture to see for ourselves that scholars, too, are subject to the Zeitgeist of their times? And are we not a little wiser because of the sociology of knowledge to know that none of us, no school of us, nor any one generation of us is ever likely to have all the answers? Once we realize that we have hardly asked all the questions, we may be able to see Enlightenment study of the Bible as a part, a remarkable part to be sure, but indeed a part of a much longer history of study of scripture. The questions we most often put to scripture about its most primitive and original meanings have been asked before and they will be asked again. But they are not the only ones to ask. Perhaps when we can gain an attitude of seeing ourselves in a line that goes back much further and deeper than two hundred years, the eighteenth century may not have to be seen as the watershed of discontinuity in Bible study it has sometimes been seen to be.[62] Such a view requires a bit more humility than we have sometimes been wont to practice.

Perhaps one of the gifts we of the SBL might celebrate in our centennial anniversary would be the lines of continuity, wherever they might lie, between ourselves and our early antecedents. Let us face it: we now know that we did not have the elephant by the tail starting in the eighteenth century. Neither has any other period of biblical study. Practicing honesty, humility, and a sense of humor[63] about our own limitations in Bible scholarship might permit us to see ourselves more clearly as beneficiaries of a very long line of students of these texts, and even to see the texts in newer lights than we today can perceive.

Such a stance might permit us to hear clearly and evaluate soberly the increasing clamor of indictments against biblical criticism, for the good uses of which this Society was founded and continues to exist. Whether we agree or not that historical and literary criticism have locked the Bible into the past or are bankrupt or corrupt or have eclipsed biblical narrative, we in this Society especially must hear the indictments for what they are really worth.[64] Perhaps we have in part shifted our faint faith from the substance of our study to the methods we use. Perhaps we have permitted the method to become an end in itself. Perhaps we have unwittingly subscribed to a hermeneutic of primitivism where only the most original of anything has been worthy of really serious attention. Perhaps we have placed faith in history or even archaeology and expected them to bear burdens they were never meant to bear. Or, perhaps, we are guilty of none of the above.

Perhaps revival of a pluralistic sense of canon and of a deep appreciation of the pluralistic texts that have been entrusted to us from many generations, and of their functions through the ages in the believing communities that have passed them on, may allow us to perceive a more limited and yet greater value of the tools of biblical criticism developed and honed over the past three centuries. Study of text and canon today focuses increasing attention upon the intrabiblical hermeneutics at every stage in biblical antiquity—how the biblical authors and thinkers themselves contemporized and adapted and reshaped the traditions they received and how those traditions functioned for them when called upon. The earliest biblical literature we have, to the latest, made points by citing or alluding to earlier traditions, whether the peculiar traditions of the community or the international wisdom of the laws, myths, legends, and proverbs of many peoples. How did Israel adapt what she received? How did Israel and the church crack open once more, each time, the shell of the old, tried and true, and make it live and derive value from it to speak to a new situation, a new problem?

We have now the tools to work on the unrecorded hermeneutics that fill the Bible from beginning to end. How did Israel and the early church from problem to problem and from time to time, passing through the five culture eras from the Bronze Age to the Hellenistic-Roman, adapt what she received? How did she depolytheize, monotheize, Yahwize, and Israeletize, or Christianize, the wisdom received from the past, whether homegrown tradition or international wisdom? *How* did they do it? The answers are lying there awaiting valid sober uses of biblical literary and historical criticism to recover them. How did Israel and the church find the value needed in a tradition without absolutizing the cultural trappings in which they were received, and without being bound by the cultural mores and givens of the past? The Bible is a veritable textbook of unrecorded hermeneutics, of the way in their time our predecessors, the biblical tradents themselves, did what it is we ourselves struggle to do.

To view our biblical antecedents as radically different from or inferior to us in this regard is to practice a kind of latter-day arrogance and hubris without warrant that cuts us off from them and impoverishes us. To deny the trappings of their insights is not to be better than they. It may but deafen us to the genius they enjoyed. We have set the Enlightenment up as a sort of humanistic resurrection experience back of which we sometimes feel we cannot go and before which there is perhaps not very much to learn. I suggest that the block is illusory, dependent upon a kind of triumphalism that we can ill afford to entertain.

We are heirs of a very long line of tradents and not necessarily more worthy of the traditions than they.

NOTES

1. See J. A. Sanders, *Torah and Canon* (1972), ix.

2. See James A. Sanders, "The Canon of Scripture," forthcoming in Compendia Rerum Judaicarum Ad Novum Testamentum, Section II: *Oral and Literary Tradition in Judaism and Christianity* (Philadelphia: Fortress Press).

3. Dominique Barthélemy, *IDBSup.*, s.v. "Text, Hebrew, history of." See the unabridged version of his original French typescript in *Etudes d'histoire du texte de l'AT* (Göttingen: Vandenhoeck & Ruprecht, 1978), 341–64.

4. M. Greenberg, "The Stabilization of the Text of the Hebrew Bible, Reviewed in the Light of the Biblical Materials from the Judean Desert," *JAOS* 76 (1956): 157–67 (also in S. Z. Leiman, ed. *The Canon and Masorah of the Hebrew Bible* [New York: Ktav Publishing, 1974], 298–326).

5. The pertinent essays by these four scholars are conveniently published together in *Qumran and the History of the Biblical Text,* ed. F. M. Cross and S. Talmon (Cambridge: Harvard Univ. Press, 1975).

6. D. Barthélemy, *Les Devanciers d'Aquila* (Leiden: E. J. Brill, 1963).

7. First expounded by F. M. Cross in "The History of the Biblical Text in the Light of the Discoveries in the Judaean Desert," *HTR* 57 (1964): 281–99, included in *Qumran;* see also the other essays by Cross in *Qumran,* esp. "The Evolution of a Theory of Local Texts," 306–20.

8. For a viable alternative to Cross's theory, see the incisive essay by S. Talmon, "The Textual Study of the Bible—A New Outlook," in *Qumran,* 321–400; see also the "central stream" theory of M. H. Goshen-Gottstein expounded in *The Book of Isaiah, Sample Edition with Introduction* (Jerusalem: Magnes Press, 1965).

9. The bibliography is already quite extensive: see M. Miller, "Targum, Midrash, and the Use of the OT in NT," *JSJ* 2 (1971): 29–82, as well as his more recent and more general article, "Midrash," in *IDBSup.*, 593–97. It is generally agreed that there was a new departure in study of midrash with the work of Renée Bloch, especially her article "Midrash," in *IDBSup.*, vol. 5 (1957), cols. 1263–81.

10. See D. Barthélemy, "Problématique et tâches de la critique textuelle de l'AT," in *Etudes,* 365–81. This essay evolved directly out of our work together for ten years on the UBS's Hebrew OT Text Project. I agree with his statement of the issues. In fact, the present chapter presupposed in a way what Barthélemy there says and attempts to go back behind the issues to the reasons one must state the problematic in that way. I want to express my profound gratitude to Fr. Barthélemy for reading the manuscript of the present chapter in first draft form and for his helpful suggestions in doing so. I owe the idea of the topic of the address to a suggestion from him during our session in Freudenstadt in August 1977.

11. M. H. Goshen-Gottstein, "Hebrew Biblical Manuscripts: Their History and Their Place in the HUBP Edition," *Bib* 48 (1967): 243–90.

12. The HUBP is explained in the introduction to Goshen-Gottstein, *Isaiah, Sample Edition,* 11–45. The UBS-HOTTP is explained in the introductions to vols. 1–5 of the *Preliminary and Interim Report on the Hebrew OT Text Project* (Stuttgart: United Bible Societies, 1973–77); see also D. Barthélemy, "Problématique." Now see D. Barthélemy, *Critique Textuelle de l'AT,* vols. 1 and 2 (Göttingen: Vandenhoeck & Ruprecht, 1982, 1986).

13. *The Aleppo Codex,* ed. M. H. Goshen-Gottstein (Jerusalem: Magnes Press, 1976).

14. *Textus* is published irregularly by Magnes Press. In addition to Goshen-Gottstein, *Isaiah, Sample Edition,* see also idem, ed., *The Book of Isaiah, Parts One and Two,* vol. 1 (Jerusalem: Magnes Press, 1975), which extends the "sample" and includes Isaiah 1—22:10 (almost), and vol. 2 (1981) to Isa. 44:28.

15. The first edition of *The Greek NT* (ed. K. Aland, M. Black, B. M. Metzger, and A. Wikgren) appeared in 1966 (Stuttgart: Württemberg Bible Society). The fourth edition (1990) will include corrections and modifications in versional evidence and in citations of the fathers.

16. D. N. Freedman, "Biblical Archaeologist," *BA* 40 (1977): 94–132, esp. 94–97. See esp. p. 97: "Therefore I propose that newly discovered inscriptions and documents be presented in a suitable format—namely, photographs, handcopies, and preliminary transcriptions as soon after discovery as is physically feasible." We heartily concur and offer the services of the Ancient Biblical Manuscript Center in Claremont to scholars for that purpose.

17. See the introduction to Goshen-Gottstein, *Isaiah, Sample Edition*, bottom of p. 12 to p. 18, and S. Talmon, "The OT Text," in *The Cambridge History of the Bible*, 1:164–70 (= *Qumran*, 8–12); see also J. A. Sanders, "Text Criticism and the NJV Torah," *JAAR* 39 (1971): 193–97. Talmon's four periods are only apparently different from ours: they actually fit into the same basic scheme.

18. In "Adaptable for Life: The Nature and Function of Canon" (chap. 1 of this book); idem, "Canon of Scripture."

19. See, e.g., P. R. Ackroyd, "Original Text and Canonical Text," *USQR* 32 (1977): 166–73.

20. Cf., e.g., I. L. Seeligmann, *The Septuagint Version of Isaiah* (Leiden: E. J. Brill, 1948), and more recently the work of D. W. Gooding, e.g., *Relics of Ancient Exegesis: A Study of the Miscellanies in 3 Reigns 2*, SOTSMS 4 (Cambridge: Cambridge Univ. Press, 1976); cf. R. P. Gordon, "The Second Septuagint Account of Jeroboam: History or Midrash?" *VT* 25 (1975): 368–93; and P. M. Bogaert, "Les Rapports du judaïsme avec l'histoire de la Septante et ses revisions," in *Tradition Orale et Ecrite*, ed. L. Dequeker (Brussels: Institutum Judaicum, 1975), 175–224.

21. See Goshen-Gottstein, *Isaiah, Sample Edition*, 17.

22. D. Barthélemy, "Les tiqqunê sopherîm et la critique textuelle de l'AT," VTSup. 9 (1962): 283–304 (= *Etudes*, 91–110); Carmel McCarthy, *The Tiqqune Sopherim* (Göttingen: Vandenhoeck & Ruprecht, 1981).

23. Talmon, "Textual Study of the Bible."

24. Barthélemy, *Les Devanciers d'Aquila*.

25. Goshen-Gottstein, *Isaiah, Sample Edition*, 15.

26. Ibid., 20–21.

27. See G. Weil's own comment in *BHS*, xiii.

28. Such as S. Baer, S. Frensdorff, C. D. Ginsburg, and Paul Kahle. See Aron Dothan's prolegomenon in C. D. Ginsburg's *The Massorah*, 4 vols. (New York: Ktav, 1975 [1880–1905]), xix; and H. Orlinsky's prolegomenon in *Introduction to the Massoretico-Critical Edition of the Hebrew Bible* (New York: Ktav, 1966 [1897]). See as well the proof by Dothan that neither Moses nor Aaron ben Asher was a Karaite in *Ben Asher's Creed*, SBLMasS 3 (Missoula, Mont.: Scholars Press, 1977).

29. Cf. G. Weil, *Initiation à la Massorah* (Leiden: E. J. Brill, 1964); idem, *BHS*, xiii–xviii; and idem, *Massorah Gedolah* (Rome: Pontifical Biblical Institute, 1971), xiii–xxvii.

30. See G. Weil, "La nouvelle edition de la massorah gedolah selon le manuscrit B 19a de Leningrad," *Note e Testi* (Firenze: Olschki, 1972), 302–40.

31. See, e.g., Lam. 3:20, where the mp *qere* should read *wĕtā-shôah*.

32. See S. Frensdorff, *Das Buch Ochlah wochlah (Massorah)* (Hannover: Hahn, 1864), and idem, *Die Massora Magna, I. Massoretisches Wörterbuch* (New York: Ktav Publishing, 1968; prolegomenon by G. Weil); C. D. Ginsburg, *Massorah;* and idem, *Introduction to the Massoretico-Critical Edition.* Orlinsky observes that the rise of archaeology pushed out the classical approach to the study of the text of the Bible but that discovery of the Dead Sea Scrolls has helped restore it. While we disagree with Norman Snaith ("The Ben Asher Text," in *Textus* 2 [1962]: 10) that Ginsburg's herculean labors are largely a monument of wasted effort, his *Massorah* is indeed difficult to use; Barthélemy calls it "le cocktail de Ginsburg" (in a private note). And Frensdorff's work was but a beginning of what he had wanted to do.

33. See above, n. 29.

34. This incidentally is Weil's own mp. Note the inexact notation at Ps. 135:3; there are, in fact, only ten masoretic psalms in L that begin with *hallelu-jah*.

35. B. W. Anderson ("Exodus Typology in Second Isaiah," in *Israel's Prophetic Heritage*, ed. B. W. Anderson and W. Harrelson [New York: Harper & Row, 1962], 177–95) notes Exodus 15 in passing, parenthetically on p. 183, but fails to see how Isa. 43:16–21 is a poetic midrash on Exodus.

36. F. M. Cross and D. N. Freedman, *Studies in Ancient Yahwistic Poetry*, SBLDS 21 (Missoula, Mont.: Scholars Press, 1975).

37. See Brevard S. Childs's Sprunt Lectures, "Canon and Criticism," of 1972 as yet unpublished (much of this appears in his *Introduction to the OT as Scripture* [Philadelphia: Fortress Press, 1979]). Sanders, "Adaptable for Life"; idem, "Biblical Criticism and the Bible as Canon" (chaps. 1 and 4, above); and idem, "Canon of Scripture."

38. This is seen esp. in the work of philologists, and in bold relief in that of Mitchell Dahood; cf. James Barr, *Comparative Philology and the Text of the OT* (Oxford: Clarendon Press, 1968), for a critique of the position. See also the discussion of the two sides of the issue, as well as of what the expression "original meaning" may itself connote, in J. F. A. Sawyer, "The 'Original Meaning of the Text' and Other Legitimate Subjects for Semantic Description," in *Questions disputées d'AT*, ed. C. Brekelmans (Gembloux: Duculot, 1974), 63–70; the debate by Dahood and Barr is resumed in the same volume, 11–62.

39. S. V. McCasland, "Matthew Twists the Scriptures," *JBL* 80 (1961): 143–48.

40. Merrill Miller's apt phrase in a paper, as yet unpublished, titled "Directions in the Study of Biblical Interpretation in Late Antiquity."

41. Much of what Jacob Neusner has written would illustrate the point: it is clearly stated in his *Development of a Legend: Studies on the Traditions Concerning Yohanan ben Zakkai* (Leiden: E. J. Brill, 1970). See also idem, *The Redaction and Formulation of the Order of Purities in Mishnah and Tosefta*, vol. 21 of A History of the Mishnaic Law of Purities (Leiden: E. J. Brill, 1977).

42. M. Goshen-Gottstein uses the metaphor of "central current" for the proto-masoretic text before 70, "with rivulets flowing side by side with it." After the destruction of the temple "the rivulets that flow by its side are almost dried up . . . but a thin trickle continues. . . ." See *Isaiah, Sample Edition*, 17. Robert A. Kraft finds a parallel phenomenon in Greek Jewish scriptures: "As a rule tendencies to tamper with the texts would tend to date from relatively early times. . . ." See his "Christian Transmission of Greek Jewish Scriptures," in *Paganisme, Judaïsme, Christianisme: Influences et affrontements dans le monde antique. Mélanges offert à Marcel Simon*, ed. André Benoit et al. (Paris: Boccard, 1978), 22.

43. Cf. G. Weil, "La nouvelle édition," 329.

44. Barthélemy, "Les tiqqunê sopherîm."

45. Talmon, "Textual Study of the Bible."

46. Miller, "Directions in Study of Biblical Interpretation."

47. In my "Biblical Criticism and the Bible as Canon" (chap. 4 of this book).

48. See Sanders, *Torah and Canon* (1972), 52; idem, "Torah: A Definition" (first part of chap. 6 of this book). See also Jacob Neusner, *First-Century Judaism in Crisis. Yohanan ben Zakkai and the Renaissance of Torah* (Nashville: Abingdon Press, 1975).

49. See Sanders, "Adaptable for Life" (chap. 1); idem, "Canonical Hermeneutics: True and False Prophecy" (chap. 5 of this book); and idem, "Canon of Scripture."

50. E. Bickerman and M. Smith, *The Ancient History of Western Civilization* (New York: Harper & Row, 1976), 113–45; Morton Smith, *Palestinian Parties and Politics that Shaped the OT* (New York: Columbia Univ. Press, 1971), 57–81.

51. See J. A. Sanders, "Paul and the Law" (second part of chap. 6 of this book).

52. See J. A. Sanders, "The Qumran Psalms Scroll (11QPs^a) Reviewed," in *On Language, Culture, and Religion: In Honor of Eugene A. Nida*, ed. M. Black and W.

Smalley (The Hague: Mouton Press, 1974), 77–99; and see Barthélemy, "Text, Hebrew, history of," 880.

53. Y. Yadin, *Megilat ha-Miqdash* (Jerusalem: Israel Exploration Society, 1978), 1:295–307.

54. Miller, "Directions in Study of Biblical Interpretation."

55. The MT of Daniel, in contrast to that of the LXX and even Theodotion Daniel, presents enigmatic readings that perhaps are due to the writer's desire to be less than clear to the general reader but convey a sense of reality through mystery to an in-group. Some passages seem to be of the character of riddle or oracle and purposely written so. Ezekiel was probably not written in this way, but much of the text lends itself to oracle-type interpretation.

56. Albert C. Sundberg, Jr., *OT of the Early Church*, HTS 20 (Cambridge: Harvard Univ. Press, 1964).

57. J. A. Sanders, "Torah and Christ" (chap. 2 of this book).

58. See S. Talmon, "The Three Scrolls of the Law that Were Found in the Temple Court," *Textus* 2 (1962): 14–27. Talmon's article is reprinted in Leiman, *Canon and Masorah*, 455–68. Greenberg "Stabilization," is pertinent here as well.

59. Infrequently this is not the case: cf., e.g., Jer. 49:19 and 50:44 where some Masoretes seem to have done what we tend to do—assimilate a *yĕ'odennu* to *yō'idennî*. See the list at the end of the Ben Ḥayyim Bible. A study needs to be made of oriental ketivs. See the notes by D. Barthélemy in *Critique Textuelle de l'AT* (see n. 12, above).

60. See Sanders, *Torah and Canon*, 116–21, and "Adaptable for Life." The diversity or pluralism in textual tradition is preserved in many ways by the several masoretic marginal traditions. When the limit of function of such traditions was reached then hermeneutics stepped in to continue the work: e.g., the step from notation of a *ḥilluf* to use of *'al tiqrē'* as a hermeneutic technique is very slight indeed. (On the *qere-ketiv* traditions indicating ancient variants, see H. Orlinsky, "The Origin of the Kethib-Qere System: A New Approach," VTSup. 7 [1959]: 184–92, and R. Gordis, *The Biblical Text in the Making* [New York: Ktav, 1972]).

61. As in *'Abot Nathan* 31; see Judah Goldin, ed., *The Fathers According to Rabbi Nathan*, YJS 10 (New Haven: Yale Univ. Press; London: Oxford Univ. Press, 1955), 126; *b. Ned.* 39b; etc.

62. Cf. H. Frei, *The Eclipse of Biblical Narrative: A Study in Eighteenth and Nineteenth Century Hermeneutics* (New Haven: Yale Univ. Press, 1974).

63. J. A. Sanders, "Canonical Hermeneutics" (chap. 3 of this book).

64. See Sanders, "Biblical Criticism and the Bible as Canon."

8
Canonical Context and Canonical Criticism

The following is one of five reviews of Brevard Childs's *Introduction to the OT as Scripture* (1979) that were published together with a response by Childs in *HBT* 2 (1980). Rarely has an introduction to Scripture commanded so much immediate attention. A similar bevy of reviews appeared in Britain in *JSOT* (1980). Individual reviews have been given major status in some journals. Professor Bernhard W. Anderson's presidential address in *JBL* (1981) was given in part to a critique of Childs's position seen in a broad context.

In my review essay I tried to provide a substantive answer to the many questions often posed as to the similarities and differences in Childs's and my understandings of the concept of canon as applied to the Bible. I took the opportunity afforded to draw a detailed tally of where we agree and where we disagree.

Of considerable importance in my mind is the sort of debate Childs and I perhaps symbolize in revitalizing the concept of canon as applied to Scripture. The inclusion of my assessment of Childs in this volume will, I hope, serve that purpose, and will help to clarify for students the really important differences between the two positions.

A concern I have that is not here addressed is that of critics who see my position as being existentialist. I regret that as it might convey to students the impression that I hold an existentialist philosophy. The discussions would really go awry if that is not corrected. I do indeed discuss the dimension of life-giving power Torah and canon have had since their inception for the believing communities that find their identity in them; but that is not "existentialism."

Brevard S. Childs has brought to fruition a perspective on biblical understanding and interpretation first suggested, to my knowledge, in an article published in 1964.[1] There he raised serious objection to a basic and fundamental tenet of modern biblical scholarship in its attempts to engage in exegesis of biblical texts. Modern scholarship assumes that it must first strike a posture of neutrality in probing a text in order to be as descriptive as possible in reading it in terms of the thought of the ancient writer and his or her ancient audience; thereafter, one may, if indicated, move to a theological understanding of the text. Childs was particularly concerned with how this "scholarly" attitude dictated the manner in which biblical commentaries have been shaped, written, and edited. No one was clear on how to move from the descriptive task to the theological one: embarrassment seemed a proper attitude, or at least none other seemed respectable for a real scholar if he or she felt he or she had to go on and "preach" or exposit.

Childs argued that "the genuine theological task can be carried on successfully only when it begins from within an explicit framework of faith,"[2] not when it begins with a neutral description of what they back there thought. "Theological exegesis is a disciplined method of research fully commensurate with its material."[3] Childs was equally critical of the scholarly attitudes of form critics in this regard and of the biblical archaeologists who claimed that their tools opened the true avenue to what really happened and thus provided a means of bypassing the biblical witness to God's redemptive purpose with Israel.

Childs made three basic points in that early article. The first was to affirm a hermeneutical circle in movement from a single text to the whole canonical witness. This he claimed was a descriptive task true to the Bible itself as canon. (It should be noted, however, that Childs back then did not yet use the word or concept of "canon": that was to come later.) His second point was that the exegete must interpret the OT in the light of the NT and vice versa;

in so doing one illumines the ontological relation of the two, the differences between which must be respected and guarded. Both testaments nonetheless witness independently and together to the one purpose of God. The correspondence between the two testaments is ontological, pointing to the reality of the one purpose of God. Typological exegesis, so pervasive in both testaments, is understood as part of the witness to the ontological relationship. Thus his third point was that the hermeneutical circle (of the dialectic between single text and whole) moved from the level of the witness in the text to the reality itself. Theological exegesis penetrates to that reality that called forth the witness.

Childs then fleshed out these ideas in *Biblical Theology in Crisis* (1970), stressing particularly the importance of the hermeneutical circle in dialectic movement between single text and full canon.[4] His position was clearly staked out: the Bible and its single texts must be understood and interpreted in full canonical context rather than in original historical context. Emphasis was laid on full literary context and what emerges from reading the Bible and its several single texts not in terms of whence and thence they arose but in terms of an inner literary relationship defined by the believing communities who shaped the canon and passed it on.[5] The picture Childs painted was of a canonical process in which ultimate, final redactors and shapers of what had been received divorced it from the history that had produced the literature in its varied formation, and, in Childs's terms, made it thus available to all the believing communities thereafter in their historical contexts.

Then in 1974 Childs gave us *The Book of Exodus: A Critical, Theological Commentary,* in which he tried to put back together what the form and tradition critics had torn asunder. The fact that Childs did a better job there of showing how the parts of Exodus discerned by criticism related to other parts of the canon than of showing us the canonical shape of the whole of the Book of Exodus need not detain us here.[6] His various short studies that appeared in the 1970s prepared us quite well for the present work. Superscriptions, idiomatic formulae, etiological tales, and the like came under review in an effort to recover their significance in the light of their function in fuller literary context rather than as the textual throwaways criticism had tended to make them.[7] And then we had *Introduction to the OT as Scripture* (1979).

I

There is no question in my mind that Childs has been responding to a very real need created by biblical criticism itself. What is that need?

Biblical criticism was generated in the excitement of application of Enlightenment insight to the question of the origins of the faith. Enlightenment within the fold of traditional religious identity unleashed intellectual honesty in ways that seemed to give new life to old truths. One could question the provenance of the most precious premises of tradition—and not be struck dead! On the contrary, a blow had been struck for honesty within the faith, and it was felt that only good could come from it. Much good has come from it, but as with all such movements problems have arisen as well.

One of the charges being leveled with increasing frequency at the guild of biblical criticism is that we have locked the Bible into the past. Protestantism may have cut the chains that had bound the Bible to the church lectern, but it proceeded to sponsor, at least to some degree, Enlightenment study of the Bible that seemed in turn to chain the Bible to the scholar's desk. It went from being the peculiar province of priests to being the special subject of scholars, who made it into a sort of archaeological tell that only experts could dig! A new breed of priest arose to replace the old. The degree of expertise needed to enter the new guild became sufficient to make it quite exclusivist. The professor of homiletics trembled to preach in chapel out of dread that her colleagues in Bible might be present. Tooling up to gain credentials in the guild took so long and began to be so expensive that many otherwise faithful folk tended to avoid the Bible in preaching, lecturing, and study. As long as liberalism and then neo-orthodoxy remained in fairly widespread consensus in Western Christianity (which had nourished historical criticism) there was a shield around the guild that protected it from such charges and even prevented it from hearing them. In the meantime skillful members of the guild were in constant demand for lecturing and writing to reveal to the faithful the fruits of their clandestine digs. It was the same in other fields and did not seem too strange in ours: every human discipline of inquiry was becoming specialist.

Except that neo-orthodoxy fell a casualty to the radical upheavals of the 1960s. But instead of another equally discrete and commanding consensus taking its place, many and varied theological postures were struck, none sufficiently cohesive enough to shield the guild from the ever-increasing charges. Several responses have been forthcoming to the charges, and I have listed those with discussion elsewhere.[8] They range from the various pneumatic and charismatic movements of left and right to structuralism, symbolism, political (Marxist) and psychological (Jungian) and language-event hermeneutics to functionalism. And they range all the way from disdain for biblical criticism to abandonment of the Bible altogether in theologizing (liberal pneumatic personal storytellers). Biblical criticism has been cited as bankrupt.[9]

There is truth in the charges, even if some have been caricatures. We in the guild cannot and must not hide behind pitiful countercharges that some of the potshots have been rhetorically overcharged. We hid behind the shields of liberalism and neo-orthodoxy long enough. It is time we reform ourselves. How can we retain the solid advances made in biblical study since the Enlightenment and yet correct what has gone wrong?

Childs has a clear answer to the question, and it is well worth hearing and to a large extent heeding. His own statement of the problem varies somewhat from the above, though it is quite congruous with it. He stated the problem brilliantly in his Sprunt Lectures in Richmond, Va., in 1972.[10] Biblical criticism in the eighteenth century in the work of Johann Salomo Semler had redefined the concept of canon "in strictly historical terms as an external ecclesiastical validation without any real significance for the shaping or interpretation of the biblical literature."[11] It had indeed. My own work brought me to a similar observation.[12] The concept of canon up to that point had meant authority and as used in church tradition was simply a concept criticism could not cope with. It reduced its semantic impact to an idea manageable by the tools of historical inquiry being developed in the guild. Childs cites his former student (and my former colleague) Gerald T. Sheppard to clear effect: "Little wonder that once the biblical text had been securely anchored in the historical past by 'decanonizing' it, the interpreter has difficulty applying it to the modern religious context."[13] To locate biblical meaning in the past is in effect to decanonize it. Biblical historical criticism in large measure succeeded in taming the concept of canon and making it a proper subject of critical study. How was this managed? How had criticism managed to decanonize the Bible?

As Childs says canon was defined in strictly historical terms. My own way of putting this is that criticism reduced canon to the last and ultimate stage in literary formation of the biblical text—how the larger literary units, the several books, got together. One could then write a history of the literary formation of the Bible in critical terms, all the way from the earliest sources discerned by criticism right up to the so-called Palestinian and Alexandrian canons.[14] Criticism was happy now, for it could write a history of the origins and development of biblical literature from J, or J's own earlier sources, to the Palestinian canon, and then do the same for the NT from Q to Chalcedon. And it was able to do it by focusing on phenomena malleable to critical search: lists of biblical books in noncanonical literature, such as Sirach, Philo, Josephus, the Talmud, Marcion, church fathers, fragments (Muratorian), and the like. But another achievement came in importing to early Judaism and Christianity the Western understanding of councils. A real breakthrough occurred when enough references were discovered to a gathering of rabbinic Jews in Jabneh or Jamnia in Palestine in the decades after the fall of Jerusalem to Rome in 70 C.E. The Western critical mind could really latch on to that. What a discovery![15] The needs of criticism were served. If the faithful still needed some notion of "authority" involved with canon, here it was: the authority was superimposed from the outside by ecclesiastic councils. It was their authority that rubbed off on the canon and sealed its content and order. The quest for other councils was soon satisfied in Christianity: there were enough of those to go around. But what of earlier councils in Judaism for the Pentateuch and Prophets? Jabneh dealt only with the Hagiographa. It took a while, but one was found: the *anshê knesset ha-gedolah* convened by Ezra in Jerusalem in the late fifth century B.C.E.![16] That took care of the Writings and the Pentateuch; the Prophets would behave until something showed up.

But it did not. Instead the Dead Sea Scrolls and other such discoveries showed up, like Nag Hammadi, for instance; and the assured results of criticism in this regard seemed less sure. Then there was the ecumenical movement that brought to consciousness the question: whose canon? If canon is reduced to the question of what books are in the canon (and what books are out) and in what order, then one had to ask which canon? Qaraites and Samaritans were still around on the Jewish side with their narrower views of canon; and triumphalist Protestants all of a sudden became aware of other Christian communions with their broader views of canon, all the way to the eighty-one the Ethiopian canon.[17] Without question the concept of canon had returned to haunt us. It would not behave.[18] Something clearly had to be done.

But wait! Along with all the discoveries of ancient and modern communities having different canons came something called the sociology of knowledge. Historical criticism had had a very definite view of authority all the time it thought it was being descriptive and neutral, to use the terms of Childs's early article. While it was consciously trying to bypass the question of authority it was unconsciously subscribing to a view of authority with the vigor of hot pursuit—the pursuit of points originally scored and the *ipsissima verba* of whoever in antiquity had made them. Not a received text but a hypothetical Urtext became the bearer of authority. Whatever could be shown to be "secondary" or "spurious" or "added by a later hand" and hence of no value in reconstructing the original moment of speech or of writing was also viewed, until recently, as of no value theologically or even homiletically. It was because of this last view that the seminary preacher dreaded seeing the Bible scholar in chapel. The latter was quite likely later to say something like: That was very nice, but you apparently did not read von Rinkeldinck's latest monograph on that passage in which he completely rewrote the text in the light of the latest discoveries at Tell el-Mishmash! The comment would have had the effect of depriving the sermon of its authoritative base. It is one thing to determine that a text has no direct value in reconstructing a particular historical moment and quite another to imply that it has no value for other purposes; but that is unfortunately what had happened in large measure.

Another problem historical criticism has spawned is that of fragmentation, even atomization, of the text. As Childs shows in this book, even as sensitive and fine a scholar as Walther Zimmerli contributes to the problem. Form and tradition criticism come in for as much scolding from Childs as the stance and view of the archaeologists. They both tend to atomize the text even as the ancient exegetes did whom they both deplore—though in quite different ways and for different reasons. If *Biblical Theology in Crisis* tended to castigate the archaeologists, especially the school of W. F. Albright and more especially the work of G. Ernest Wright who epitomized biblical theology in this country, *Introduction* does the same for the form and tradition critics. While Childs recognizes that Zimmerli, in contrast to most other scholars, takes seriously the so-called secondary passages in what he calls amplification of the Ezekiel text, he nonetheless reserves some fairly sharp words for the result. He accuses Zimmerli of having "missed the significance of the canonical process in which the experience of Israel with the use of its authoritative writings has been incorporated into the text itself as part of the biblical witness." He feels Zimmerli "disregards this fundamental canonical decision by substituting a pre-canonical stage in the texts' development for the normative canonical text, and by judging a significant part of the canonical text as merely commentary." "Zimmerli's method of working from a reconstructed *Grundtext* [foundational text] to which has been appended commentary runs the danger of losing the inner dynamic of the full canonical passage. To divide a passage historically into stages often destroys the synchronic dimension of the text. A literary entity has an integrity of its own which is not to be identified with the sum of its parts."[19]

Childs is largely right. Even with the efforts increasingly made in the past thirty years to rehabilitate "later hands" in the texts, through redaction criticism and focus on the *Nachleben* (continuing life) or *Nachgeschichte* (later appearance) of certain "messages," the penchant for attributing a greater authority to (often hypothetically reconstructed) "original" cores and forms is still in us. Whether they should be dismissed as Childs tends to seem to say is another matter and will be addressed below.

And so we stand accused of locking the Bible into the past by our subscribing subconsciously to a kind of primitivism (the earliest or the original bore the authority); by subscribing to a kind of fragmentation of the text (to get back to the original we had unregrettably to tear the text apart); and by reducing the concept of canon to what was manageable in the historian's shop and would yield to its tools.

II

Childs's response has been to focus on the concept of canon in understanding scripture. He stresses the observation that the Bible as a whole is far more than the sum of its parts. The phrase most aptly associated with Childs's work is "canonical context," and by this he means literary context, not historical. On the contrary, that to which he most objects in criticism is its fragmentation of the text and its basic tenet or dogma that each fragment can be understood properly only in its original historical setting. He sees in this Enlightenment move an usurpation of the question of authority: we have destroyed the text as molded by the early communities in the canonical process and then manipulated the pieces according to our own best lights brought in from outside the text. Criticism has bypassed the canon going back up the stream of "history" and pinned the fragments discerned by criticism to this, that, and the other historical moment from which each supposedly originated. Childs is especially critical of form and tradition criticism in this regard, his own basic training as a student.

But it must be made as clear as possible that Childs is not against use of the tools of literary criticism in this manner. Much light, he feels, comes by proper use of all we know in this regard. What he strongly objects to is leaving the question of authentic meaning of the text at that point of work on it. Some of Childs's own best work has been in tradition criticism as may be seen in articles[20] and in these books in which he lodges his protest, but he is intent on showing that one must now move beyond all that to discern the further meanings of those fragments or pericopes when they were indeed put together in the manner received. They say other things in canonical context than what they said originally as smaller units in conjunction with a particular historic moment. Nay, more! They say yet other things when read in *full* canonical context. The canon is full of many dialectical theological conversations going on at all times within its covers. The historical context that is really important is that of the present (whenever) reader. The present reader with his or her particular concerns and problems should read any passage totally aware of the full shape of the larger context in which it is found, the book where located, and even the entire canon.[21]

Awareness of the theological movements framed by canonical context provides one with the hermeneutics necessary for reading the passage under eye. Childs allows for some limited pluralism in this regard when he speaks of dialectical movement within the larger text.[22] But what he seems to be affirming is that the Bible when read in canonical context provides some basic uncontested theological statements, even doctrines, in the light of which each passage should be read. Each passage apparently should be read by the hermeneutics of the whole, and those hermeneutics are clearly theological statements: God is Creator, Elector, Sustainer, Judge, Redeemer and Re-Creator. And no passage should be read, or applied by the present reader, without that affirmation clearly in mind.

Isaiah, perhaps, provides Childs's strongest example. Isaiah was finally shaped in such a way that one must read it as a literary whole to discern its full canonical message. He makes much of the editors adjoining Second Isaiah without superscription or indeed mention of any historical context. While Cyrus is definitely there, and Childs would never take it out of the text as some historical critics have done who wanted to date it late, Cyrus does not matter that much. What matters is what the full Book of Isaiah says, when it is altogether whole, about God's Word and its function in the believing community. God is both Judge and Redeemer at all times, not a Judge in preexilic times and a Redeemer in exilic times. And so God is for the present person or community that reads Isaiah at any time. And so Isaiah should be read at any time, no matter which portion, by lectionary or otherwise.

Childs sees canon as God's Word. This should be seen as an issue of his long debate through the 1960s with G. Ernest Wright, whose canon within the canon was a story or recital about the God who acts in history.[23] Childs constantly devalues the mighty acts of God for that throws one right back to the historical contexts of antiquity when God acted. God's Word is for all time. Typology is put in its place in this manner. The problems with typology are exacerbated by stress on God's acts rather than on his Word which returns not void, the overarching theme finally of the Book of Isaiah in its wholeness.

Childs levels the same criticism at a Zimmerli (for instance) as he did at a Wright: they both located an inner canon within the canon that was authoritative, to which all accretions were commentary. Childs stresses that commentary in this sense is not to be found in the Bible: all that follows canon may be thought of as commentary, but nothing that is in it (in the sense of being secondary or less authoritative). Wright's canonical recitals as core of canon and Zimmerli's *Grundtext* as literary core both denigrate some portions of the biblical text and lift up others as authoritative.

Childs does not confuse Wright and Zimmerli in terms of what they did to arrive at their positions; it is just that Childs feels they are both wrong. By emphasizing that the recitals can be verified in large measure by history and archaeology and hence are "true," Wright bypassed canon per se and Israel's own witness to its faith. His real canon was archaeologically verified "history" that he imported to the Bible, according to Childs. By emphasizing that a *Grundtext* can be isolated and verified by the best tools of literary analysis, especially tradition criticism, and hence was the original insight of a passage, Zimmerli also bypasses canon per se and the full experience of the early communities of faith that shaped the whole passage as received and heard and believed over a period of time—again by-passing Israel's own witness to its faith. That Word that speaks out of the text again and again may have gotten its start with, say, Ezekiel; but Ezekiel the prophet is not and was not canonical. The Ezekiel *book* is canonical and had many contributors, without any one of which the text is not yet canonical.

This brings us to another element of Childs's view of the canonical process: the relation of text or tradition and community. That which is canon comes to us from ancient communities of faith, not just from individuals. One of the solid observations of what I prefer to call canonical criticism and what Childs prefers to call canonical perspective or stance was also a basic observation of form criticism: the whole of the Bible, the sum as well as all its parts, comes to us out of the liturgical and instructional life of early believing communities. Childs often insists that nothing there can be seen as "fact" plus interpretation. It is all interpreted, by definition. By the same token, it is all finally a community product. The tools of criticism can help us discern perhaps the literary history of a text from kernel to final form, but it is the final form, according to Childs, that is canon—and nothing in its history of formation.[24] Childs also stresses the function of scripture in believing communities, both ancient and modern. The final shape was determined by how the text functioned in the community along its path toward canonical text. The understandings of the communities, of the tradition as layered in the texts, are an integral part of canonical text. Says Childs, "The modern hermeneutical impasse which has found itself unable successfully to bridge the gap between the past and the present has arisen in large measure by its disregard of the canonical shaping."[25] "A basic characteristic of the canonical approach in regard to both its literary and textual level is its concern to describe the literature in terms of its relation to the historic Jewish community rather than seeing its goal to be the reconstruction of the most original literary form of the books, or the most pristine form of a textual tradition."[26] The canonical shaping took place in community determined by how the tradition being shaped functioned in community. The tradition or text that was moving toward canonicity was always in dialogue with the community. The community shaped the text as it moved toward canon and the text or tradition shaped the communities as it found its way along its pilgrimage to canon.

The final element I want to emphasize in Childs's schema is the form of the text. I have been doing this all along since it is so integral to his position, but it needs focusing. In a manner somewhat similar to the structuralists, Childs calls canon only the text in its full and final canonical form. This includes not only the contributions of the later editors, the superscriptions, the subscriptions, and all the redactional seams, but even all that could possibly fall outside such a literary history of a text. He cites R. Rendtorff to the effect that "the present form of the Pentateuch can be attributed neither to traditional connections made on the oral stage nor to the literary strands of the Pentateuch, whether to J or P. A hiatus remains between the shape given the material by the last literary source and its final canonical shape."[27] This is what the communities contributed to and this is what they passed on. The canonical perspective is not just a redactional perspective. It moves on beyond redaction criticism.

III

There is much in Childs's position with which I agree. Historical criticism in its handling of the Bible has bypassed the ancient communities that produced it and shaped it. It has focused, in good modern Western fashion, on individual authors. Liberals and conservatives alike have done the same: the one simply attributes less of a text to the early "author" than the other. They both located authority almost solely in individuals and original speakers: conservatives claim the individual said all the words of a book or passage while liberals peel away accretions. But they have both bypassed the communities in one way or another. And historical criticism has been primitivist, locking the Bible into the past, even decanonizing it thereby, as Sheppard aptly put it. And criticism has in large measure tended to fragmentize the text, though redaction criticism has corrected the tendency to some extent. Finally, criticism has felt free to rewrite the text in the light of what it could bring to study of the text in an effort to reconstruct an Urtext. Rewriting the Bible with such conviction caused a shift of locus of authority from what the early believing communities received, shaped, and passed on, to what scholars were convinced was said or written in the first place. What perhaps had started as a historian's exercise to see what the history of formation of a passage or book or literary corpus had been, became a focus of authority. This became so much the case that Bible translations done in this century, and especially those done in the 1930s through 1960s, reflected the new topos of authority. Many rewrote the Bible.[28] Matters had clearly gone too far.

It was time to move beyond redaction criticism and criticism's focus upon individual geniuses to the early believing communities that found, in their new contexts, value enough in what some of those geniuses had said, thought, and written, to apply what they received to their own situation—adapting it as need be, and going on to recommend it to their children as well as to neighboring communities. It was time to focus upon communities rather than upon "editors," or rather, to focus on the communities in which these editors participated and which they served. Many "editors" have undoubtedly done much editing that was never passed on. There were undoubtedly many geniuses whose works we have never seen, or see now only because of modern discoveries, simply because the ancient communities—without malice aforethought—did not find value in them and did not commend them to others or to the next generation. We know of some of these for two reasons: some Eastern Christian communities had more in their "canons" than the Western; and modern archaeology, accidental, clandestine, or scientific, has recovered others from long burial.

Because of loss of attention to the early communities that shaped and passed on what they found of value, and therefore loss of attention to why they did so, criticism followed a radical and major shift in epistemology that accompanied the Enlightenment and hence caused a radical and major shift in ontology of canon. Whereas up to the Enlightenment it was the Bible that generation after generation had shed light on the world and helped the believing communities and the faithful to understand their problems and find solutions to them, after the Enlightenment criticism tried to bring light from the world to understand the Bible and the problems it found in it. This observation is not to deny that there were problems: there are discrepancies, anomalies, anachronisms, and inconsistencies in the text. There can be no retreat from the excitement of honesty the Enlightenment brought to biblical study. That is not the point. The point is that focus on those problems and quest for solutions to them brought about a radical shift in epistemology and ontology of canon that lost sight of why those early communities had canonized the text in the first place. My own way of putting it is as follows. There had been a relationship between tradition, written or oral, and community, a constant, ongoing dialogue, a historical memory passed on from generation to generation, in which the special relationship between canon and community resided. There was a memory that this particular body of tradition had at crucial junctures throughout the centuries of that relationship given life to the communities—just as the communities had given life to it by passing it on and keeping it alive. Torah, and then Christ, was viewed as the way, the truth, and the life. One searched Scripture because in it one found even eternal life (John 5:39). Why? Because in the very conception and birth of canon was the historic event of death and resurrection of the community of faith when it otherwise should have passed from the scene of history like everybody else.[29]

That had happened in the sixth century B.C.E. when the concept of canon in this sense arose (though it had a prehistory that gave it momentum), and it happened time and again thereafter with the message of the Gospels giving the old idea a fresh boost and even a new dimension. The communities and the canon (of whatever length) understood each other: they gave each other life. The fact that their understanding of canon was no longer historically "accurate" from our perspective is beside the point. The believing communities were no longer historically "accurate" either. Neither was the same as at the beginning. Each had adapted to ever-changing situations, but they understood each other; and up to the Enlightenment the relationship had never been broken even though it had gone through numerous adjustments. Childs puts all this differently, but in these observations we largely agree.

It was time to focus on the early communities that received and shaped the traditions and the application of them into canon. Criticism had skipped over this crucial link, jumping from redaction to conciliar decision. There was a tacit recognition of community in the quest for decision-making councils; but it was wrongheaded for it assumed authority was brought to canon by an ecclesiastic or community body, rather than arising out of an ongoing intimate relationship between canon and community that a council could but ratify. Whatever Josephus meant by popularity being a criterion of canonization, it at least means that no single council of men undoubtedly sitting in the midst of one set of problems (those uppermost in their minds) could foist off onto the communities some esoteric literature. At most they affirmed what the communities, scattered in space and drawn out in time, in their corporate wisdom (including the geniuses and leaders as well as followers and faithful) found valuable and gave life.[30] It was time in study of Scripture to vitalize what Childs calls the canonical process and what I call the periods of intense canonical process.

On all this Childs and I largely agree. We also both sponsor an emphasis now on the function of canon rather than on its form or structure. The point is not that literary form is unimportant. Neither of us has any desire to denigrate the excellent, continuing work of form criticism. The future of structuralism will undoubtedly be in the way form critics, like Rolf Knierim, have adapted the better observations of the structuralists. Stress on function in the believing communities is the proper province of focus on canon. When a tried and true tradition is called upon by a tradent for the sake of his or her community, we ask how it functioned for them. What was the purpose of the *relecture*, what was its effect, and how was the tradition or scripture resignified when cited? Study of canon should not focus too much on its structure since there have been so many different canons both in the past and still in the present, depending on which believing community is under purview. Beyond a certain core the lists vary considerably in terms of both content and order. Focus on function has brought a felicitous review of the import of canon and its prehistory. It is indeed adaptable for life.[31]

We also agree on the full text of a canon, of whichever community. Here

Childs is quite insistent. The expression "full canonical context" will always be associated with his position. We both agree that the terms "spurious," "secondary," and "not genuine" should be dropped from serious biblical study. They may have started out having a valid function, but they have become symbols of criticism's peculiar doctrine of authority: only the original is authentic. Seeing how the early communities shaped what they received and resignified for addressing their later situations and problems is very important to understanding how and why we have a canon in the first place. Redaction criticism is not enough. If what the several geniuses did right on up to the final editor did not speak to the people and address their needs we would either not have their work or we would be digging it up in holes in the ground in the Near East. Not only so, but the matter of juxtaposition of the larger units, right on up to the various sequences of books, may often have evolved, as Rendtdorff rightly sees, out of a history of corporate liturgical and instructional life of the communities. Of course, some individuals perceived the communities' needs better than others and what they did in the shaping of canon was more enduring than what others did, but focus on individuals in that process is no longer sufficient in itself.

IV

But there are crucial differences between us, so crucial that we both feel it important that students not bracket our work on canon beyond a certain point. One of the beautiful things that happened in my last year of teaching at Union Theological Seminary in New York, before moving to Claremont, was that the seminary invited Childs down in the spring of 1977 from Yale to have an open conversation on canon. I think we both enjoyed celebrating the differences between us as much as the agreements. Not that they are not genuine differences—on some points we differ sharply—but because I think we both see ourselves in a very long line of tradents and neither of us is under the impression that truth will falter if we listen to each other. I feel a deep kindred spirit with Bard Childs. Our roots go deep in the faith. I truly believe that he, too, is a monotheizing pluralist; and that is, as all my students know, the highest compliment I can pay the man.[32]

My greatest problem with Childs's position is his divorcing the development and growth of canonical literature from its historical provenances. When Childs says "context," he means literary context; when I say it I most often mean historical context. He focuses almost exclusively, in his work on canon, on the final form of the text. To do that, he has to choose one text, and he has chosen the MT. That is already an immense problem for me. It is to read back into canonical history a post-Christian, very rabbinic form of the text. By "very rabbinic" I mean a text unrelated to the Christian communities until comparatively late. While Jerome learned a lot from his Bethlehem rabbi, the Vulgate is a far cry from the MT! Focus on the MT leaves the NT, whose Scripture was the Septuagint, out in the cold for the most part. Childs devotes a full chapter to this problem;[33] but he does not solve it, because his problem is a prior one, his insistence on a text at a single frozen point, and that is simply not my view of canon. Far from it. Canon, by its very nature, is adaptable, not just stable. One must keep in mind all the texts and all the canons and all the communities. While Childs speaks of a canonical process he apparently means those moments in past history precisely between the final redactors and the stabilized text of the MT only. By canonical process I mean both that and all the history of function of canon before that and ever since. To distinguish the early history to which Childs refers, I speak of periods of intense canonical process.

This is in large part the reason I have chosen to use the phrase canonical criticism, rather than canon criticism, precisely because the same thing is going on now in the believing communities as went on back then. Another reason I use it is to try to account for the phenomenon of canon itself; it is the link between those early believing communities that produced the canon and the present ones in which it continues to function. Canonical criticism in my view is both a subdiscipline, albeit new and developing, of biblical criticism, and the way I think we can best and most carefully and most judiciously unlock the Bible from the past, into which criticism has tended to seal it, and unchain it from the scholar's desk. That is, we must give it back to the current believing communities, but give it back responsibly, that is, with the scientific thoroughness of recognition of its proper *Sitz*.

Childs does not want to use the term "criticism" at all. He feels that to use the word relegates what he is doing to the category of another technique, as he puts it, in humanistic study of the Bible.[34] I have no such fear. On the contrary, I view what is happening as evolving out of critical study of the Bible and as the next stage in its development. We are moving on, still fully employing all the valid tools of criticism to date, to bring also into focus the next stage of formation of canon, its reception and shaping in the several believing communities before the periods of intense stabilization.[35] Not only so, but I feel that it may be an important way for the guild of biblical critics to respond to the charge that we have locked the Bible into the past, precisely by recognizing that as a guild we did have a particular, even narrow, view of authority, and that we can reform ourselves as historians and scientists. We simply were not being as scientific and as thorough as we thought we were in our "objective" work. The solution to the problem of giving the Bible back to the churches is not only for scholars to do more continuing education and do more writing normal folk can understand, though these are important; but it must include our confessing the error of our ways and then going on to construct a history of function of canon that links past to present. Childs is at his best when he does a history of interpretation right on through church and synagogue history, and I mean this aspect of his work in part when I speak of a history of function of canon.[36]

But that point leads to my strongest objection to Childs's work. He focuses on one form of stabilized Scripture, and what he calls its inner theological dialectic and conversation, and dissociates it from history altogether. That is,

I do not see any really clear evidence that what he claims is canonical context functioned as such in any believing community until perhaps the Reformation. One might possibly extrapolate from a few pieces of intertestamental literature evidence that portions of the Bible were read as a continuous story, such as Jubilees, the Genesis Apocryphon, some of Philo's retailing, and other such paraphrases, and that canonical context of larger units was so honored. But it is not clear that any of the writers of such documents derived the hermeneutics by which they read the text from canonical context. On the contrary, each such retail displays hermeneutics imported from elsewhere. The speeches in Acts and the recital in Hebrews 11 would support Wright's views considerably more than demonstrate Childs's thesis, and there is nothing in Paul to encourage it. Nothing in the pesher or midrashic literature goes so far. Origen? Hardly. It would not be until the Reformers' commentaries arrived on the scene that one could argue such a point, it seems to me. I honestly cannot see that what Childs claims in this regard ever really happened. One is tempted to see in Childs's canon a Reformation perspective both in its MT vs. LXX (Vulgate) form and in his insistence on full context.

Childs indicates a canonical shape that few if any subsequent tradents heeded. On the contrary, careful study of the history of text and canon during the period of canonical process and immediately thereafter indicates a shift in ontology of canon and the rise of new kinds of hermeneutics in all the denominations of Judaism that practically prove that very few tradents, if any, read Scripture in the way Childs theorizes.[37] The shift in ontology can best be signaled by seeing it as a move away from viewing scriptural traditions primarily as stories, and hence from viewing Scripture as story, to treating Scripture as oracle.[38] The NT is a product from the period of the shift, containing both lengthy recitals of holy history and numerous examples of the newer view of Scripture as oracle. Even when one says that Matthew viewed himself as the Christian Ezra and wrote his Gospel with that model in mind, or when one says that Luke viewed himself as the Christian Deuteronomist, or when one says Paul viewed himself as the new Jeremiah, none of these indicates they read Ezra-Nehemiah, or Deuteronomy–1–4 Kingdoms, or Jeremiah, in Childs's full canonical context.[39] These are modern theories that have some limited validity, but they do not bear out Childs's thesis. Nor does he claim such. In a genuine effort to test Childs's thesis, and with the hope he was right, my students and I thought precisely of the above kinds of hypotheses about the composition of the NT, and proceeded to probe in that direction. But in no case did it work out in Childs's favor. Certainly there was evidence that some NT writers sometimes thought in larger terms than isolated passages: C. H. Dodd had shown that in *According to the Scriptures: The Sub-Structure of NT Theology.*[40]

But it is not the same. Ezra may have been taken as a model by Matthew in thinking of himself as a scribe trained for the kingdom of heaven, but it would have been Ezra, the human figure that emerges from Scripture, not what he may have written. What Johannes Munck meant by Paul's self--

understanding being that of the Christian Jeremiah was limited to Paul's understanding of his vocation being expressed in Jeremiah's terms of his own call.

Luke presented the best test. If those of us are right who see Luke as shaping his Gospel in terms of Deuteronomy and the Deuteronomic history (1–4 Kingdoms), here would have been the support we needed for Childs's thesis. For Luke is remarkable in this regard. Of all the NT writers, he appears to have read Scripture in larger literary units than anyone else. But close scrutiny indicates that Luke's interest was not in an overall thesis presented (only) by the Deuteronomist but rather in presenting Jesus as fulfilling Deut. 18:15. Luke thus arranged what he received in his special section by *Stichwörter* derived from Deuteronomy 1—26. But it would be very difficult to say that Luke presents evidence of having read Deuteronomy in canonical context in the manner Childs describes. Luke was very interested in the ethic of election expressed not only in Deuteronomy but as received from Scripture generally, but that can be discerned in selected short passages as well: it cannot be securely introduced as evidence of his reading Scripture in full canonical context.

For the sake of argument one might want to grant Childs Luke and a few others in the period, but the overwhelming evidence simply points in another direction. Precisely concurrent with the final shaping of OT Scripture was the shift in viewing Scripture from that of story to that of oracle. The bulk of the evidence is in the direction of reading Scripture in very short literary units, or fragmentizing it. God was thought to speak through each passage and each verse, and if one could cite a passage from each section, Torah, Prophets, and Writings, one scored big.[41] The Habakkuk Pesher from Qumran Cave 1 evinces no interest whatever in reading Habakkuk in canonical context. Each verse was taken as divine oracle speaking to this, that, and the other Essene historical context. Habakkuk had to be disjointed in order to speak to the new historical context, and whatever verse or phrase did not fit the *new context* was simply bypassed. All Scripture was resignified in this manner in order to derive light from it for the new situations.

And herein lies another anomaly in Childs's thesis. How can one be so concerned with rehabilitating the function of Scripture in the believing communities when he effectively denies the importance and humanity of those very communities by ruling out ancient historical contexts in discerning ancient texts—not only the original ones but the subsequent historical contexts through the periods of intense canonical process? One cannot deal effectively with the question of canon by ignoring the very important work being done in the early histories of resignification or *relecture*, as the French say, of Scripture. One has to work continually in historical criticism, insofar as possible in each sequential generation, to trace the history of shaping of canon up to full stabilization of text and canon.[42] Where is the force of argument in favor of the importance of believing communities when one argues for dissociating Scripture from historical contexts?

One certainly can and should view Scripture synchronically as well as diachronically. And one can surely theorize about a hypothetical moment when a final canonical redaction gave the text the shape it finally attained—in order to see it then synchronically. But to dissociate it from history altogether as though that final canonical redaction had a timeless theology in mind for all generations and centuries to come is unrealistic. It is an overreaction to the excesses of historical criticism. One should work both synchronically and diachronically. As one moves through the history of formation of text and canon diachronically, one should work on each stage synchronically. And that requires all the tools of biblical exegesis and historical criticism at one's command for each period of formation.

The overwhelming evidence points to the moment of final shaping as not particularly more important than any other. The hard fact is that once text and canon were stabilized, a new ontology of Scripture arose with new modes and techniques of hermeneutics to crack it open once more.[43] When the text was still fluid before stabilization and it was still viewed primarily as sacred story, a *peshat* exegesis and hermeneutic were sufficient. But once it got frozen into the state Childs wants apparently to absolutize, other types of hermeneutic arose to break it open for application to new circumstances to derive light from it and to find life in it. Final stabilization was but a stage in the history of formation of Scripture, and an elusive one at that. The believing communities, the actual ones in history, apparently did things quite a bit differently from the way Childs suggests. And if one is truly going to honor those believing communities, one has to engage in full historical criticism at each stage of shaping.

Another anomaly in Childs's argument occurs in studying his excellent efforts at rehabilitating so-called later additions, including superscriptions and the like. Childs seems to argue that these indicate the shaping process. But I cannot find where Childs deals with the obvious question arising out of such observations. Does not most such editorial work indicate the intense interest of such redactors in date lines and historical contexts? They seem to be saying fairly clearly, if the reader wants to understand the full import for his or her (later) situation of what Scripture is saying, he or she had best consider the original historical context in which this passage scored its point. Childs may be right to some extent that the editors of the Psalter wanted their readers to view David as an example of the way God can deal with any leader or any person, but the way they did it was to draw attention to historical situations in which David supposedly composed his songs. One cannot read the Torah or the Prophets without the clear impression from the text that one had best know the historical contexts into which Moses and the prophets said what they had to say. Only wisdom literature gives the appearance of being unrelated to historical context but even there some of the ancient redactors and tradents insisted on a particular author who wrote in a particular historical framework (whether criticism says they were right or not).

How available to future generations of believers is Scripture when the historicity of the ones that gave it to us is denied? Childs is right about so much that he says that it is disturbing to me that he leaves so many such questions unanswered. Yes, biblical criticism has fragmentized the text, but that simply means that we are in a long line of tradents who did the same in their day and way. Yes, biblical criticism has too much gone back behind Scripture as canon to the points scored at early stages in its formation to seek its authority. This is perhaps his strongest point.

V

In contrast to Childs's contention, I want to say loud and clear that I consider biblical historical and literary criticism a gift of God in due season. It is only when it is abused or taken as an end in itself, or when it does not keep issues of authority clear, that it generates problems. It has generated such problems, and I, with Childs, feel that the proper antidote to those ills is a revival of the concept of canon as applied to Scripture. But in contrast to Childs I am convinced that the revival must be seen as a proper extension, in due season, of biblical criticism. Criticism, which began in the Enlightenment, is now evolving to its next stage of development after redaction criticism. It is also my conviction that only by developing this further subdiscipline within the guild of criticism can the guild respond adequately to the charges noted at the beginning of this chapter or can biblical criticism redeem itself and become scientifically thorough.

Elsewhere I spell out the task of canonical criticism with its concepts and method.[44] Suffice it here to say that it has already discerned characteristics that must be taken into account for full appreciation of Scripture as canon: those salient characteristics are repetition or *relecture* with concomitant resignification for the later believing community; multivalency of canonical literature—its ability to say different things in different contexts; pluralism or canon's own built-in self-critical and self-corrective apparatus; its adaptability-stability quotient with concomitant built-in textual restraints on resignification; and finally, and perhaps most important of all, its unrecorded hermeneutics discernible throughout canon by means of proper use of historical and literary criticism. The Bible is full of unrecorded hermeneutics recoverable by use of a triangle of interrelationship of ancient traditions or texts repeated in particular historical contexts of the believing community by use of certain hermeneutics.[45]

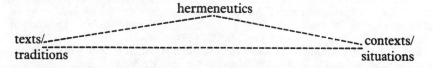

hermeneutics

texts/ traditions — contexts/ situations

Canonical criticism focuses on the function of Scripture in the believing communities. Its exact structure, or length and order of contents, is not unimportant but is secondary. It was produced by early believing communities, handed down by believing communities, and still has its only proper *Sitz im Leben* in the continuing believing communities. Canon owes its life to its dialogue with those believing communities; and the believing communities owe their life to their dialogue with it. The kinds of repetition of text and tradition in ever-changing contexts, the evidence of its multivalency or pregnant ambiguity, the evidence of its adaptability-stability factor and the power of the hermeneutics that helped shape and reshape its traditions are all still operative in the continuing believing communities today. The canonical process that started way back with the first case of repetition long before Scripture was fully penned continues today in the believing communities that find their identity in it, as well as indications for their life styles. It provides a paradigm for *how* to learn from the communities' traditions and for *how* to learn from the rest of the world as well. Just as the biblical tradents not only reapplied community traditions to ever-changing contexts but also adapted international wisdom and made it their own, so modern believing communities continue to do the same. Canon provides the paradigm or the guidelines for how to carry on.

NOTES

1. Brevard S. Childs, "Interpretation in Faith," *Int.* 18 (1964): 434ff.
2. Ibid., 438.
3. Ibid., 440.
4. *Biblical Theology in Crisis* (Philadelphia: Westminster Press, 1970).
5. Childs's focus has varied since *Biblical Theology in Crisis*. There he seemed to stress the inner dialectic of canonical themes within the OT and between the testaments. In *The Book of Exodus: A Critical, Theological Commentary* (Philadelphia: Westminster Press, 1974) he was constrained by the commentary form to focus on the larger literary units within a single book (even though he failed in it to suggest what the canonical shape of the book as a whole was). And in his *Introduction to the OT as Scripture* (Philadelphia: Fortress Press, 1979) he focuses almost entirely on the hermeneutical shape of each individual book, constrained again, perhaps, by the introduction form.
6. Childs, *Exodus.* See my review in *JBL* 95 (1976): 286–90.
7. Brevard S. Childs, "A Traditio-Historical Study of the Reed Sea Tradition," *VT* 20 (1970): 406–18; "Psalm Titles and Midrashic Exegesis," *JSS* 16 (1971): 137–50; "The OT as Scripture of the Church," *CTM* 43 (1972): 709–22; "The Etiological Tale Re-examined," *VT* 24 (1974): 387–97; "Reflections on the Modern Study of the Psalms," in *Magnalia Dei: The Mighty Acts of God. Essays on the Bible and Archaeology in Memoriam G. E. Wright*, ed. F. M. Cross (Garden City, N.Y.: Doubleday & Co., 1976), 377–88; "Sensus Literalis: An Ancient and Modern Problem," in *Beiträge zur alttestamentlichen Theologie*, Festschrift W. Zimmerli (Göttingen, 1976); "The Canonical Shape of the Prophetic Literature," *Int.* 32 (1978): 46–55.
8. J. A. Sanders, "Biblical Criticism and the Bible as Canon" (chap. 4 of this book). See Gerhard Maier, *The End of the Historical-Critical Method* (St. Louis: Concordia Publishing House, 1977), and Peter Stuhlmacher, *Historical Criticism and Theological Interpretation of Scripture* (Philadelphia: Fortress Press, 1977).
9. Walter Wink, *The Bible in Human Transformation: Toward a New Paradigm for Biblical Study* (Philadelphia: Fortress Press, 1973), 1.

10. "Canon and Criticism," as yet unpublished, though much of what Childs did there appears in his *Introduction* (cf. p. 17).

11. Childs, *Introduction*, 45.

12. J. A. Sanders, "Adaptable for Life: The Nature and Function of Canon" (chap. 1 of this book).

13. Childs, *Introduction*, 79.

14. The work of Albert C. Sundberg has thrown serious doubt on the concept of a separate Alexandrian canon in the sense criticism needed it: see *The OT of the Early Church*, HTS 20 (Cambridge: Harvard Univ. Press, 1964).

15. A discovery shown false by Jack P. Lewis, "What Do We Mean by Jabneh?" *JBR* 32 (1964): 125–32.

16. L. Finkelstein, "The Maxim of the Anshe Keneset ha-Gedolah," *JBL* 59 (1940): 455–69.

17. R. W. Cowley, "The Biblical Canon of the Ethiopian Orthodox Church Today," *OstKSt* 23 (1974): 318–24; S. P. Kealy, "The Canon: An African Contribution," *BTB* 9 (1979): 13–26.

18. It should be noted that Childs does not address all these problems. I feel he might modify his position if he did.

19. Childs, *Introduction*, 367–70.

20. See Childs's excellent "Traditio-Historical Study."

21. See above, n. 5.

22. Childs, *Biblical Theology in Crisis*, 149–219.

23. See George Ernest Wright, *The OT and Theology* (New York: Harper & Row, 1969), and my review in *Int.* 24 (1970): 359–68; and Childs's *Biblical Theology in Crisis* and my review in *USQR* 26 (1971): 299–304.

24. Contrast James Barr's view of inspiration that would "apply to the formation of tradition that finally comprised Scripture rather than to the formation of Scripture" (*The Bible and the Modern World* [New York: Harper & Row, 1973], 130–31); and see my review, "Reopening Old Questions About Scripture" (1974).

25. Childs, *Introduction*, 79.

26. Ibid., 96–99.

27. Ibid., 132. This observation seems to be congruous with the thesis of S. Talmon, "The Textual Study of the Bible—A New Outlook," in *Qumran and the History of the Biblical Text*, ed. F. M. Cross and S. Talmon (Cambridge: Harvard Univ. Press, 1975), 321–400.

28. Such as the first edition of the *JB* (the subsequent editions of *JB* in French have become more responsible to the extant texts), NEB, NAB, and others. Contrast now the recent *Traduction Oecuménique de la Bible* (Paris: Cerf, 1976) and *Die Einheitsübersetzung der heiligen Schrift* (Stuttgart: Katholische Bibelanstalt, 1974). Contrast also the *New Jerusalem Bible* (1985) and the revised *New English Bible* (forthcoming, 1989).

29. J. A. Sanders, *Torah and Canon* (1972), 7–8.

30. Sanders, "Adaptable for Life."

31. Ibid.

32. Despite his skepticism about it: Childs, *Introduction*, 57.

33. Ibid., 96–99, 659–71.

34. Childs, "Canonical Shape," 54; and *Introduction*, 56–57.

35. J. A. Sanders, "Text and Canon: Concepts and Method" (chap. 7 of this book).

36. See esp. Childs's *Exodus*.

37. Sanders, "Text and Canon" (section VII of chap. 7 of this book).

38. A point well made by Merrill Miller in an as-yet-unpublished paper, "Directions in the Study of Biblical Interpretation in Late Antiquity."

39. O. Lamar Cope, *Matthew: A Scribe Trained for the Kingdom of Heaven* (Washington, D.C.: Catholic Biblical Association, 1976); C. F. Evans, "The Central Section of

St. Luke's Gospel," in *Studies in the Gospels*, ed. D. E. Nineham (Oxford: Oxford Univ. Press, 1955), 37–53; J. A. Sanders, "The Ethic of Election in Luke's Great Banquet Parable" (1974); Johannes Munck, *Paul and the Salvation of Mankind* (Richmond: John Knox Press, 1959).

40. C. H. Dodd, *According to the Scriptures: The Sub-Structure of NT Theology* (London: James Nisbet & Co., 1952).

41. A technique sometimes called *hariza*. See A. Goldberg, "Petiha and Hariza," *JSJ* 10 (1979): 213–18.

42. Elsewhere we respond more fully (see chap. 9, below) to two of Childs's concerns expressed in such a way as to indicate uncertainty on his part. In *Introduction*, 56–57, he speaks of our insistence on working as fully as possible on the histories of the periods of intense canonical process, with all the tools of criticism, as "speculative." All historical reconstruction is speculative to some extent, and the Persian period perhaps more than most. But to use this as excuse to give up entirely and to absolutize in great degree a particular form of literature unrelated to the trials and tribulations and other facets of history of the believing communities that shaped it would be to me both intolerable in terms of our common claims about function of Scripture in those communities, and very limited in terms of concept of canon. To call the work of quest for the hermeneutics of the faithful, who found value in these traditions and texts enough to create the very concept of canon, speculative is evidence of uncertainty of one's own position—especially when that position stresses function of canon among those faithful.

The other concern is expressed in *Introduction*, 589, where Childs calls the quest for points scored by the resignification of traditions in antiquity, "a romantic understanding of history," might perhaps best be left to fall of its own weight. Must we not look for the Word or point made by these words (in text and tradition) so as not to confuse the two? Childs's best support for his whole position is perhaps in the Reformers. But I know of no Reformer who focused on text without historical context as appears to be the case in Childs's position.

43. See Sanders, "Text and Canon."

44. J. A. Sanders, *Canon and Community* (1984).

45. J. A. Sanders, "Canonical Hermeneutics: True and False Prophecy" (chap. 5, above, pp. 89ff.).

9

From Sacred Story
to Sacred
Text

The following chapter was originally written for and delivered at the international conference on "Sacred Texts: The Hermeneutics of Religious Literatures in a Post-Holocaust Age," held October 17 to 19 at Indiana University in Bloomington in 1982. It was later adapted for delivery at the School of Theology in Claremont as the first annual Knopf-Hill Lecture on November 20, 1984. It is published here for the first time.

This chapter synthesizes my interests and hence makes an appropriate conclusion to this book of pilgrimage; hence the title of the book. Here I have attempted to bring together what is pertinent about text and canon, Dead Sea Scrolls, canonical hermeneutics, and comparative midrash or the *Nachleben* of biblical traditions and their function in later literature, including the NT. It expresses my concern about the relation of canon to ancient believing communities as well as to current believing communities, Jewish and Christian, but especially the latter in which I have some responsibility. Finally, it suggests how I understand the Bible as canon may function as a prophetic voice to the world today.

In its original format the piece concluded with the seventeen results that might ensue if Christian churches could learn to read the Bible on its own terms, that is, with its own theocentric, monotheizing hermeneutics. But those were presented in *Canon and Community* (1984), 74–76. Some of the observations made in "Text and Canon: Concepts and Method" (see chap. 7) about the masoretic phenomenon are pressed back to the Deuteronomic phenomenon. The notes contain cross-references to my earlier works, several of which appear in this volume, because this contribution may be read as an epitome, for the time being, to the pilgrimage.

Since the following was written, indeed after this book was sent to press, a student suggested that I review Walter Ong's *Orality and Literacy* (New York: Methuen Inc., 1982; 3d printing, 1986). It was a felicitous suggestion. Upon putting it down I thought how much I wish I had had that kind of support in mind in writing not only what follows but also in a good bit of what we are attempting to do. Most of the Bible, as Ong recognizes, came out of the tension he so well describes between orality and textuality; each had and has its own cultural support system and each was and is distinct to a great extent. While agreeing with just about all he says (writes) I would focus on two areas of that tension Ong does not: the problems noted in the following chapter when an essentially oral culture (Jews in exile) wrestled with a written text (Deuteronomy) deriving from an earlier, far different milieu (ancient Judah at home); and the problems attendant on the oral reading of the early biblical texts in ancient believing communities, most of whose members were illiterate and "heard" the readings in and through their entrenched orality (how else could they?). How much of that orality, or community discussion of received texts read aloud and discussed, is embedded in the later (NT?) biblical literature? Werner Kelber (*The Oral and Written Gospel* [Fortress Press, 1983]) addresses some of the issues very well indeed, but one suspects that the discussions have only just begun.

Early Judaism of the Second Temple Period witnessed within its scattered communities in the Mediterranean and Persian worlds a significant shift in understanding its own common traditions, as well as the international wisdom that it had adapted and was adapting to its needs. That shift may be characterized as the move from sacred story to sacred text. The history of text transmission, as well as the history of community attitudes toward the texts, that stretched from the Deuteronomic phenomenon to the masoretic phenomenon, has been considerably revised over the past twenty years. Our understanding of what happened seems to be coming closer to the reality of situation.

The dramatic revival of the Mosaic view and understanding of Judah's origins and identity, celebrated in the Josianic Reformation and the so-called discovery of the scroll of Deuteronomy in 621 B.C.E., marked the beginning or at least the first truly important event in that history. Deuteronomy effectively triumphed over all other ancient understandings of those origins and that identity. By the time of Ezra's return from Babylonia to Jerusalem two centuries later the triumph was complete. Deuteronomy and the Deuteronomic movement cast light backward and forward. It effectively Mosaized the traditions about the origin of Jerusalem. The old history about how David had taken the city, without firing a shot, and made it the capital not only of Judah but of the united kingdom, would continue to be told and recited: but henceforth it would be heard in the light of Moses' last will and testament in the plains of Moab in which it was he who first legitimized that place God would choose to have his name invoked. Moses would have designated it as willed by God well before David took it from the Jebusites. The all-powerful Davidic traditions would henceforth be contained and largely limited to the Books of Samuel, Isaiah, and the Psalter until the Chronicler issued another revisionist history about the time, apparently, of Ezra. It is, in fact, quite possible that the Chronicler's revision of that history was composed as a counterbalance to the powerful effect that the Genesis-to--

Deuteronomy Torah was already having in Judaism, as may be seen in the old histories being reviewed and culminating in the Deuteronomic history with the Books of Kings. The Chronicler's references to many ancient writings dating to before Deuteronomy and the Deuteronomic history were clearly an effort to lend non-Deuteronomic but ancient authority to the Chronicler's revisionist history.

But even before Deuteronomy was to triumph so magnificently in terms of the canonical shapes of the Torah and subsequent history, it had started a trend of thinking about the value of community texts that was never to end. There are lines of prehistory to the Deuteronomic phenomenon, to be sure, but an incomparable boost was given by Deuteronomy to the notion of a sacred text that would be felt for centuries to come. There had been sacred texts prior to Deuteronomy, such as the tablets of the law and whatever else may or may not have been in the Ark of the Covenant. All cults and cultures apparently had such. In Israel, history writing may or may not have received considerable impulse in the time of Solomon, but none such had the dramatic impact of Deuteronomy. Oral traditions about the people's origins and identity apparently had greater authority in the pre-Deuteronomic era, as may be seen in the prophetic and hymnic literature, than written texts. Those traditions were clearly fluid and adaptable to the needs and uses conceived by the prophets and psalmists of the Iron Age. They could be poured into many different forms, such as oracles, songs, narratives, didactic stories, hymns, and parables.

But once they were poured onto the written scroll discovered by Hilkiah's workmen in the temple in 621 in the form of the last will and testament of Moses, they entered into another dimension of tradition history that would eventually see Judaism embrace the concept of sacred texts as the core of her very existence.

On the positive side, that embrace caused an extensive review in the exile of all the traditions the survivors could collect from the prewar days, especially about the old times before their ancestors had settled in the land. They did not save them all, as the many references to nonextant works of the early days clearly show. But they saved those that became repeatable and recitable, that were of value to enough of the communites in exile, precisely to tell them who they were if they chose, as a remnant indeed did choose, *not* to assimilate either to Babylonian or Persian identity and culture. Such an intensive review undoubtedly caused considerable literary activity so that most of what they reviewed, and were to keep, came to be written down in an acceptable form. As Frank M. Cross has put it, there was a renaissance in the sixth century B.C.E. of interest in the Bronze Age, precisely of the time when their ancestors were scattered about in Mesopotamia just as they now were. But there also would have been an intensive review in exilic reflection on the oracles and messages of the prophets, early and late from the prewar days. They valued and wrote down what made sense and offered true hope of a transcendent sort in their new situation and were not like Gilead's superficial and worthless balm, precisely the messages of the so-called false prophets. In fact, they came to call their core history in the land "Early Prophets," and they came to call "Latter Prophets" those who had arisen precisely in the period of the power flows between their being under Egyptian hegemony prior to the mid-eighth century and under that of Persia after the middle of the sixth century.

The review and the literary activity in exile were of a vital sort and they issued in the essential shaping of Torah and the early collection and shaping of the Prophets. The process would not be completed in the sixth century, but the molds and the dies were cast. After all, as Ezekiel put it, old Israel and Judah had died and a New Israel had been resurrected: Judaism was here to stay as the transformed people of God. Eventually other types of literature would also hit a kind of tenure track, of value to the believing communities, sufficient to form a tertiary or third collection of texts also to become sacred for all the people. But not yet a while: that would take considerably longer as would the final stabilization of the prophetic corpus.

Deuteronomy had taken the preexilic prophetic view of Israel's origins and identity and institutionalized it. Moses, who had surely been a community organizer, a revolt leader, a good defensive military strategist, and a lawgiver, was now focused upon as prophet. As Joseph Blenkinsopp has shown, Deuteronomy lifted the role of prophet in Israel's history to a level above that of king and priest.[1] The honorary title was extended eventually all the way back to David and even Abraham. The Qumran psalter would say that David had written 4,050 psalms through prophecy. It had been the prophetic ability not only to say that God was signifying the disasters of the power flows from Egypt to Assyria to Babylonia, and finally to Persia, as punishment for the people's sins and the crucible in which God was transforming the people into his New Israel, but that he also had sent prophetic eyewitnesses to tell them of that transcendent signification of their suffering, in advance of its doing so! Whatever else others might have said in attempts to understand what was happening, the so-called true prophets had prepared the people in advance or at least a significant remnant of the people, and given them the vision by which to see world events and their own disintegration as but part of a process of transformation. They had gone to the wall in their belief in God as universal Creator, Redeemer, and Re-Creator. He was the God of death, as well as of life, and could signify death and give it meaning in a further dimension. That vision provided the eyes for the review of all the traditions that affirmed that God was not stumped by the phenomenon called death, even the death of a whole people as a nation. Eventually they would affirm that same sovereignty of God over death for individuals.

But not yet. For now it was important to be able to say to those who mocked the faithful, both from within and from without, that God had not let them down, or been defeated by Marduk. On the contrary, God had signified the defeat of his people both as punishment for sin and as a redemptive re-creation of them in his new Israel—Judaism. Deuteronomy caught up the prophetic view of history and institutionalized it. It also stabilized that view in the form of a written text.

And that brought with it both bad news and good news. Deuteronomy started out as a stable text. It did not have the advantage of earlier traditions that were fluid and could be adapted into whatever form was needed to meet whatever need was perceived. A frozen text written for one set of problems can create new ones when read in a totally different situation. And this is what apparently happened when the prophetic ethic of election became institutionalized in its Deuteronomic form. Deuteronomy was written to challenge the domestic policies of Manasseh that had been dictated by the pressures of Assyrian domination. Manasseh wisely pursued a policy of broad flexibility toward the Assyrian merchants, diplomats, and tourists who freely came and went plying their trade and exerting their undisguised pressures on the habits and customs and traditions of Judahites and refugee Israelites who lived in the south. He successfully kept the Assyrian wolf from coming down on the southern fold and totally assimilating what was left of the Israelite venture on earth. He was paying a heavy price for it, but at least they did not get crushed like their northern cousins. Manasseh could do what he did for Judah's continuity of identity by relying heavily on the Davidic and royal ethic of election and Judahite self-understanding for his foreign and domestic policies.

Royal theology viewed God as the faithful promisor who would keep his word no matter how much the people might err or be pressured into accepting alien ways. This was the once-saved-always-saved point of view and it provided the Judahite governments of the seventh century with the ability to sway but not be broken by the Assyrian foreign policy of total integration of conquered peoples. The price was that of allowing the danger of influence from Assyrian beliefs and life style.

Deuteronomy was written to challenge this policy which was becoming dangerously risky. And it did so not on the basis of royal theology, as Isaiah had tried unsuccessfully to do in the eighth century, but on the basis of Mosaic theology and traditions. Josiah found the moment in history of respite from Assyrian pressure sufficient to have his reformation and vigorously reintroduce the Mosaic vision and practice. The prediction made by the man of God in 1 Kings 13 was fulfilled by Josiah in 2 Kings 23. There had been the eyewitness quite early on to say what God intended. He also honored the bones of the man of God who, though he had not passed the test of the old prophet concerning prophetic life style, had faithfully communicated the message. God's message cannot be contaminated by the sin of the messenger. We have indeed received this sacred text through earthen vessels. (Once again "Errore hominum providentia divina" applies.)

Deuteronomy's challenge to Manasseh's policies, when later read in the totally different context of dispersion and exile, apparently said something quite different from what was originally intended. The different eyes to see and ears to hear brought on by the destitution of 586, by which the many old traditions were reviewed in exile and appreciated, also meant a different reading of Deuteronomy from what had been intended. Deuteronomy had so stressed the conditioned nature of the divine promises in the covenant that it effected a needed reformation in the prewar days. But that very stress, read in dispersion when there was no longer a government or army or city or temple, appeared to say something quite different. It appeared to say that individuals who obeyed God's commands would be blessed while those who disobeyed would be punished. This was apparently then read to say that if one was blessed one must have been obedient, but if one suffered, one must have sinned. This whole misreading of the frozen text of Deuteronomy and indeed of the Mosaic theology generally is still with us today, as pastoral counselors know. The Book of Job was written in large part to say a loud no to such readings. Much since, including a good bit of Jesus' teachings, has been directed to rectify the reading.

Stabilized texts, and especially those that become sacred texts are in grave danger of such misreadings unless the appropriate hermeneutics are applied to bring out the dynamic analogy relative to text and sociological and historical context. The move from the Deuteronomic phenomenon to the masoretic is in part a history of efforts to get those texts to say what they do not apparently say, precisely to bypass a *peshat* reading. The importance of both context and hermeneutics to understanding a text has brought me elsewhere to suggest the value of the triangle as a tool both in attempting to reconstruct the original points scored by the text, in its original or early historical contexts, at the layers of formation of the text in antiquity, but also in order to score the same canonical points in the current historical contexts in which and for which the text is contemporized and resignified.[2] The tool of the triangle is particularly valuable when there is the conscious desire to avoid misreadings of frozen texts, as in the case of Deuteronomy read after 586 B.C.E. in exile. The triangle can assist a desire to attempt to score the same points that were originally scored within the historical time span that the ancient believing communities authored, composed, edited, and shaped a given biblical passage.[3] This much we can learn, from the Deuteronomic phenomenon, on how to read an ancient text.

The stabilization of the Torah was apparently compressed into a remarkably short period of time, in contrast to the Prophets and Writings and even the NT literature. I have suggested that a new law seems to be emerging in textual study of both testaments: the older the texts or versions the less likely they were copied accurately.[4] While this was true to a limited extent for the Pentateuch, as may be seen in the variants in the Samaritan Pentateuch and the LXX as well as in the Qumran literature, the Torah apparently enjoyed a foreshortened process of stabilization over against the rest of biblical literature. Our experience on the United Bible Societies' Hebrew OT Text Project bears this out. Such an observation is part of the ongoing discussion in comparative studies, especially in the Hellenistic and Roman periods, where time and again it is observed that there was nothing in Greek literature that functioned in Greek cults or culture quite like Torah for Judaism.

I have suggested elsewhere that it was the exilic experience of death and resurrection, for the Jewish remnant that did not assimilate to either Babylonian or Persian identity and culture—precisely those that experienced and needed the formation of a body of literature called sacred—that made the Torah function for those believers in the very distinct way that it apparently did.[5] That experience of death and life was made possible in exile by reviewing and repeating and reciting a selected grouping of old preexilic traditions that provided the vision and conviction necessary to endure. And that select group of traditions which has provided that renewed life came to be called "Torah"—the old word that had in preexilic times meant prophetic oracle or teaching or priestly instructions. It had proved its life-giving power to those who had read and reread its traditions in that way. It was to be called the *sefer ḥayyim* (Book of Life) for that reason.

But it was also later to be called *ha-sefer shekol bo* (The Book with Everything in It), both epithets being eventually applied to the *Tanach* (Hebrew Bible) as a whole. How did it get the reputation for having everything in it necessary to live life out, even to the fullest? The answer to that question lies along the route from the Deuteronomic phenomenon to the masoretic. Just about the time prophecy was thought to have ceased there was Torah available to take the place of the prophet. One could consult it as one used to consult an oracle or a prophet. "Ha-yesh davar me-adonai," Zedekiah asked Jeremiah (Jer. 37:17): Is there a word from the Lord? But when there was no Jeremiah where did one turn for a word from the Lord? To that which was eventually to be called the Word of God. But how could it provide a fresh new torah or word of guidance in a brand new context, if it was becoming more and more stabilized?

At first the answer apparently lay in the limited tolerance of variants, as attested by the manuscripts of the Hebrew Bible and versions in the period of textual fluidity. This would have been the case in the early period before the proto-masoretic viewpoint of a really stable text gained command of the process. But it was the gradual shift in understanding the very nature of the text that meant it could be read in certain ways sufficient to secure the fresh torah or word of guidance needed. And that shift was a move from sacred story to sacred text. The word "story" in this sense is not restrictive: that is, it does not designate a limited literary form, but rather an attitude in the mentality of the believing communities. History and story derive from the same Greek root, and basically the Torah and Early Prophets provide a story line from the mythic dimensions of prehistory through the middle Bronze Age down to the close of the Iron Age. The superscriptions provided in the corpus of the Latter Prophets provide the necessary co-relation between the various events of that history and the prophetic efforts to indicate how God was signifying those events in terms of judgment and hope for Israel and the nations. It is only in the *Ketuvim* (Writings) that we find some totally nonstory literary forms, but by the time the communities accepted Proverbs, Ecclesiastes, and the Song as sacred, the shift in attitude toward the text was complete.

That shift must be fully appreciated to grasp its significance. I have elsewhere suggested that it was in part a response to certain sociopolitical stimuli and pressures, the most compelling of which was the immense problem that evolved out of the Hellenistic challenge.[6] As Bickermann, Smith, Hengel, and others have pointed out, Judaism under Persia, while apparently fraught with problems of religious and perhaps even racial prejudice for a people scattered throughout the empire, nonetheless was able to manage a life style of obedience to the laws in Torah within rather moderate adjustments of interpretation.[7] But when Judaism faced the radically different European cultures of the Hellenistic period there developed a Torah crisis that had to be met. The old Bronze and Iron Age laws of Torah simply did not provide enough guidance to meet the challenge. Proto-Pharisaic Judaism responded in two ways; the introduction of *Torah she-bĕ-ʿal-peh* (oral Law), the belief that God had given Moses many laws that were not written down but were passed on by memory through Joshua, the prophets, and sages; and second, the introduction of the idea of verbal inspiration with the attendant new hermeneutic techniques whereby to get the text to say more or other than its *peshat* meaning. If the words were inspired then the structure and syntax of the whole could be bypassed and words and phrases could be extricated from here, there, and yon in the text to yield the necessary new torah, now called halachah, to meet the new situation. A third and more radical solution was that of the apostle Paul who declared the laws of Torah abrogated but the story in it holy, eternal, and good.[8]

Having a highly stable text such as that of Torah, following in the line of the Deuteronomic phenomenon, meant that Judaism was stuck with a code containing outdated laws unless some means could be devised to legislate new laws using the Torah as a kind of constitution. And those means were found in the two ways suggested. When the Hellenistic challenge was joined, Judaism found itself with problems for which there were no laws in a *peshat* reading of Torah, and laws for which there were no longer problems in an increasingly urbanized existence. The move to the concept of verbal inspiration was not difficult given the early understanding of a stable written text of traditions and laws called precisely "Torah." The very name encouraged viewing the text as a kind of prophetic oracle or priestly instruction. And if the words and not just the story or ideas in it were sacred and inspired then the number of new combinations of those words and phrases was indeed limitless. The seven *middot* (hermeneutic rules) of Hillel, the thirteen of Ishmael, and the eventual thirty-two *middot* of later tradition provided the guidelines on what was permissible in terms of rearranging those words and phrases to secure the new halachah in terms of the new needs.

The need to be able to do the rearranging, taking words and phrases out of the original context and creating a whole new literary context by reading them together, was imperative enough to have the whole new mode of reading the text institutionalized. In preexilic times narrators, prophets, and psalmists did it openly and freely, drawing upon oral traditions from different contexts and reciting them together to address needs of that time. Redactors apparently arranged the sequence of some of the oracles and addresses in a book like Isaiah by *Stichwörter*. The new way of reading the text had its prehistory and its antecedents. The *middot* called *gezerah shavah* and *asmakhta* permitted interpreters and midrashists of the Torah and Prophets and Writings to continue to do likewise.

But precisely because of the need to do it, controls had to be instituted. And those controls came in two ways, by the observance of the *middot*, and the increasing belief in the sacredness of every word in the text. The standardization process, described first by Moshe Greenberg but refined by Dominique Barthélemy with rather overwhelming evidence, which took place over the course of the first centuries B.C.E. and C.E., was complete by the end of the first century for Judaism.[9] It would not be so for Christianity for some time to come. The latter not only preserved many Jewish works from early Judaism that Pharisaic-rabbinic Judaism sloughed off in the course of the first century, but it also clung to the old Greek and other translations of the Law, Prophets, Psalms, and many other writings that had been effected well before the period of stabilization and standardization. It would not be until the fourth century C.E., which began with the nationalization of a great portion of Christianity and ended with the work of Jerome and his debates with Augustine over the nature of the sacred text—whether Hebraica Veritas or LXX and the Vetus Latina based on it—that a serious move toward stabilization and so-called accurate copying would take place.[10]

In Judaism, by contrast, the movement toward the masoretic phenomenon was assured. Precisely because it was now the text itself that was sacred, and each word in it inspired, rigid controls had to be adhered to. By the time of the work of the Ben Asher family verses and words would be counted and a very strong *seyyog* (fence) would be constructed around the sacred text in every margin, lateral, top, and bottom, as well as in the end-pages. As Christian Ginsburg reminded S. Baer, there was and is no canon of the masora; and as those of us who work in text criticism know, there are errors in the various masorot; nonetheless, the very phenomenon of the masora must be seen as the end result of the trajectory we have traced from its inception in the Deuteronomic phenomenon. A tremendous new appreciation for the masoretic phenomenon and its antecedents and prehistory has come since the discovery of the Qumran literature that dates to the period of textual fluidity prior to full stabilization and standardization. But the reasons for our gratitude were not the reasons for these phenomena. The move in early Judaism to the concept of a sacred text came about not because of scholarly desires to be accurate but because of the needs of the believing communities.

The believing communities of today, however, have no fewer needs than those of antiquity. The challenges come today not because of Assyrian or Babylonian threats, or Persian biases and prejudices, Hellenistic distractions, or Roman oppression. Challenges come today because of other threats, biases, prejudices, distractions, and oppression. Some of these have evolved out of the Enlightenment. Humanity lives today on a shrinking globe between its immense pride and its horrendous fear. We are all children of the Enlightenment and harbor deep within us, no matter how conservative or orthodox some may think they are, some belief in humanism. The sixteenth to eighteenth centuries are said to have constituted a resurrection experience for humanity behind which we cannot go. Humanity, it is said, has come of age. We are all there is of us, some say. That is the pride. But there is also the fear. One of the results of the Enlightenment is the mushroom cloud. We are so mature as humanity that we have invented the means to offer up the planet as a whole burnt offering on no altar whatever. And we have so come of age as children of the Enlightenment that, as Morris Abrams says, the twentieth century will be known, if we survive it, as the century of massacres, beginning with the pogroms in Eastern Europe, the Turkish slaughter of the Armenians, the mass murders sanctioned by the state in Germany in the 1930s and 1940s, the massacres of the Ibos and other tribes in Africa, South Asia, Southeast Asia, and the Near East. Adolf Hitler, Edward Teller writes in a recent article in the *Los Angeles Times*, caused fifty million deaths in a decade.

We live in a post-Holocaust age; but perhaps we also live, God forbid, in a pre-holocaust age. This is A.B. (After the Bomb) 42 (since August 1945). This planet survives on a thin thread of grace. James Reston, the abiding optimist, takes courage in the fact that we did not blow ourselves up already in the 1950s. Rather we find ourselves facing not only that continuing fear but others as we race in a little under thirteen years to the turn of the millennium. Whether we make it depends on the strength of that thread of grace. God knows we humans seem to continue to find ways to weaken it if not sever it.

Our ancestors in the faith also faced extinction. Not on the global level we face, no, but extinction nonetheless. The Bible seems to be full of stories and accounts of Israel being at the end of its existence, but finding itself recapitulating and transcending each "end." Abraham was ninety-nine years old and Sarah ninety, besides being barren, when the next generation of the promise finally was born. And this is but a sign of the kinds of stories and accounts that follow in the canonical story. The Bible seems to be at its best when it shows how God can take certain death and educe further life out of it. *Hu' memit vehu' mehayyeh* (he brings to death and he brings to life). Much of that which made it into the canon, of all the ancient literature available, goes to the wall, as it were, with the realism of life lived at the eastern end of the Mediterranean, a life lived on the land-bridge amongst three continents constantly desired by any neighboring government that could work up surplus economy enough to field an army. They all wanted Palestine.

Canonical criticism asks how it was that the succeeding generations read

their tradition, oral or written, and read their socio-political-historical context, so as to be able to recapitulate and transcend the successive crises and
even moments of death, as it were, with their identity intact. Many peoples
survived in flesh and blood but assimilated and hence died as peoples.
Judaism alone with its old traditions that became Torah and Prophets survived, albeit in a transformed state. How?

The answer to that question lies in ferreting out of the Bible the unrecorded hermeneutics that lie between so many of the lines of it. Canonical
criticism has a major interest in just that task. Wherever a tradition is cited,
whether in oral form or in written, there is presented the opportunity to
discover by what hermeneutics the author or tradent caused that tradition to
function in the new situation. What we have discovered is that the Bible,
Hebrew and Greek, is remarkably consistent in presenting a theocentric,
monotheizing hermeneutic. The theocentric focus can be demonstrated
rather consistently. Only in some wisdom literature is there an anthropo-
centric hermeneutic, but even there for the most part the transformation that
Coert Rylaarsdam noted years ago has taken place; in the canon the fear of
God is the very beginning of wisdom. It is clear that Paul in the course of
working out his Christology in his epistles used a theocentric hermeneutic in
constructing it out of his Scripture. The hermeneutics by which he worked
out his ecclesiology still need further work and might at times indicate a
christocentric hermeneutic. But that which ends up in the canon subscribes
rather consistently to a theocentric hermeneutic. The teachings of Jesus as
presented in the Gospels pursue a theocentric hermeneutic rather vigorously.

And one can tentatively say that that which ends up in the canon also
suggests a monotheizing hermeneutic, even in the literature of the Persian
and Hellenistic-Roman periods, despite some of the idioms borrowed from
those cultures. Some passages and writers of the Bible pursue a monotheizing
hermeneutic more or less well. Second Samuel 24 says God incited David to
take a census and God punished him for doing so, while 1 Chronicles 21 says
Satan had incited him to do so. Second Samuel goes to the wall, as it were,
while Chronicles puts the onus on Satan. Even so, Satan is not an independent deity with his own power: there he is but a member of the heavenly
council doing his job, as in the prologue to the Book of Job. The Synoptic
evangelists marshal demons to tell what for them was the truth, as in Mark
1:24 and Luke 4:34 where the spirit of the unclean demon confesses that
Christ was the Holy One of God. Elsewhere in the NT principalities and
powers express realistic encounters with evil, but the burden of proof would
fall on those who would see any passage in the NT subscribe to polytheism in
any form.[11] The Trinitarian formula became the church's way of monotheizing in a general culture of rampant polytheism as Cyril Richardson and Jane
Schaberg have shown, just as the concept of the heavenly council was the way
OT thinkers and writers had of monotheizing in the midst of general cultural
polytheism in the Iron Age and Persian period. One could not simply keep

repeating *ehad hu'*, *ehad hu'* (he is One). One also asked, *Mi kamokha ba'elim, adonoi* (who is like you among the gods, O Lord)?

To monotheize in a context of polytheism, whether it was Iron Age types of polytheism, Persian dualism, or Hellenistic polytheism, is the principle paradigm the Bible as canon exercises and recites. To monotheize is not just to believe that there is only one God of all creation and of all peoples. On the contrary, the canonical commandment to monotheize is not only the first of Ten Commandments, it is first in terms of the challenge it presents to the modern mind. For truly we are polytheists in our modes of thinking every bit as much as the ancients, including most Israelites. Our situation is perhaps worse in that because of the Judeo-Christian roots of Western civilization we think we are monotheists whereas we fragmentize truth in most of our modes of thinking. To pursue the oneness of God or the Integrity of Reality is perhaps the greatest challenge the human mind and spirit have ever encountered.

Whenever we ask the question of how a good God could ask Abraham to sacrifice his son, or how God could harden the heart of Pharaoh, or send a lying spirit in the mouths of King Ahab's court prophets, or commission an Isaiah and Jesus (Mark 4) so to preach that the people may become blind and deaf and senseless so that they cannot repent, we are polytheizing. It is our normal bent so to do. Monotheizing requires vision, a perspective, a hermeneutic by which we read not only these struggles of our ancestors in the faith but also our own world and ourselves in that world—texts and contexts. It requires believing that Mot and Abaddon have indeed been retired, put on a pension, and added to the heavenly council or heavenly choir, but we do not really believe. Like Abraham and Sarah we cannot really believe these annunciations of transcendent ability to redeem our lostness. We find ourselves between the Assyrian destruction and the Babylonian imminent threat, and we live between the pride and the fear. We read of God's promise to Noah, "I set my bow in the cloud." But we cannot believe it. As Dean Joseph Hough of the School of Theology at Claremont says, that cloud now has the shape of a mushroom. We have done it to ourselves, and we are scared. We are far more impressed by the cloud than by the rainbow. We live in a post-Holocaust, and potentially a pre-holocaust period, and we ask how a good God can allow such inhumanity to humans, such slaughter and such downright evil.

Polytheizers that we are we would have preferred God to soften Pharaoh's heart and invite Moses into the palace for a cup of tea while he dictated an emancipation proclamation for the Hebrew slaves. That would have been nice and tidy, but we would have no Torah. We might even have established a stele of stones or some monument for archaeologists to find near Goshen expressing gratitude to Pharaoh for his emancipation proclamation, but we would have no Torah. The Bible is not a soft-shoe act. The so-called false prophets thought of God in that way, but not those that end up in the canon. This canon is God's emancipation proclamation for all God's world.

In my work on true and false prophecy (see chap. 5) I reported that a review of the disputation passages in the Prophets, with an eye to the hermeneutics used by the various debating parties, indicated that the canonical prophets always read and contemporized the traditions they cited by a hermeneutic of God as both universal Creator of all peoples and Redeemer of Israel—not just one or the other. The so-called false prophet was inclined to say that the God who had brought Israel out of Egypt, guided her in the wilderness, and brought her into the land was capable of keeping Israel safe in the land. The so-called true prophets, those whose sayings we have in the Bible, if the historical context indicated prophetic critique and challenge to the people's thinking, on the contrary said that the God who had brought them out of Egypt, guided them in the wilderness, and brought them into the land was capable of taking Israel out of the land. God is not only Redeemer in a particular story of a particular people, in the Bible God is also universal Creator of all peoples. To emphasize God as Redeemer in reading a passage or tradition is to stress the freedom of the grace of God; to emphasize God as Creator of all is to stress the freedom of the God of grace. They must be held in tension and not let one collapse into the other.

A hermeneutic that theologizes in reading a passage, and attempting to signify it for a new historical context, is one that asks not what the passage says we should do but asks what the passage says God can do in such a situation as the story depicts. The Joseph story says that we sold our brother into slavery but that God could redeem even that dastardly deed so that the brother we sold to Pharaoh became prime minister when we needed bread. That is theologizing. To moralize would be to derive the moral that we should sell more brothers into slavery so that we will be sure to have bread when we need it! Obviously it is absurd, but I draw it out to show what we do when we moralize only in reading the text. To moralize would be to say that perhaps we, too, should be a murderer and fugitive from justice so God can call us like Moses to free his people. It is obviously absurd and yet we moralize more often than not in reading the Bible and hence cannot read it honestly. Then to go on and monotheize is to affirm, morning by morning, despite our unbelief, that God can work through Pharaoh's recalcitrance to effect a true liberation, or even Isaiah's early preaching of unconditioned consolation so that the people not engage in a facile-type repentance, or through his servant Nebuchadnezzar to effect Judah's death and Judaism's resurrection (Ezek. 37).

Understanding the bulk of Isaiah 28 to pertain to the siege of Jerusalem by Sargon II, taking that as the context, I might suggest two different ways one could read Isa. 28:16, *ha-ma'amin lo' yahish* (he who believes is not in a frenzy). By the hermeneutic of God the Redeemer and peculiar God of Judah, the phrase might mean that he who believed would not be in a frenzy because he believed that God would defend them and deliver them before the destruction of the city. By the hermeneutic of God the universal Creator of all as well as Redeemer of Israel, the phrase might mean that he who believed would not be in a frenzy because he believed that God was capable of taking even an Assyrian siege-stone being catapulted perhaps that moment into the city and make it into a precious cornerstone of a new foundation upon which a whole new construction would be built using justice as the line and righteousness as the plummet. Someone apparently objected to such seeming blasphemy and reminded Isaiah of the traditions (we know) from 2 Samuel 5 of how God had arisen to help David fight the Philistines on Mount Perazim and had been angry against the Philistines in the valley of Gibeon. Isaiah responded that he fully agreed about the truth and validity of the tradition. God was indeed a Holy Warrior; he never disputed it. But this time God was to be commandant of the Assyrian troops entering the city.

We, ourselves, being polytheists and hence singularists, do not like such apparently blasphemous readings of Scripture in which Isaiah and the other preexilic prophets engaged. Or, we tend to reject the implication of their message that the sins of the people could have been so great. Like Job's friends we do not understand how a good God can let such a thing happen to Job unless his sins had been horrendous. Do we think that the Galileans whose blood Pilate mingles with their sacrifices were worse sinners than all the other Galileans because they suffered thus? Jesus answered the question with a clear no. Or do we think that those eighteen upon whom the tower in Siloam fell and killed them, do we think that they were worse offenders than all the others who dwelt in Jerusalem? Jesus also answered that question with a clear no (Luke 13:1–5), indeed with the same clear no of the Book of Job to the friends who misread the Deuteronomic ethic of election.

It is the faith of the Bible that God can take whatever evil we do or is done to us and redeem it. He can signify power flows and even the awful destruction that one people can wreck on another.

There is no claim that we can signify such. The claim is, rather, that the Integrity of Reality can reach in and through the worst we do to each other precisely because God is universal Creator as well as Redeemer. Suffering and death do not stump God, even the crucifixion of the best you have known. *Hu' memit vehu' meḥayyeh* (he brings to death and brings to life). The monotheizer knows that God is the God of death as well as of life. The old creation battles between the gods as well as the eschatological battles between the gods of life and death have been transcended. But we find it hard to believe. Like Abraham we may find ourselves in a posture of great piety with our foreheads to the ground, but still we may not believe. We know it is over.

Well, it was not. But we like Abraham, in the ambiguity of Reality, seem to find ourselves with a knife in our hands. And it is not until we go to the wall apparently and raise the knife that we are permitted to hear the heavenly voice. "Abraham, Abraham, do not touch the lad or do anything to him whatever for now I know you fear God." Polytheists do not like that. We would rather revere God. After all God is love. But the monotheizer knows, when he or she engages in the monotheizing struggle against our own forms of polytheism, that to fear God is to direct the emotion of fear to the one place it can be redeemed—by the Creator-Redeemer God in the Integrity of

Reality. We permit ourselves to fear airplanes, freeways, earthquakes, and the mushroom cloud, but not God because God is supposed to be nice according to whatever cultural standards.

Living as we do between the pride and the fear, it would appear that the question we have today is very much the same question frequently faced in the Bible. Do we believe we have placed ourselves beyond the reach of God to redeem? Frankly, yes, we do. Only by faith can we say otherwise, a faith instructed by these sacred texts. My thesis is that if we can learn to read the Bible on its own terms in the light of the hermeneutics the biblical authors and tradents themselves used in their understanding of God, we may find it once more to be the prophetic voice we so desperately need to hear. There is no guarantee from such a reading that the Babylonians will fail to breach the walls, none whatever. On the contrary, people's hearts, Egyptian, Babylonian, or otherwise, are hardened to their own self-interest as our own elections remind us. And thus it has ever been. The Bible does not promise continuity as we would like it, or decency or great wisdom on the part of governments or peoples.

But it does say that there is an integrity to Reality which we, like the three blind persons around the elephant, cannot perceive on our own. How can there be any integrity to a Reality that hardens Pharaoh's heart or lets his son be crucified or lets madmen become dictators? There is no evidence for it that we can gather. We do not have the instruments.

But we can try to use a theocentric monotheizing hermeneutic to read these sacred texts and the world about us, so that we can attain the vision of that Integrity that is both Creator and Redeemer. God cannot be viewed as a puppeteer or master chess player. Such idioms in the Bible should not be absolutized. Rather God as Creator and Redeemer responds with purpose to the crises we create. There is an integrity to Reality that by faith we can affirm if we monotheize, that is, refuse to indulge in polytheistic good-guy/bad-guy thinking in reading the Bible, reading history, or reading our current situations. If God is universal Creator then we are all God's children; and if the same God is Redeemer, or respondent to our problems, then we are all a part of God's Integrity—our good points and our bad, our strengths and our weaknesses, our wisdom and our stupidity—and "they" are a part of God's Integrity as well.

Hope, that seemingly illusive but absolutely necessary factor in human existence, can only be found in the assurance that we, each of us and all of us humans on this globe, are caught up into the Integrity of Reality that is beyond our comprehension but alone gives life meaning.

NOTES

1. Joseph Blenkinsopp, *Prophecy and Canon* (Notre Dame, Ind.: Notre Dame Univ. Press, 1977), 80ff.

2. J. A. Sanders, "Canonical Hermeneutics: True and False Prophecy" (chap. 5 of this book); idem, *Canon and Community* (1984), 77–78.

3. See now Robert Wilson, *Sociological Approaches to the OT,* GBS (Philadelphia: Fortress Press, 1984).

4. J. A. Sanders, "Text and Canon: Old Testament and New" (1981), 373–94.

5. J. A. Sanders, *Torah and Canon* (1972); and "Adaptable for Life: The Nature and Function of Canon" (chap. 1 of this book).

6. J. A. Sanders, "Text and Canon: Concepts and Method" (chap. 7 of this book).

7. See, e.g., Elias Bickerman and Morton Smith, *The Ancient History of Western Civilization* (New York: Harper & Row, 1976), 113–45; and Martin Hengel, *Judaism and Hellenism,* 2 vols. (Philadelphia: Fortress Press, 1974; reprinted in 1 vol., 1981), 1:107ff.

8. J. A. Sanders, "Torah and Paul" (chap. 6 of this book).

9. D. Barthélemy, *IDBSup.*, s.v. "Text, Hebrew, history of."

10. Sanders, "Text and Canon."

11. Luke 10:17–20 illustrates the point: the mention of Satan in v. 18 is immediately followed by the assertion that Christ has power over the enemy, Satan, and that he has even given that power to lowly fishermen from Galilee! Satan has no power unless humans grant it to him which "belief in the devil" seems indeed to do.

Epilogue

The journey into a critical understanding of the Bible as canon is by no means complete. The pilgrimage of taking the Bible back to church as canon with the best and enduring results of biblical-historical and literary criticism will and must continue. The alternative to reading the Bible critically in the university study cannot be fundamentalism, but there must be recognition on the part of those who read it critically that there is a dimension to the Bible as the churches' book that transcends similar study of other literature. The Bible, of whatever canonical content, has its true *Sitz im Leben* in church or synagogue, not in the scholar's study. The Bible has tremendous value, as archaeologists and other historians have shown, for reconstructing history; and it has other secular values. But it has another dimension that gives it a qualitative difference from being only a source book. Despite its considerable pluralism it came out of early believing communities over a two-thousand-year period and it still belongs there.

"In a postliberal age a fresh case must be made for the Bible's integrity, if this can be done—and if the proper hermeneutical implications can be drawn."[1] I feel that it can be done and that the journey here described is our best hope for discerning the Bible's integrity and its own hermeneutic. Its integrity, as often stressed in this volume, is the Integrity of Reality (see the Prologue), that is, God. God is the Bible's unity and integrity. And the basic hermeneutic sought is in its own canonical hermeneutics, those by the ancient contributors and communities bridged gaps between earlier authoritative traditions, and wisdom, and their own times and contexts.

My position stresses the full historical process whereby the canon grew, developed, and was shaped, and in which its canonization continues. A full comprehension of the process of the shaping of the Torah is clue for understanding canon. Canonical criticism sees validity in all the subdisciplines of biblical criticism and views them all as complementary, but moves on beyond tradition and redaction criticism and focuses on the periods of intense canonical process, after the last individual geniuses had done their work, when the several believing communities either found life-giving value in this or that literature received, or did not. Those periods of intense communal selectivity were in point of historical fact moments of death and resurrection for Israel after the destruction of the first temple in the sixth century B.C.E., and for Judaism and Christianity after the destruction of the second in the first century C.E.

Canonical criticism recognizes the pluralism in the Bible and celebrates its diversity by underscoring biblical criticism as the means of discerning points scored by ancient "texts" in ancient "contexts." Within that pluralism, it seeks the shape of the canon, not only in the interrelationship of its various parts, but more important, in its own canonical hermeneutics. In the canonical process, discerned through the responsible use of the tools of biblical criticism, we are now able through the method of canonical criticism to discern the hermeneutics in antiquity in the crucial moments of adapting older traditions (texts) to new situations (contexts) to derive life-power from them, to continue the community's essential identity and not assimilate to the dominant culture of the time, precisely what fundamentalism does.[2] Study of the function of the OT in the NT is but a stage of this much longer study of such re-presenting of authoritative traditions well back into OT times, and on into synagogue and church.

Canonical criticism considers seriously the possibility that the hermeneutics employed within the Bible, even when not recorded in it as text, may be just as canonical for the ongoing believing communities today as anything explicit in its literature, precisely for going on and doing likewise with community authoritative traditions and with international wisdom today, as they did then. The same process or pilgrimage continues today. Careful, responsible, critical study of the Bible in terms of its dialogue through the ages with those communities of faith that bequeathed it to us provides the paradigm for the same dialogue to continue among their heirs today.

NOTES

1. Albert C. Outler, "Toward a Postliberal Hermeneutics," *TToday* 42 (1985): 287; cited also in an as-yet-unpublished paper by Robert W. Wall of Seattle Pacific University, "Ecumenicity and Ecclesiology: The Promise of the Multiple Letter Canon of the NT."

2. As argued in a paper I read before the General Assembly Council of the Presbyterian Church (USA) in Denver on March 15, 1986, "The Mission of the Called People of God."

Select Bibliography in Canonical Criticism

Achtemeier, Paul J. *The Inspiration of Scripture: Problems and Proposals*. Biblical Perspectives on Current Issues. Philadelphia: Westminster Press, 1980.

Ackroyd, Peter R. "The Open Canon." *Colloquium: The Australian and New Zealand Theological Review* 3 (1970): 279–91.

———. "Original Text and Canonical Text." *USQR* 32, nos. 3–4 (1977): 166–73.

Aland, Kurt. *The Problem of the NT Canon*. CST 2. Westminster, Md.: Canterbury Press; London: A. R. Mowbray, 1962.

Anderson, Bernhard W. "Tradition and Scripture in the Community of Faith." *JBL* 100, no. 1 (1981): 5–21.

Appel, Nicolaas. *Kanon und Kirche: Die Kanonkrise im heutigen Protestantismus als kontroverstheologisches Problem*. KKTS 9. Paderborn: Bonifacius-Druckerei, 1965.

———. "The NT Canon: Historical Process and Spirit's Witness." *TS* 32, no. 4 (1971): 627–46.

Bailey, Lloyd R. "The Lectionary in Critical Perspective." *Int.* 31, no. 2 (1977): 139–53.

———. *The Pentateuch*. Nashville: Abingdon Press, 1981.

Barr, James. *The Bible in the Modern World*. New York: Harper & Row, 1973.

———. *Holy Scripture: Canon, Authority, Criticism*. Oxford: Clarendon Press, 1983.

———. *Old and New in Interpretation: A Study of the Two Testaments*. New York: Harper & Row, 1966; rev. ed., forthcoming.

———. *The Scope and Authority of the Bible*. Philadelphia: Westminster Press, 1981.

Barstad, Hans. "Le canon comme principe exégétique: autour de la contribution de Brevard S. Childs à une 'herméneutique' de l'AT." *ST* 38, no. 2 (1984): 77–91.

Barth, Karl. *God Here and Now*. Translated by Paul M. van Buren. New York: Harper & Row, 1964.

Barthélemy, Dominique. "Text, Hebrew, history of." In *IDBSup*.

Barton, John. "Classifying Biblical Criticism." *JSOT* 29 (1984): 19–35.

Beckwith, Roger. *The OT Canon of the NT Church and Its Background in Early Judaism*. Grand Rapids: Wm. B. Eerdmans, 1985.

Best, Ernest. "Scripture, Tradition and the Canon of the NT." *BJRL* 61, no. 2 (1979): 258–89.

Beumer, Johannes. "Zur Vorgeschichte des neutestamentlichen Schriftkanons nach den Zeugnissen des frühen Christentums." *Königsteiner Studien* 18 (1972): 145–66.

Biblical Theology Bulletin 14, no. 3 (1984). Five articles by Jacob Neusner with introduction by James A. Sanders.

Blenkinsopp, Joseph. *Prophecy and Canon: A Contribution to the Study of Jewish Origins.* University of Notre Dame Center for the Study of Judaism and Christianity in Antiquity 3. Notre Dame, Ind.: Univ. of Notre Dame Press, 1977.

Brueggemann, Walter. *The Creative Word: Canon as a Model for Biblical Education.* Philadelphia: Fortress Press, 1982.

Campenhausen, Hans von. *The Formation of the Christian Bible.* Translated by J. A. Baker. Philadelphia: Fortress Press, 1972.

Canon and Authority: Essays in OT Religion and Theology. Edited by George W. Coats and Burke O. Long. Philadelphia: Fortress Press, 1977. Articles by Peter R. Ackroyd, Bernhard W. Anderson, Ronald E. Clements, George W. Coats, Paul D. Hanson, Rolf P. Knierim, Burke O. Long, James A. Sanders, Wayne Sibley Towner, and Gene M. Tucker.

The Canon and Masorah of the Hebrew Bible: An Introductory Reader. Edited by Sid Z. Leiman. LBS. New York: Ktav Publishing, 1974. Articles by J. P. Audet, J. Bloch, G. D. Cohen, I. H. Eybers, D. N. Freedman, L. Ginzberg, M. Haran, P. Katz, J. P. Lewis, G. F. Moore, J. A. Sanders, A. C. Sundberg, Jr., and S. Zeitlin.

Le Canon de l'AT: sa formation et son histoire. Edited by Jean-Daniel Kaestli and Otto Wermelinger. Geneva: Labor et Fides, 1984. Articles by S. Amsler, D. Barthélemy, G. Bavaud, G. Bedouelle, P. Fraenkel, E. Junod, J.-D. Kaestli, F. Nuvolone, H.-P. Rüger, J. A. Sanders, and O. Wermelinger.

Carroll, Robert P. "Canonical Criticism: A Recent Trend in Biblical Studies?" *ExpTim* 92, no. 3 (1980): 73–78.

_____. "Childs and Canon." *Irish Biblical Studies* 2 (1980): 211–36.

Childs, Brevard S. *Biblical Theology in Crisis.* Philadelphia: Westminster Press, 1970.

_____. "The Canonical Shape of the Prophetic Literature." *Int.* 32, no. 1 (1978): 46–55.

_____. *Introduction to the OT as Scripture.* Philadelphia: Fortress Press, 1979.

_____. *The NT as Canon: An Introduction.* Philadelphia: Fortress Press, 1985.

_____. "On Reading the Elijah Narratives." *Int.* 34, no. 2 (1980): 128–37.

_____. *OT Theology in a Canonical Context.* Philadelphia: Fortress Press, 1986.

"The Childs Proposal: A Symposium with Ralph W. Klein, Gary Stansell and Walter Brueggemann." *Word & World* 1, no. 2 (1981): 105–15.

Clements, Ronald E. *OT Theology: A Fresh Approach.* London: Marshall, Morgan & Scott, 1978.

Colwell, Ernest C. *New or Old? The Christian Struggle with Change and Tradition.* Philadelphia: Westminster Press, 1970.

Dulles, Avery. "Scripture: Recent Protestant and Catholic Views." *TToday* 37, no. 1 (1980): 7–26.

Dunn, James D. G. "Levels of Canonical Authority." *HBT* 4, no. 1 (1982): 13–60.

Evans, Craig A. "The Isaianic Background of Mark 4:1–20." *CBQ* 47 (1985): 464–68.

_____. "Paul and the Hermeneutics of 'True Prophecy': A Study of Romans 9—11." *Bib* 65 (1984): 560–70.

Farmer, William R., and Denis M. Farkasfalvy. *The Formation of the NT Canon: An Ecumenical Approach.* Theological Inquiries: Studies in Contemporary Biblical and Theological Problems. New York: Paulist Press, 1983.

Fishbane, Michael. *Biblical Interpretation in Ancient Israel.* Oxford: Clarendon Press, 1985. Reviewed by J. A. Sanders in *CBQ* 49, no. 2 (1987).

Freedman, David Noel. "Canon of the OT." In *IDBSup.*

Fuller, Reginald H. "What Is Happening in NT Studies?" *Saint Luke's Journal of Theology* 23, no. 2 (1980): 90–100.

Gamble, Harry Y. *The NT Canon: Its Making and Meaning.* Philadelphia: Fortress Press, 1985.

Gottwald, Norman K. "Social Matrix and Canonical Shape." *TToday* 42, no. 3 (1985): 307–21.

Hahn, Ferdinand. "Die heilige Schrift als älteste christliche Tradition und als Kanon." *EvT* 40, no. 5 (1980): 456–66.

Hammer, Paul L. "Canon and Theological Variety: A Study in the Pauline Tradition." *ZNW* 67, nos. 1–2 (1976): 83–89.

Hoffman, Thomas A. "Inspiration, Normativeness, Canonicity, and the Unique Sacred Character of the Bible." *CBQ* 44, no. 3 (1982): 447–69.

Horizons in Biblical Theology 2 (1980): 113–211. Articles by Bruce C. Birch, Brevard S. Childs, Douglas A. Knight, James L. Mays, David P. Polk, and James A. Sanders.

Hunt, Harry. "An Examination of the Current Emphasis on the Canon in the OT Studies." *SWJT* 23, no. 1 (1980): 55–70.

Interpretation 29, no. 4 (1975): 339–405. Articles by David L. Dungan, Friedrich Mildenberger, James A. Sanders, and Albert C. Sundberg, Jr.

Jacob, E. "Principe canonique et formation de l'AT." VTSup. 28 (1975): 101–22.

Journal for the Study of the OT 16 (1980): 2–60. Articles by James Barr, J. Blenkinsopp, H. Cazelles, Brevard S. Childs, Bonnie Kittel, George M. Landes, R. E. Murphy, and Rudolf Smend.

Kalin, Everett R. "The Inspired Community: A Glance at Canon History." *CTM* 42, no. 8 (1971): 541–49.

Kealy, Sean P. "The Canon: An African Contribution." *BTB* 9, no. 1 (1979): 13–26.

Keck, Leander E. "Scripture and Canon." *Quarterly Review* 3, no. 4 (1983): 8–26.

Leiman, Sid Z. *The Canonization of Hebrew Scripture: The Talmudic and Midrashic Evidence.* Transactions of the Connecticut Academy of Arts and Sciences 47. Hamden, Conn.: Archon Books, 1976.

Lemaire, André. *Les Ecoles et la formation de la Bible dans l'ancien Israel.* Orbis Biblicus et Orientalis 39. Fribourg: Editions Universitaires, 1981.

Lemcio, Eugene E. "Ephesus and the NT Canon." *BJRL* (forthcoming 1986).

———. "The Gospels and Canonical Criticism." *BTB* 11, no. 4 (1981): 114–22.

———. "The Parables of the Great Banquet and Wedding Feast: History, Redaction and Canon." *HBT* (forthcoming 1986).

Lewis, Jack P. "What Do We Mean by Jabneh?" *JBR* 32, no. 2 (1964): 125–32. Also in *The Canon and Masorah of the Hebrew Bible: An Introductory Reader,* 254–63. Edited by Sid Z. Leiman. LBS. New York: Ktav Publishing, 1974.

Lightstone, Jack N. "The Formation of the Biblical Canon in Judaism of Late Antiquity: Prolegomena to a General Reassessment." *SR* (1979): 135–42.

Mays, James L. "Historical and Canonical: Recent Discussion about the OT and Christian Faith." In *Magnalia Dei: The Mighty Acts of God. Essays on the Bible and Archaeology in Memory of G. Ernest Wright,* 510–28. Edited by Frank Cross Moore, Werner E. Lemke, and Patrick D. Miller, Jr. Garden City, N.Y.: Doubleday & Co., 1976.

McKim, Donald K., ed. *The Authoritative Word: Essays on the Nature of Scripture.* Grand Rapids: Wm. B. Eerdmans, 1983.

Murphy, Roland E., Albert C. Sundberg, Jr., and Samuel Sandmel. "A Symposium on the Canon of Scripture." *CBQ* 28, no. 2 (1966): 189–207.

Das Neue Testament als Kanon: Dokumentation und kritische Analyse zur gegenwärtigen Diskussion. Edited by Ernst Käsemann. Göttingen: Vandenhoeck & Ruprecht, 1970. Articles by Kurt Aland, Oscar Cullman, Gerhard Ebeling, Gerhard Gloeg, Ernst Käsemann, Werner Georg Kümmel, and Willi Marxsen.

Ohlig, Karl-Heinz. "Zur Theologie des Kanons der Heiligen Schrift: Uberlegungen anhand der Geschichte des Kanons." *ThG* 16 (1973): 74–83.

Orlinsky, Harry M. "The Canonization of the Bible and the Exclusion of the Apocrypha." In *Essays in Biblical Culture and Bible Translation*, 257–86. New York: Ktav Publishing, 1974.

Osswald, E. "Zum Problem der hermeneutischen Relevanz des Kanons für die Interpretation alttestamentlicher Texte." *Theologische Versuche* 9 (1977): 47–59.

Östborn, Gunnar. *Cult and Canon: A Study in the Canonization of the OT*. UUÅ 10. Uppsala: Lundequistska, 1950.

Outler, Albert C. "The 'Logic' of Canon-Making and the Tasks of Canon-Criticism." In *Texts and Testaments: Critical Essays on the Bible and Early Church Fathers*, 263–76. Edited by W. Eugene March. San Antonio: Trinity Univ. Press, 1980.

Pedersen, Sigfred. "Die Kanonfrage als historisches und theologisches Problem." *ST* 31, no. 2 (1977): 83–136.

Priest, John F. "Canon and Criticism: A Review Article." Review of Brevard S. Childs, *Introduction to the OT as Scripture*. In *JAAR* 48, no. 2 (1980): 259–71.

Rendtorff, Rolf. "Zur Bedeutung des Kanons für eine Theologie des Alten Testaments." In *Wenn nicht jetzt, wann dann? Aussätze für Hans-Joachim Kraus zum 65. Geburtstag*, 3–11. Edited by Hans G. Geyer, Johann Schmidt, Werner Schneider, and Michael Wernrich. Neukirchen-Vluyn: Neukirchener Verlag, 1984.

Roberts, Bleddyn J. "The OT Canon: A Suggestion." *BJRL* 46, no. 1 (1963): 164–78.

Sand, Alexander. *Kanon: Von den Anfängen bis zum Fragmentum Muratorianum*. HDG 1. Freiburg: Herder, 1974.

Sanders, James A. "Adaptable for Life: The Nature and Function of Canon." In *Magnalia Dei: The Mighty Acts of God. Essays on the Bible and Archaeology in Memory of G. Ernest Wright*, 531–60. Edited by Frank Cross Moore, Werner E. Lemke, and Patrick D. Miller, Jr. Garden City, N.Y.: Doubleday & Co., 1976 (= chap. 1 of this book).

———. "The Bible as Canon." *CCen* 98, no. 39 (December 2, 1981): 1250–55. Also in *Le Canon de l'Ancien Testament*.

———. "Biblical Criticism and the Bible as Canon." *USQR* 32, nos. 3–4 (1977): 157–65 (= chap. 4 of this book).

———. "Canon and Calendar: A Lectionary Proposal." In *Social Themes of the Christian Year: A Commentary on the Lectionary*, 257–63. Edited by Dieter T. Hessel. Philadelphia: Geneva Press, 1983.

———. *Canon and Community: A Guide to Canonical Criticism*. GBS. Philadelphia: Fortress Press, 1984.

———. "Canonical Context and Canonical Criticism." *HBT* 2 (1980): 173–97 (= chap. 8 of this book).

———. "Canonical Hermeneutics in the Light of Biblical, Literary and Historical Criticism." *Proceedings of the Catholic Theological Society of America* (1985): 54–63.

———. "Cave 11 Surprises and the Question of Canon." First published in *McCQ* 21 (1968): 284–98; reprinted in *New Directions in Biblical Archaeology*, 101–16. Edited by David Noel Freedman and Jonas C. Greenfield. Garden City, N.Y.: Doubleday & Co., 1969. Also in *The Canon and Masorah of the Hebrew Bible: An Introductory Reader*, 37–51. Edited by Sid Z. Leiman. LBS. New York: Ktav Publishing, 1974. (References in this volume are to the Freedman and Greenfield edition.)

———. "The Ethic of Election in Luke's Great Banquet Parable." In *Essays in OT Ethics* (J. Philip Hyatt, in Memoriam), 245–71. Edited by James L. Crenshaw and John T. Willis. New York: Ktav Publishing, 1974.

———. "From Isaiah 61 to Luke 4." In *Christianity, Judaism, and Other Greco-Roman Cults: Studies for Morton Smith at Sixty*. Part 1: New Testament, 75–106. Edited by Jacob Neusner. SJLA 12. Leiden: E. J. Brill, 1975.

———. *God Has a Story Too: Sermons in Context*. Philadelphia: Fortress Press, 1979.

———. "Habakkuk in Qumran, Paul, and the OT." *JR* 39, no. 4 (1959): 232–44.

———. "Hermeneutics." In *IDBSup*. (= chap. 3 of this book).

———. "Hermeneutics in True and False Prophecy." In *Canon and Authority: Essays in OT Religion and Theology,* 21–41. Edited by George W. Coats and Burke O. Long. Philadelphia: Fortress Press, 1977 (= chap. 5 of this book).

———. "Reopening Old Questions About Scripture." Review of James Barr, *The Bible in the Modern World.* In *Int.* 28, no. 3 (1974): 321–30.

———. Response to "The Gospels and Canonical Criticism" by Eugene C. Lemcio. In *BTB* 11, no. 4 (1981): 121–24.

———. "Text and Canon: Concepts and Method." *JBL* 98, no. 1 (1979): 5–29 (= chap. 7 of this book).

———. "Text and Canon: Old Testament and New." In *Mélanges Dominique Barthélemy: Etudes bibliques,* 373–94. Edited by Pierre Casetti, Othmar Keel, and Adrian Scheuber. Orbis Biblicus et Orientalis 38. Fribourg: Editions Universitaires; Göttingen: Vandenhoeck & Ruprecht, 1981.

———. *Torah and Canon.* Philadelphia: Fortress Press, 1972; 7th printing, 1986.

———. "Torah and Christ." *Int.* 29, no. 4 (1975): 372–90 (= chap. 2 of this book).

———. "Torah and Paul." In *God's Christ and His People: Studies in Honor of Nils Alstrup Dahl,* 132–40. Edited by Jacob Jervell and Wayne A. Meeks. Oslo: Universitets-forlaget, 1977 (= second part of chap. 6 of this book).

Sarna, Nahum. "Bible: The Canon." In *EncJud,* vol. 4.

Schrage, Wolfgang. "Die Frage nach der Mitte und dem Kanon im Kanon des Neuen Testaments in der neueren Diskussion." In *Rechtfertigung: Festschrift für Ernst Käsemann,* 415–42. Edited by Johannes Friedrich, Wolfgang Pöhlmann, and Peter Stuhlmacher. Tübingen: J. C. B. Mohr (Paul Siebeck); Göttingen: Vandenhoeck & Ruprecht, 1976.

Schweizer, Eduard. "Kanon?" *EvT* 31, no. 7 (1971): 339–57.

Sheehan, John F. "The Historical Method and Canonical Criticism: A Place on Which to Stand in Doing Biblical Theology." In *Theology and Discovery: Essays in Honor of Karl Rahner,* 337–57. Edited by William J. Kelly. Milwaukee: Marquette Univ. Press, 1980.

Sheppard, Gerald T. "Canon Criticism: The Proposal of Brevard Childs and an Assessment for Evangelical Hermeneutics." *Studia Biblica et Theologica* 4, no. 2 (1974): 3–17.

———. "Canonization: Hearing the Voice of the Same God through Historically Dissimilar Traditions." *Int.* 36, no. 1 (1982): 21–33.

Smart, James D. *The Strange Silence of the Bible in the Church: A Study in Hermeneutics.* Philadelphia: Westminster Press, 1970.

Smith, Jonathan Z. "Sacred Persistence: Towards a Redescription of Canon." In *Approaches to Ancient Judaism: Theory and Practice,* 11–28. Edited by William Scott Green. Brown Judaic Studies 1. Missoula, Mont.: Scholars Press, 1978.

Smith, Morton. *Palestinian Parties and Politics that Shaped the OT.* New York: Columbia Univ. Press, 1971.

Smith, T. C. "Canon and the Authority of the Bible." *Perspectives in Religious Studies* 1 (1974): 43–51.

Smith, Wilfred Cantwell. *Belief and History.* Charlottesville: Univ. Press of Virginia, 1977.

———. *Faith and Belief.* Princeton: Princeton Univ. Press, 1979.

Spina, Frank. "Canonical Criticism: Childs versus Sanders." In *Interpreting God's Word for Today: An Inquiry into Hermeneutics from a Biblical-Theological Perspective,* 165–94. Edited by Wayne McCown and James E. Massey. Anderson, Ind.: Warner Press, 1982.

Stemberger, Gunter. "Die sogenannte 'Synode von Jabne' und das frühe Christentum." *Kairos* N.S. 19, no. 1 (1977): 14–21.

Stuhlmacher, Peter. *Historical Criticism and Theological Interpretation of Scripture: Toward a Hermeneutics of Consent.* Translated with an introduction by Roy A. Harrisville. Philadelphia: Fortress Press, 1977.

Sundberg, Albert C., Jr. "Canon of the NT." In *IDBSup*.

————. *The OT of the Early Church*. HTS 20. Cambridge: Harvard Univ. Press, 1964.

Tate, Marvin E. "Promising Paths toward Biblical Theology." *RevExp* 78, no. 2 (1981): 169–85.

Tradition and Theology in the OT. Edited by Douglas A. Knight. Philadelphia: Fortress Press, 1977. Articles by Peter R. Ackroyd, James L. Crenshaw, Michael Fishbane, Hartmut Gese, Walter Harrelson, Arvid S. Kapelrud, Douglas A. Knight, Robert B. Laurin, and Walther Zimmerli.

Wainwright, Geoffrey. "The NT as Canon." *SJT* 28, no. 6 (1975): 551–71.

Wall, Robert W. "Eschatologies of the Peace Movement." *BTB* 15 (1985): 3–11.

————. "Introduction: NT Ethics." *HBT* 5 (1983): 49–94.

West, J. King. "Rethinking the OT Canon." *RelLife* 45, no. 1 (1976): 22–32.

White, Leland J. "Biblical Theologians and Theologies of Liberation—Part I: Canon—Supporting Framework." *BTB* 11, no. 2 (1981): 35–40.

Whybray, R. N. "Reflections on Canonical Criticism." *Theol.* 84 (1981): 29–35.

Wilson, Gerald. *The Editing of the Hebrew Psalter*. Chico, Calif.: Scholars Press, 1985.